I Am in Fact a Hobbit

Also by Perry C. Bramlett

C. S. Lewis: Life at the Center
Touring C. S. Lewis' Ireland and England (with Ronald W.
    Higdon)
The C. S. Lewis Readers' Encyclopedia (contributor)
A C. S. Lewis Spiritual Reader (forthcoming)

I Am in Fact a HOBBIT

An Introduction to the Life and Work of
J. R. R. Tolkien

by Perry C. Bramlett
with a reflective chapter by Joe R. Christopher

Mercer University Press

ISBN 0-86554-894-3
MUP/P262

© 2003 Mercer University Press
6316 Peake Road
Macon, Georgia 31210-3960
All rights reserved

First Paperback Edition.
(Also available in hardback)

∞The paper used in this publication meets the minimum requirements of American National Standard for Information Sciences—Permanence of Paper for Printed Library Materials, ANSI Z39.48-1992.

Library of Congress Cataloging-in-Publication Data

    Bramlett, Perry C.
    I am in fact a hobbit : an introduction to the life and works of J.R.R. Tolkien / Perry C. Bramlett.— 1st ed.
        p. cm.
    Includes bibliographical references and index.
    ISBN 0-86554-894-3 (alk. paper)
    1. Tolkien, J. R. R. (John Ronald Reuel), 1892-1973. 2. Fantasy literature, English—History and criticism. 3. Authors, English—20th century—Biography. 4. Anglicists—Great Britain—Biography. 5. Middle Earth (Imaginary place) I. Title.
    PR6039.O32 Z585 2002
    823'.912--dc21

                                                2002151071

TABLE OF CONTENTS

Preface	vi
1. Tolkien: An Overview of His Life and Career	1
2. *The Hobbit* and Other Works for Children	26
3. *The Lord of The Rings*	56
4. *The Silmarillion*	76
5. Poetry	88
6. Works of Scholarship	104
7. Other Lectures, Stories, Art, Letters	134
8. *Unfinished Tales* and *The History of Middle-Earth*	153
9. The Impact of Tolkien's Writings— A Personal Reflection by Joe R. Christopher	182
Appendixes	
1. Chronology	191
2. Published Works	199
3. Resource Bibliography	213
4. Journals, Newsletters, Societies, and Archives	229
5. Tolkien on the Internet	234
6. A Listing of Recordings by and about Tolkien and His Works	236
Index	247

Preface

This has been an almost impossible book to write, partly because, as a well-known scholar and writer told me months ago, "Tolkien is a remarkably difficult subject for writing about concisely." I was also told a book like this *could* be useful, but that today's Tolkien fans "tend no longer to buy books about him, especially not since the glory days of the sixties and early seventies," and that "few now buy anything *by* Tolkien except the *Hobbit* and the *Lord of the Rings*. Why buy printed books?" he said, "when there are Tolkien web sites, for free?" Finally (and thankfully) he told me that other works by Tolkien, and works about him, are still well worth writing, publishing, and reading.

Thanks in part to the success of and the tremendous sales revenues and publicity generated worldwide from the new Tolkien movie the *Lord of the Rings: The Fellowship of the Ring* (visually stunning and very enjoyable), it appears now there is another "Tolkien boom" similar to what took place in the sixties and seventies. People new and old are becoming involved with Tolkien and what he wrote: reading and rereading, "chatting" on the Internet, and buying art and movie posters and character figures and games and calendars and other assorted memorabilia. The *Hobbit* and the *Lord of the Rings* are receiving the most attention of Tolkien's works just as before, and these enduring classics surely deserve it...and more.

This book is a basic introduction only, a "nuts and bolts" survey of Tolkien's life and works. It is meant for the general reader of Tolkien, the person who desires to know him a little better and wants to go past the movie and fanzine hype. The literature about him, both scholarly and popular, is so enormous that it would take a much larger book (or books) to interact adequately with the literally hundreds of detailed studies, interpretations, synopses, investigations, and analyses of Tolkien and his works that have been written (many of them excellent), starting over a half century ago. In this work I chose not to concentrate solely on the *Hobbit* and the *Lord of the Rings*, both of which have had more than their share of scrutiny. I have given comparable space, or as close to that as possible, to Tolkien's other published works, including his lesser-known works for children, his oft-neglected poetry, his academic essays and talks, the posthumous Middle-earth writings edited by his son, his collected treasure-trove of letters, and some other "obscure" pieces. My hope is that this book will "whet the reader's appetite" for *all* of Tolkien, and inspire him or her to read what is now currently popular…and then go beyond.

Someone wrote that a writer of genius is a person "who sees the world and is able to make other people see it in a different light…life is not the same after reading them as it has been before." Reading J. R. R. Tolkien is like exploring a great and wonderful library, and the interested reader who takes him seriously and goes "deeper and further" will not view life through the same lenses again, and at the same time will be thoroughly entertained.

I am grateful to many for their encouragement and friendship during the writing of this book. It has been very challenging and difficult, but at the same time always a stimulating education and inspiring journey, which has not ended. Some of these friends and colleagues include Dr. Marc Jolley of Mercer University Press, who initiated this project, Mr. Wayne Hammond, Dr. Ronald Higdon, Dr. Evarose Gutmann, Rev. Fred Lane, Mr. Todd Miller,

Mr. Harold Maier, and Dr. Murray Adams. My wife Joan, not surprisingly, has been more steadfast and patient than ever. Dr. Joe Christopher wrote for me a superb personal reflection on Tolkien, and I deeply appreciate him taking time away from his busy schedule to do so.

This book is dedicated to Kathryn Lindskoog, who understands more about writing well than anyone I know.

Tolkien:
An Overview of His Life
and Career

In a now famous letter, Tolkien told an American writer who had asked for information about him (which he "would not mind our knowing"), that he did not like giving "facts" about himself, primarily because it would "distract attention" from an author's works, if the works were worthy of attention. He then proceeded to give a few significant facts about himself, and among these were that he was born in 1892 and lived his early years in the "Shire" in a pre-mechanical age, he was a Roman Catholic Christian, he was a hobbit in all but size (Tolkien was a little more than five feet eight inches tall), he liked gardens, trees, and unmechanized farmlands, he smoked a pipe and liked good plain unrefrigerated food (especially mushrooms), he had a simple sense of humor, he went to bed late and got up late, he traveled little, and he loved what was left of Wales and the Welsh language.[1]

---

[1] This letter to Deborah Rogers was dated 25 October 1958, and was first included in Rogers, *J. R. R. Tolkien: A Critical Biography* (New York: Hippocrene Books, 1980) 125; next in Humphrey Carpenter, ed., *The Letters of J. R. R. Tolkien* (Boston: Houghton Mifflin, 1981; 2000) 288-89.

Readers all over the world know that Tolkien's works are indeed worthy of attention, and many would also say that they deserve all the good attention they receive. In England, Tolkien was recently voted "author of the century," and the *Lord of the Rings* was voted "book of the century." This was no accident, since it has been said that one way to judge an author is to look at his or her reception by the reading public. On the surface, Tolkien led a rather uneventful academic life, but that life was the energy that fueled his creative imagination, and no other author of the last 100 years has so captured the imagination and hearts of his readers. His "uneventful academic life" has been well chronicled by others, but hopefully the overview given on these pages will stimulate anew and help bring to Tolkien a new generation of readers.

Early Life

John Ronald Reuel Tolkien (from the German *tollkühn*, "foolhardy") was born in Bloemfontein in central South Africa, 3 January 1892. Tolkien's near ancestors came to England in the early 1800s and tradition claimed that his great uncles were born in Berlin. At the time of his birth, Bloemfontein ("fountain of flowers") was a small city of less than 4,000, and in Tolkien's brief three-year stay there it was the capital of the former Afrikaner republic called the Orange Free State, now Free State.

Ronald (or John Ronald, then later "Tollers" or "J. R. R. T" at Oxford) was the eldest son of Arthur Reuel Tolkien, a branch manager of Lloyds Bank of Africa, and Mabel (daughter of John Suffield), both formerly of Birmingham in the West Midlands of England. Mabel, born in 1870, became engaged to Arthur in 1888, but did not marry him till 1891 because of Arthur's low salary at Lloyds in Birmingham. In 1889 he sailed for South Africa, and Mabel joined him two years later, as Arthur's new position as a manager carried with it a substantially larger salary and the use of a house.

Bloemfontein was not yet fifty years old when the Tolkien family took up residence, and the city was still experiencing growing pains. Although there were churches, a hospital, a library, a club for European residents, a tennis club, and several shops, the town was sparsely populated, very dusty, and not a pleasant place to live. The family lived on Maitland Street, just off the town market square on the Bank of Africa grounds, and the household was provided a maid, nurse, two servants, and a houseboy.

The terribly hot South African summers and (mostly) unpredictable cold, dry winters proved unsuitable for Mabel and Ronald, and the boy was often sick.[2] There were also problems with the local wildlife. The family home was very close to open plains, and wild dogs, jackals, snakes, and even lions sometimes threatened their security. Once a wild monkey climbed over their security wall and ate three of Ronald's pinafores, and the child was also bitten by a tarantula. Although he later said this incident left him with no particular aversion to spiders, the memory stayed with him, and the theme of large, venomous spiders occurs in the *Hobbit* and the *Lord of the Rings*.

Mabel, Ronald, and his younger brother Hilary (born 1894) were on a visit to England in 1896 when Arthur died of a severe hemorrhage caused by rheumatic fever. Mabel and the boys moved back to England and settled in the little town of Sarehole Mill (the inspiration for the Shire), near Birmingham, where they lived from 1896 to 1900. Mabel tutored the boys in natural history, art, Latin, and French, which Ronald did not care for. He did show a natural inclination for drawing, particularly if his subject was a

---

[2] Tolkien later recalled that his first Christmas memory of Bloemfontein was "of blazing sun, drawn curtains and a drooping eucalyptus." See Carpenter, *Letters*, 213.

landscape or tree.³ Mabel also encouraged her sons to read, and Ronald enjoyed works such as *Alice's Adventures in Wonderland*, the "Curdie" books of George MacDonald, the Arthurian stories, and the Fairy books of Andrew Lang. He was especially enthralled with Lang's *Red Fairy Book* and the tale of Sigurd the dragon-slayer. He wrote his first story, about a dragon, around this time. His mother aroused his first interest in words and languages by pointing out that he had to say "a great green dragon" instead of "a green great dragon." He wrote no more stories for years afterwards, immersing himself in language instead.

In 1900 the family moved to the Moseley district of Birmingham, near a railroad, and the boys were sent to King Edward's School. Ronald desperately missed the Sarehole countryside but became proficient at Latin at King Edward's, and he also began his lifelong appreciation of the Welsh language, from the names on the trucks in the coal yard near where he lived.

Christianity played a vital role in Mabel's life after Arthur's death, and after visiting an Anglican church, she and the boys attended St. Anne's Catholic Church in the city. She converted to Roman Catholicism in 1900, ostracizing her family, particularly her father, a Unitarian, and her uncle, an Anglican. In 1902 Mabel attended the Birmingham Oratory Church (founded by John Henry Newman) and met its rector, Fr. Francis Morgan, who became a lifelong friend of the family. The boys attended the less expensive St. Phillips Grammar School for a while, then Ronald returned to King Edward's, where he studied Old English, the great philological love of his life. In 1903 Mabel was diagnosed with diabetes, and in the summer of 1904 she moved to a cottage at the Birmingham Oratory Retreat on the outskirts of the city. She died of complications due to diabetes on 14 November 1904, when Ronald was thirteen. At her request, he and Hilary were brought

---

³ Tolkien said often that he loved trees, and that he found mistreatment of them "hard to bear." In all his works he "took the part of trees as against their enemies." See Carpenter, *Letters*, 220, 419; other references 321, 420.

up as Roman Catholics by Fr. Morgan, who became their legal guardian.

The boys lived with their Aunt Beatrice Suffield in the Edgbaston district, and their time there was far from congenial. Beatrice destroyed Mabel's personal papers and letters, and was often distant and never considerate. The boys sought refuge at the Oratory, and it became their home away from home. They would serve mass for Fr. Francis and eat breakfast in the refrectory, go to school (Hilary was now at King Edward's), then after school spend as much time as they could at the church. Ronald studied Old Norse and Gothic, discovered *Sir Gawain and the Green Knight*, and started to invent his own languages. The school's headmaster, Robert Gilson, encouraged his students to study classical linguistics, and another teacher, George Brewerton, introduced Ronald to Anglo-Saxon. One of Ronald's best friends at school was Christopher Wiseman, whom he met in 1905, and they remained friends for life.

In 1908, the boys moved to a dingy boarding house near the Oratory, where they lived on the second floor. There Ronald met another lodger who lived on the first floor, a pretty nineteen-year-old named Edith Mary Bratt. Edith was an orphan and a talented pianist who had previously attended a girl's boarding school that specialized in music. She and Ronald became friends immediately, and in the summer of 1909 they declared their love for each other. Fr. Francis discovered their relationship in late 1909 and moved Ronald to another house. He was deeply distressed that Ronald had neglected his studies and was conducting a "discreet love affair" with a woman three years his senior. In March 1910 Edith moved to Cheltenham (Gloucestershire, in the eastern Cotswolds) where she stayed with family friends, and although she and Ronald wrote to each other, they did not meet again for nearly three years.

Ronald began to write poetry, and some of his poems contained themes he would later incorporate into his mythology, such as woodland fairies. He also read and was entranced by the

Finnish *Kalevala*, and identified with the unlucky Kullervo, who was the inspiration for the story of Túrin. He and Wiseman became close friends with Robert Gilson (son of the headmaster) and Geoffrey Smith, and these four became the nucleus of a reading group known as the "T.C.B.S.," or "Tea Club (of the) Barrovian Society." This fellowship lasted until two of the members (Gilson and Smith) were killed in World War I. The encouragement of his friends in the T.C.B.S. inspired Ronald to express his deepest emotions in poetry, and these found their way into his mythology.

Oxford Years–Early Period

Ronald won a scholarship to Oxford in 1910 and left King Edward's in 1911. That summer he and Hilary and ten others (including his aunt, Jane Neave) vacationed in Switzerland. Before coming home, he bought some "touristy" postcards, and on one of them was a painting by the German artist Josef Madlener (1881–1967) called "The Mountain-spirit" (*Der Berggeist*), and it showed an old man with a white beard and wearing a cloak sitting on a rock by a tree and talking to a faun. Ronald kept the postcard, and years later he wrote on it: "Origin of Gandalf."

He had continued writing to Edith, and on his 21st birthday, no longer bound to Fr. Francis, he wrote her again and proposed on 3 January 1913. Edith replied and informed Ronald that she was engaged to George Field, the brother of a school friend. Five days later he traveled to Cheltenham to see her, and by the end of the day she agreed to marry him. A year later she converted to Catholicism, a sacrifice Ronald remembered and placed in the story of Arwen and Lúthien. They were married on 22 March 1916 at the Catholic church in Warwick and honeymooned for a week in Clevedon, Somerset, the same little town where Coleridge brought his bride in 1795.

Ronald enlisted after England entered the war in August 1914 but was permitted to finish his studies at Exeter College, Oxford. While at Exeter, he was active in college life and played rugger, joined the college Essay Club and Dialectical Society, and took part in a debating society. He also started his own club, which he called the Apolausticks, "those devoted to self-indulgence." Mostly freshmen, the members of the club wrote papers, had discussions and debates, and held extravagant dinner parties. Tolkien was happiest in groups like this where he could talk and laugh with friends, discuss books, and smoke—he was already addicted to pipes and tobacco.

His special interest at Exeter was philology,[4] and this meant he attended lectures and classes taught by Joseph Wright, Deputy Professor of Comparative Philology. Wright was a renowned linguist, a self-made man who wrote language primers and eventually published a six-volume English dialect dictionary. Tolkien learned enthusiasm from Wright, who encouraged him to show initiative and study Celtic. Tolkien instead delved deeply into medieval Welsh, which continued to interest him his entire life.[5] He obtained First Class Honours in English Language and Literature from Exeter in 1915. It was in character that his one surviving traceable entry in the Junior Common Room Suggestions Book was a request for the purchase of "a good English dictionary." While at Exeter the *Book of Lost Tales* began to develop in his mind, and he wrote several poems, including "You and Me and the Cottage of Lost Play." Later his earliest

---

[4] "Philology" was defined by the *Oxford English Dictionary* (1936) as "the study of the structure and development of language" and "the science of language, or linguistics." The word was used by Chaucer in 1386 and originally was a generic term meaning "the study of literature, in a wide sense, including grammar, literary criticism and interpretation, the relation of literature and written records to history."

[5] In a 1955 letter to W. H. Auden, Tolkien said he was fascinated with Welsh names and in them found "an abiding linguistic-aesthetic satisfaction." See Carpenter, *Letters*, 213.

mythological writings took shape in a paper delivered to the college Essay Club in 1920.

After graduation from Oxford he began military training at Bedford and Staffordshire and was commissioned as a second lieutenant, and during the war he fought with the 11th Lancashire Fusiliers on the Western Front in France (Flanders). Just after his marriage, he was sent to France on 4 June 1916, and a little over a month later learned that his boyhood friend Robert Gilson had been killed at the Battle of the Somme; Tolkien saw action there on 14 July. His other friend from the T.C.B.S., Geoffrey Smith, was killed on 1 July. In October, Tolkien was afflicted with trench fever and invalided home; he was in and out of hospitals for the rest of the war. During his hospital stays he completed much of the *Book of Lost Tales* and a "Gnommish Lexicon." He and Edith also conceived a child, and John Francis Reuel Tolkien was born 16 November 1917.

After the war, Tolkien and his family moved to Oxford (50 St. John's Street) and he worked for the *New English Dictionary*, housed a few blocks away in the old Ashmolean Building on Broad Street.[6] His work was primarily concerned with etymology ("the historically verifiable sources of the formation of words and development of their meaning"), and the definitions of nouns, as he was not very good with verb usage and definition. Years later, when working with his own invented languages, he spent most of his time on etymology, developed the nouns, and largely ignored the verbs. He said that during his two years with the *Dictionary* he learned more than at any other comparable time in his life. Another child was conceived, and Michael Hilary Reuel Tolkien was born 22 October 1920.

In the summer of 1920, he was appointed Reader in English language at Leeds University. That same year he wrote a "Father Christmas letter" to his children, a custom that continued until

---

[6] Now the Museum of the History of Science and the first purpose-built museum in England.

1943. In 1922 he was joined by E. V. Gordon, a Rhodes Scholar from Oxford whom he had tutored. Soon after Gordon's arrival, Tolkien began work on a new Middle English glossary, which was published in 1922. Looking for a significant piece of work, Tolkien and Gordon decided to write a revision of *MS Cotton Nero A*, the British Museum's manuscript of *Sir Gawain and the Green Knight*, written around 1400. In 1925 their new edition was published, with Tolkien writing the text and Gordon supplying the notes. In 1924, he and Edith had another child, Christopher Reuel Tolkien, who was born 21 November. During this time Ronald wrote and told many stories to his children; some of these were later published as *Roverandom*.

In 1925, he was elected Rawlinson and Bosworth Professor of Anglo-Saxon at Oxford in a stunning upset of his old tutor at Exeter, Kenneth Sisam. The two men were tied after the election, and the deciding vote for Tolkien was cast by the Vice-Chancellor, Joseph Wells. He was elected a Fellow of Pembroke College and immediately set out to improve the "language" side of the syllabus. As a full professor he was required to give a minimum of thirty-six lectures a year, but being the perfectionist he was, in his second year he gave 136 lectures and classes.[7] He enlisted another professor, Charles Wrenn (later an Inkling) to help him, but through the end of the 1930s he gave at least seventy-two or more lectures each year. His position also involved supervising post-graduate students and examining (give tests or examinations) within the university. He also worked as a freelance examiner for colleges throughout Britain.

---

[7] Although Tolkien often mumbled and was inarticulate when he spoke, his students were fascinated by his dramatic persona. The author J. I. M. Stewart (Michael Innes) later recalled that Tolkien "could turn a lecture into a mead hall in which he was the bard and we were the listening guests," and W. H. Auden wrote Tolkien years later and told him his "voice was the voice of Gandalf" when he recited *Beowulf*. See Humphrey Carpenter, *J. R. R. Tolkien: A Biography* (Boston: Houghton Mifflin, 2000) 138.

On 11 May 1926 he met Clive Staples (Jack) Lewis of Magdalen College, while both attended an English faculty meeting at Merton College. At first both men were wary of each other. Lewis said later that he had been warned never to trust a Catholic and a philologist, and Tolkien was both. Ronald knew that Lewis was on the "Lit" side of the syllabus and could be a potential enemy in reform. But they soon became fast friends, primarily because both loved beer, good stories, and laughter. Tolkien sent his "Lay of Leithian" for Lewis to read later in 1926 and wrote the "Sketch of the Mythology" to explain it. By 1927 Ronald had talked Lewis into attending the Coalbiters, a group that read and discussed the Icelandic sagas. On holidays in 1927 and 1928 he drew pictures for the Silmarillion stories and read E. A. Wyke-Smith's the *Marvellous Land of Snergs*, later an "unconscious source book" for hobbits.

Although Tolkien was by all accounts a good father and husband, there were some marital problems and tensions through the years. Edith, while a very talented pianist and vocalist, had not been given a good all-around education at the girl's boarding school. Earlier she wanted a career as a piano teacher and possibly as a soloist, but after her marriage to Tolkien, and because the family needed no extra income, her career hopes gradually faded. In that Victorian era, it was "expected" that a middle-class wife would stay at home and raise the children—to work outside of the home would mean the husband could not earn enough for the family to live comfortably. Tolkien did not encourage her to attempt intellectual or social activities, because he (like many males in that society) did not believe these were a necessary part of a wife's duties. And Edith was shy and felt uncomfortable in the male-dominated bastion of Oxford academic life, especially in the presence of Tolkien's professor friends.

She had enjoyed living in Leeds, where people occupied modest homes, life was more informal, and his students often visited for tea. But back in Oxford, life suddenly became very formal again, and it did not help that they moved often and never felt quite settled. Another problem was Tolkien's work load. Although he was always loving and considerate (especially about her health) and would help her with domestic responsibilities, Edith often felt that she was second to his academic work and writing. He seemed to "come alive" only when he was in the company of his friends and when he was working at home on his mythology. When Lewis visited, the children enjoyed him because he gave them presents (usually books) and talked openly to them. Edith became a little jealous of Lewis, because around her he was shy and awkward, and she could not understand the bond of affection Tolkien had for him.

Another problem for them was Catholicism. Edith had converted in order to please Ronald, but as the years went by she attended mass infrequently. This was due partly because she resented Tolkien's insistence on regular confession, and she had never been comfortable confessing her sins and deepest feelings to a male priest. This led to much discord, but in 1940 she and Tolkien had a reconciliation, and from then on, although she never attended mass as often he did, she did not show outward resentment and became more involved in church social life.

They did lead somewhat separate lives at home, as he would work late after she had gone to bed so he could stay at his desk without interruption. She often helped him with the typing and proofing of manuscripts and was usually the first person he would read them to. Two of these in particular were "Leaf by Niggle" and *Smith of Wootton Major*. They learned to share friends, some of them with academic connections, such as Rosfrith Murray, daughter of Sir James Murray, the original editor of the *Oxford English Dictionary*. Other regular visitors to their home included several of his students such as Simonne d'Ardenne, Elaine Griffiths, and Mary Salu. These students became almost like members of the family and were as much a part of Edith's life as they were of Tolkien's. Friendships with female students gradually helped Edith gain a sense of acceptance into her husband's world, and she became almost a surrogate mother to several of them. But the primary source of happiness for both, and the most positive part of their marriage, was their care for the children, on whom they lavished love and attention. They were involved in virtually every detail in the lives of the children, and later their grandchildren, and never hesitated to openly show affection to them all, both at home and in public.

There was never a scandal or even the hint of one in the Tolkien marriage, and their close friends and family knew that despite their differences, the love between them was going to grow stronger and endure. Edith was basically shy, but as she grew older she gained self-confidence, partly based on Ronald's fame and prosperity, but also because of, according to her children, "her own inner strength of character."[8] Edith and Ronald slowly learned to communicate and express their emotions, to rely on each other and center on their family, and their marriage lasted for over fifty years.

Tolkien's only daughter Priscilla was born in 1929, and in that same year he published an essay in *Essays and Studies*, volume 14, on the Middle English narrative poem the *Ancrene Wisse*. He also worked on a number of other projects in the next few years, including the "Annals of Beleriand" in 1929 and the "Quenta Noldorinwa," the "Annals of Valinor," and the "Aotrou and Itroun" all in 1930. He also started telling the hobbit stories to his children in 1929, and by 1931 began writing it. He continued to be active in college life and in 1930 proposed a revision of the English School Syllabus, which was passed in 1931. The rift between the factions of the English School had widened since the first war, with the "Lit" group insisting that "Lang" students spend many hours studying Milton, Shakespeare, Chaucer, and others (while neglecting Anglo-Saxon and Middle English), while the "Lang" faction made sure that "Lit" students spent an inordinate amount of time studying English philology and other obscure

---

[8] John Tolkien and Priscilla Tolkien, *The Tolkien Family Album* (Boston: Houghton Mifflin, 1992) 86.

linguistic courses. Tolkien determined that this would have to change, and he also ensured that Icelandic was added to the syllabus.

Oxford Years—Middle Period

On 19 September 1931, after a long conversation with Tolkien and Hugo Dyson, C. S. Lewis started his conversion to Christianity, which Tolkien recorded in his poem "Mythopoeia." Lewis and Tolkien spent a great deal of time together, and Tolkien would read aloud parts of the *Silmarillion*, which Lewis urged him to publish. Tolkien said later that Lewis was long his "only audience," and that from him he got the idea that "his stuff" could be more than just a private hobby. The Inklings were formed in 1932 and would meet for lunch on Tuesdays in the Eagle and Child ("Bird and Baby") pub in downtown Oxford, and later on Thursday evenings, usually at Lewis's rooms at Magdalen College. The "Inklings" name came from a short-lived Oxford literary society, and Lewis, Tolkien, and friends took it as their own. Other charter members who attended regularly before and after World War II included Lewis's brother "Warnie," an Army major; R. E. Havard, Lewis and Tolkien's physician; Hugo Dyson; and Lewis's solicitor Owen Barfield, who attended infrequently. Barfield was also a noted philosopher and author, and his *Poetic Diction* (1928) was a primary influence on both Lewis and Tolkien.[9]

Lewis's first book on Christianity was the autobiographical the *Pilgrim's Regress* (1933), and its publication irritated Tolkien, who, because of his private nature, thought Lewis rushed his ideas into print. In the mid-1930s Tolkien wrote "Errantry," "The Fall of Arthur," and *Farmer Giles of Ham*. Beginning around 1934 he

---

[9] For an excellent short study of *Poetic Diction* and Barfield's influence on Tolkien, see Verlyn Flieger, *Splintered Light: Logos and Language in Tolkien's World* (Grand Rapids MI: Eerdmans, 1983).

wrote more Silmarillion material, including "The Lhammas" and "Ambarkanta." The *Hobbit* was nearing completion by 1935, finished by October 1936, and eventually published in 1937. Tolkien also offered *Mr. Bliss* to his publishers, but the children's book was rejected because its color pictures were too costly to print.

He delivered his landmark lecture "Beowulf: The Monsters and the Critics" to the British Academy in late November 1936, and it was published the next year. In the late 1930s Lewis approached Tolkien and suggested they write space stories, with Lewis doing "space travel" and Tolkien writing "time travel." Lewis published *Out of the Silent Planet* in 1938, and Tolkien began work on "The Lost Road," which led to "The Fall of Númenor" and "Etymologies." In "The Lost Road" a father and son travel back in time to the land of Númenor, Tolkien's Middle-earth creation modeled after Atlantis.[10] After the publication of the *Hobbit*, Tolkien's publisher wanted more "hobbit stories," and Tolkien revised and submitted "Leithian," "Quenta Silmarillion," "The Lost Road," *Farmer Giles of Ham*, and others. These were rejected by Allen & Unwin, who still wanted more "hobbit material" for anticipated legions of fans. In December 1937 Tolkien started work on the *Lord of the Rings*. He worked steadily on the massive work until 1938, when Christopher became ill. At this time his oldest son John was studying theology in Rome, and Michael was a student at Trinity College, Oxford.

During the time of the writing of the *Lord of the Rings*, Tolkien was also very busy with academic duties, including the steady grind of examining and marking papers. He was ill frequently, and the terrors of the war caused interruptions. He wrote a preface for *Beowulf and the Finnesburg Fragment* in

---

[10] Humphrey Carpenter wrote that the origin of the story had its genesis in an "Atlantis haunting" nightmare Tolkien had while in his childhood, a "dreadful dream of the ineluctable Wave...towering over the green islands." See *Biography*, 173.

1940, published a private translation of *Sir Orfeo* in 1944 for a wartime undergraduate class, and wrote the short story "Leaf by Niggle" for the *Dublin Review*.

Meanwhile, Lewis was publishing several books a year, and new Inkling Charles Williams was writing books and plays and lecturing to undergraduates at Oxford. During this time there was a religious awakening at the University, thanks in large measure to Lewis's radio talks, later published as *Mere Christianity*. During the war, Tolkien gave up his car and became an air-raid warden while Lewis joined the Home Guard and his brother Warnie was called to active service. Tolkien still worked on the *Lord of the Rings*, and read E. R. Eddison's fantastical novels in 1942. Eddison was invited to Inklings meetings, and Lewis came to admire him as a writer of genius. Tolkien enjoyed his novels (except his character portrayals) for their "sheer literary merit."[11]

Tolkien bogged down in the *Lord of the Rings* in 1943 and expressed his depression and feelings in "Leaf by Niggle," triggered when a neighbor cut down her tree. Lewis persuaded Tolkien to start writing again in 1944, and he wrote with great inspiration, sending his work for Christopher to read while stationed in South Africa. The *Lord of the Rings* lay dormant for nearly two years, while Tolkien thought about and revised "The Lost Road." Lewis published *Perelandra*, the second of his "space novels" in 1943, and he and Tolkien considered collaborating on a book about language, which was never initiated.

Six days after the war ended (May 1945), Charles Williams died. Although Tolkien did not admire Williams's writings and was not influenced by him, he did love him as a person and Christian. On the day of Williams's death, he wrote a short letter to his widow, expressing his sympathy and telling her of his love for Charles and the grief he felt at his passing. The Inklings

---

[11] Eric Rucker Eddison (1882–1945) was a noted British fantasy writer and Old Norse scholar. His most popular work was *The Worm Ouroboros* (1922), now considered a masterpiece.

continued and became an Oxford institution, attracting several second-generation members. Thursday evening meetings were sometimes cheered with gifts of food from admirers (mostly in the United States), and several times the group was sent ham dinners from an American doctor in Maryland. During the Christmas holiday of 1945, Tolkien began work on "The Notion Club Papers," which was inspired in part by the Inklings. That same year his son John was ordained a priest in the Catholic church.

In early 1946 Tolkien resumed his work on the *Lord of the Rings*, and it was read to the Inklings by Christopher. With money scarce, Tolkien sold his home on 20 Northmoor Road (Headington, a few miles from Lewis) because it was too large and all the children except Priscilla had grown up and left. They moved to a smaller home on Manor Road owned by Merton College in the spring of 1947 and lived there for about three years. That same year Christopher was sometimes forbidden to read to the Inklings from the *Lord of the Rings* when Hugo Dyson attended, because of his dislike for "hobbitry." (Lewis did not read his Narnian stories to the Inklings because Tolkien did not like them.) Also in 1947 Tolkien rewrote the "Riddles in the Dark" chapter of the *Hobbit* to coordinate it with events in the *Lord of the Rings*.

The *Lord of the Rings* was "finished" in 1948. Tolkien was then able to resume his professional writing, and he published several pieces for *English Studies* and other academic journals. In 1949 he typed the *Lord of the Rings*, and the last Inklings meeting was held on 20 October of that year, although some of the group still continued to meet at the Eagle and Child.

From 1945 to 1959 Tolkien was Merton Professor of English Language and Literature at Oxford and a Fellow at Merton College. During this time there was a gradual cooling of his friendship with C. S. Lewis. The reasons for this have been debated, but some were Lewis's criticism of Tolkien's non-alliterative poems in the *Lord of the Rings*, Tolkien's dislike of the Narnian stories (1950–1956) and the fact that Lewis drew some of his ideas for them from Tolkien's mythology; that Lewis wrote them all in seven years, while the *Lord of the Rings* took Tolkien about fourteen; Lewis's quick ascent from convert to "popular theologian" for the masses; that Lewis never became a Catholic and remained Anglican; Lewis's friendship with Charles Williams, and later, Lewis's marriage to Joy Gresham. Lewis and Tolkien still remained friends, but the old intimacy never returned after the war. Tolkien continued to attend Inklings meetings, but Christopher was often asked to read passages from the *Lord of the Rings* (when Dyson was absent), as Lewis claimed he read better than his father. This was an accurate assessment, as Tolkien, though very articulate, still tended to "lecture to himself" while speaking fast and mumbling at the same time. Christopher later gained a reputation as the second best lecturer at Oxford next to Lewis, who always commanded large crowds whenever he spoke, especially to undergraduates and church groups.

Oxford Years–Later Period

Tolkien, Edith, and Priscilla moved in 1950 from Manor Road to another home owned by Merton College on Hollywell Street. This seventeenth-century semi-detached house with a large number of rooms boasted a small garden and high "medieval" wall that divided it from the New College gardens. It was angled back from the street, prompting Christopher to remark that it looked like "someone leaning back after a good dinner." On 22 June 1952 Tolkien offered the *Lord of the Rings* to Allen & Unwin, who sent Raynor Unwin to Oxford to secure the manuscript; the contract was signed in November. He had to stop work on the *Silmarillion* to complete the *Lord of the Rings* and check the proofs, and continued to revise and rework his manuscript even after the book was sent to type. At this time Tolkien found his neighborhood too noisy, so he and Edith moved back to Headington, to 76 Sandfield Road, where they stayed until 1968.

Volume One of the *Lord of the Rings* was finished by April 1953 and Volume Two soon after, with Christopher drawing and editing the maps. Tolkien bogged down in the appendices and finally finished them two years later, in May 1955. During this time he was able to complete some academic work, including his essay on Beorhtnoth and a philological piece, "Middle English 'Losenger'" for a French journal. He gave a lecture on *Sir Gawain* in August 1953, worked on the *Ancrene Wisse*, and in 1954 received honorary doctorates from the Catholic University of Dublin and the University of Liège. On 29 July 1954, Allen & Unwin published the *Fellowship of the Ring*, and the *Two Towers* followed on 11 November.

Partly due to the influence of Tolkien, C. S. Lewis became Professor of Medieval and Renaissance English at Magdalene College, Cambridge, in 1954.[12] He would travel (usually by train) to Cambridge during the week, then spend weekends and Mondays at the Kilns in Oxford. He continued to visit with his friends at the Eagle and Child, but Tolkien attended few meetings. Tolkien finally finished the appendices to the *Lord of the Rings* in 1954 and afterwards went to Italy on holiday. He presented the O'Donnell Lecture "English and Welsh" in Oxford on 21 October 1955, the day after Allen & Unwin published the *Return of the King*. Lewis by this time was involved with the American writer Joy Davidman Gresham, and married her in January 1956 without telling Tolkien and many of his other friends. This probably was the final break in their close friendship. Tolkien was puzzled and even angered by the relationship, and being very conservative, could not understand why Lewis would even consider marrying a divorced woman. He may have also resented the fact that Joy, through no fault of her own, "intruded" on his relationship with Lewis, even though it was not the same as it had been. Ironically,

---

[12] Tolkien said later that it took "a lot of diplomacy" for Cambridge to persuade Lewis to accept the chair. See Carpenter, *Letters*, 351.

Edith, along with Katherine Farrer, became one of Joy's few friends at Oxford.[13]

In 1956 Tolkien received his first royalty check for the *Lord of the Rings*, a sum of £3,500. Marquette University (Milwaukee, Wisconsin) offered to purchase the manuscripts to the *Lord of the Rings* for $5,000, and they were delivered the next year. Tolkien visited Holland in the spring of 1958, and that year Joy Lewis was diagnosed with cancer. Tolkien retired from teaching at Oxford in June 1959 at the age of sixty-seven, and brought his books back from the college and converted his garage into an office-library. Allen & Unwin supplied him with a temporary secretary to answer his fan mail for the *Lord of the Rings*, which was selling steadily (but unspectacularly) in England in hardcover. In 1962 his translations of *Sir Gawain and the Green Knight* was published, and the *Ancrene Wisse* was finished. Edith became ill with arthritis, and she and Joy were in the hospital together in May 1960. This brought on a reconciliation with Lewis, and Joy died on 13 July 1960.

In 1961 Tolkien's aunt Jane Neave (Mabel Tolkien's younger sister) asked him for a "small book about Tom Bombadil," which resulted in the publishing of the *Adventures of Tom Bombadi*. The *Ancrene Wisse* was finally published in 1962, and Tolkien worked on his Númenorean stories, revised some of his early poems, and worked on "The Bovadium Fragments," a satire about Oxford that was never published. In the summer of 1963 Lewis suffered a heart attack and retired from his post at Cambridge, and Tolkien was awarded an Honorary Fellowship at Exeter College and an Emeritus Fellowship at Merton. On 22 November Lewis died, and Tolkien described his feelings as like an old tree "that was losing all its leaves," like an "axe-blow near the roots." He regretted the

---

[13] Katherine Farrer (1911–1972) was the wife of the noted Anglican theologian and preacher Austin Farrer. She was best known for her detective stories, including *The Missing Link* (1952), and *Gownsman's Gallows* (1957). She and Joy became such good friends that Joy typed the manuscript for the latter novel.

separation of friendship that both had endured, served at a memorial mass in Lewis's honor, and attended the funeral at Lewis's church, Holy Trinity (Headington), where Austin Farrer presided. Several weeks later he told his son Michael that he was still preoccupied with Lewis's death.

In early 1964 Allen & Unwin showed a real interest in publishing the *Silmarillion*, and did publish *Tree and Leaf*. In 1965 Tolkien was asked by an American publisher to write a preface for George MacDonald's the *Golden Key*, which he turned into *Smith of Wootton Major*, published the next year. In 1965, Ace Books announced its intention to publish an unauthorized version of the *Lord of the Rings* in paperback, taking advantage of a loophole in copyright law. Allen & Unwin asked Tolkien for revisions, hoping to copyright it again, but he revised the *Hobbit* instead, not finishing the revisions until August. Ballantine published the "authorized" paperback editions of the *Lord of Rings* (unrevised) in August, but not before Ace had published their editions a few weeks prior. The resulting publicity over these publications started the Tolkien "boom" in America, which spread to England, and Tolkien and his books became internationally known.

Last Years

Because so many people from all over the world, including members of the various Tolkien societies and reading groups, were swamping Tolkien with fan mail, he felt in desperate need of a permanent secretary. His last academic work was the *Jerusalem Bible* (1966), for which he helped in the translation of Jonah. He and Edith celebrated their golden wedding anniversary on 22 March 1966 at Merton College, for which pianist and composer Donald Swann and soloist William Elven ("a name of good omen!" Tolkien said) performed Swann's Tolkien song-cycle the *Road Goes Ever On*. He continued to work on the *Rings* stories and accounts, including "The Palantíri," "The Disaster of the

Gladden Fields," "Cirion and Eorl," "Fords of Isen," and others, including linguistic works. That summer Professor Clyde S. Kilby from Wheaton College (Illinois) came to visit and help him with the *Silmarillion*.[14]

Late that year he was interviewed by a former student, Daphne Castell, who asked him what his favorite passages were from the *Lord of the Rings*. He told her two places in the story "stayed in his mind" longer than others. One was the point at which the cock crowed in the pause before the great battle of Pelennor Fields, when Gandalf was about to confront the King of the Nazgûl—the cock crowed, "welcoming the morning," then the horns of the riders of Rohan sounded. The other was when Gollum returned after making a bargain with Shelob, saw Sam and Frodo asleep, and for a moment "the evil and malice died out of his face." Miss Castell recorded that Tolkien told her that Gollum here "is about to repent," that Sam waking up spoiled his chance, but Gollum had no chance, "because he'd been evil too long."[15]

Edith suffered badly with arthritis, and the two-story home on Sandfield Road became too much for her to manage. Tolkien continually had to deal with unwanted intrusions on their privacy from fans, so in June 1968 they moved to Bournemouth, a seaside resort town they had visited often, on England's south coast about 100 miles from London. Edith loved it, and was far happier there than in Oxford, because for the first time in her life she had a lot of friends. On their holidays they stayed at the old Victorian Miramar Hotel, and the social scene there was unintellectual, affluent, and very friendly. They moved to a bungalow on Lakeside Road, very near the hotel and Sacred Heart Catholic Church, where they worshiped. They enjoyed central heating and separate bathrooms (for the first time), and also had a new kitchen and a verandah,

---

[14] Professor Kilby later published an account of that summer in a delightful little book, *Tolkien and the Silmarillion* (Wheaton IL: Harold Shaw, 1976).

[15] Castell, "The Realms of Tolkien," *New Worlds SF* 50 (November 1966): 143–54. This article was reprinted on the Internet ("Fantastic Metropolis") at www.sfsite.com.

where they could sit and smoke and talk in the evenings. The house had a large garden, and near the back of it was a gate that opened to a small wood leading to the ocean. Their neighbors would take them to church, there was domestic help readily available, and the Miramar was close enough to visit and renew old acquaintances. The garage was converted into a study, and Allen & Unwin finally did provide Tolkien with a secretary, Joy Hill, who visited regularly and became a close friend of the family.

By this time Tolkien was making a lot of money, as sales of the *Lord of the Rings* and the *Hobbit* had exploded. He was generous with his newly-acquired wealth and anonymously gave large amounts to his parish church in Headington in the last years. He also provided well for members of his family. He bought a house for Priscilla, a car for another of the children, gave a cello to a grandson, and paid school fees for a granddaughter. But he watched every penny, remembering his early days of heavy expense and little income, and was not extravagant in his purchases. He and Edith did not buy electrical "gadgets" for the house, nor did they ever own a television, a washing machine, or a dishwasher. But he did indulge in some extravagances, particularly new clothes for himself (he loved new shoes) and Edith, and expensive dinners with wine when they would shop in Oxford.

After three years at Bournemouth he still periodically worked on the *Silmarillion*, but would often become tired and not work for days. In the middle of November 1971, Edith was rushed to the hospital with an inflamed gallbladder, and after a few days of severe illness and pain, she died in a nursing home on Monday, 29 November at the age of eighty-two. After Tolkien recovered a bit, he decided to return to Oxford, and Merton College provided him with a flat at 21 Merton Street very near the college. Charlie Carr, the college scout, and his wife Mavis lived in the basement, and in addition to acting as caretakers for Tolkien and attending to the flat, they would invite him to meals with their family and cook for him if he was ill or did not want to dine at the college. The Carrs became his closest friends and confidants, and he was a great favorite of their own children and their granddaughters.

In the last eighteen months of his life Tolkien stayed as active as possible. He visited his children and grandchildren, took Priscilla and grandson Simon on holiday, visited his old T.C.B.S. friend Christopher Wiseman, spent several weeks with his son John at his parish at Stoke-on-Trent, and visited his brother Hilary, living on his farm at Evesham. He also received many academic honors and invitations, which made him very happy. He received and turned down several invitations to speak at American universities and receive doctorates. In 1972 he visited Buckingham Palace to receive the C.B.E. (Commander of the British Empire, the highest "civilian" award in England) from the queen, and in June 1973 was awarded an Honorary Doctorate from the University of Edinburgh; while there he and Priscilla stayed with his old friend Professor Angus McIntosh, a former student. The most personally gratifying award came from the University of Oxford, which in June 1972 awarded him an honorary Doctorate of Letters, not for the *Lord of the Rings* but for his "contributions to philology." The speech in his honor was given by his old friend and fellow Inkling Colin Hardie, who included several references to Middle-earth and concluded his talk with the hope that Tolkien would continue to produce (the) "Silmarillion and scholarship."[16]

Tolkien told his friend and former student Mary Salu that he expected to live for a long time, based on the longevity history of his ancestors. But in late 1972, after suffering severe indigestion on several occasions, he was advised by his doctors to go on a diet and drink no more wine. He was often lonely, and although he received callers regularly and kept up a regular schedule of short walks in the Botanic Garden near where he lived, meetings with his solicitor, drives to church, and visits to Edith's gravesite in

---

[16] The Scotsman Colin Hardie (1906–1998) was Fellow and classical tutor at C. S. Lewis's Magdalen College, and from 1967 to 1973 was Public Orator at Oxford University.

Wolvercote cemetery, his family and close friends noticed that he had changed. He often seemed depressed and distant, and it was evident that he was aging quickly. On Tuesday, 28 August 1973, he traveled to Bournemouth to visit Denis and Jean Tolhurst, the doctor and his wife with whom he and Edith had become friends with at Sacred Heart Church. On Thursday he joined in the celebrations for Jean's birthday, but did not feel well, although he did drink some champagne. During the night he was in severe pain, and the next morning was taken to a private hospital where he was diagnosed with an acute bleeding ulcer. At first his prognosis was positive, but by Saturday it had worsened and he contracted a chest infection. On early Sunday morning 2 September 1973, Ronald Tolkien died, aged eighty-three.

His requiem mass was held in Oxford with his son John as chief celebrant, at the Church of St. Anthony of Padua on Headley Way in Headington, where he had attended for many years. Tolkien was buried beside Edith in Wolvercote cemetery, and his gravestone reads, "Edith Mary Tolkien, Lúthien, 1889–1971; John Ronald Reuel Tolkien, Beren, 1892–1973."

Biographical Resources

For a complete treatment of Tolkien's life and career, the reader should consult the standard biographies by Humphrey Carpenter, *The Inklings* (1979), and *Tolkien: A Biography* (2000; formerly *Tolkien*, 1977). These works, especially the latter, are likely never to be superseded, and Carpenter provided meticulous detail in chronicling the life of Tolkien, particularly dates, times, places, friends, and influences. Also extremely valuable are Tolkien's collected letters, edited by Carpenter. These provide much insight to him as a man and artist, to his thoughts and emotions concerning his own work, to the genesis and continual creation of his Middle-earth tales, and his reactions to what he accomplished. The letters also provide valuable information about his thoughts and ideas about religion, Christianity, and politics, his own foibles and eccentricities (often humorous), and his love for and advice to his children. An older work by Deborah Rogers, *J. R. R. Tolkien: A Critical Biography* (New York: Hippocrene Books, 1980), is still a very good resource for reading and understanding Tolkien, and was written in a highly entertaining and eclectic style. A recent work edited by Joseph Pearce, *Tolkien: A Celebration*, contains several excellent essays about Tolkien's Catholic Christianity, his personhood, and his friends. The discerning Tolkien reader should try to obtain a copy of the *Proceedings of the J. R. R. Tolkien Centenary Conference* (ed. Patricia Reynolds & Glen H. Goodknight), held at Oxford's Keble College in 1992. This resource contains over sixty well-written essays about Tolkien and his career and writings, including a chronology of his life by Nancy Martsch.

The Hobbit and Other Works for Children

Tolkien evidently did not have a high opinion of the *Hobbit*, particularly after its publication (1937) and during the time of his continued work on the *Silmarillion* and the writing and publishing of the *Lord of the Rings*. In a December 1937 letter to G. E. Selby he wrote: "I don't much approve of the *Hobbit* myself, preferring my own mythology...with its consistent nomenclature...and organized history...to this rabble of Eddaic-named dwarves..."[1] In later correspondence with W. H. Auden, Tolkien told the poet that the *Hobbit* was "unhappily meant" as a children's story and that it contained some of the "silliness" of certain children's books he had read in his childhood. And in a draft of a letter (April 1959, never sent) he said that the *Hobbit* was "published hurriedly and without due consideration," and was not addressed specifically to children as an audience, but came out of his made-up stories for his own children. He further added that the *Hobbit* was a "first essay or introduction" to the *Lord of the Rings*.[2]

---

[1] Christopher Tolkien, ed., *The Return of the Shadow* (Boston: Houghton Mifflin, 1988) 7.

[2] Humphrey Carpenter, *The Letters of J. R. R. Tolkien* (London: Allen & Unwin, 1981) 297–98.

And he remembered only some of its origins: "All I can remember about the start of the *Hobbit* is sitting correcting School Certificate papers in the everlasting weariness of that annual task forced on impecunious academics with children. On a blank leaf I scrawled: 'In a hole in the ground there lived a hobbit.'"[3] Tolkien could not remember exactly when he wrote these words, although once he said it was after 1930. But his eldest sons John and Michael remembered hearing parts of the story read to them and their younger brother Christopher by their father between 1926–1930, and Michael wrote imitation hobbit stories ("apocryphal Hobbitry") that he dated 1929. He later guessed that his father started writing the story sometime between the summer of 1928 and continued it into 1929. John later told the BBC that his father read to them parts of the story for several Christmases, and Christopher remembered hearing it read to the boys in their winter "reads" after tea in the evening.[4]

Enough of the story had been written by late 1932 or early 1933 that Tolkien showed it to C. S. Lewis. In an early 1933 letter to his friend Arthur Greeves, Lewis mentioned that he had delighted in reading it, that it was "good" except the end (Lewis's version did not have Tolkien's later added chapters), and that there was a question to whether or not the story would succeed with "modern children." Tolkien's former student Elaine Griffiths remembered Tolkien lending her an early typed copy of the *Hobbit*, and that she read it with "enormous pleasure" and thought it was wonderful. In 1936, when she worked for Allen & Unwin, Griffiths, while working on a translation of *Beowulf*, was visited in Oxford by her friend Susan Dagnall, who also worked for the

---

[3] Ibid., 215.

[4] Humphrey Carpenter puts the date in 1930 or 1931, stating that the version of the story the boys heard may have been have been oral, or "impromptu tales." See *J. R. R. Tolkien: A Biography* (Boston: Houghton Mifflin, 2000) 181. This was verified by Tolkien in a letter dated 16 July 1964, when he said he invented and told stories to his children and sometimes wrote them down. See Carpenter, *Letters*, 346.

publisher. Griffiths recommended the *Hobbit* to Dagnall, who met Tolkien and took a borrowed copy of the story back to London.

Dagnall read and approved the story, then returned it to Tolkien, suggesting that he finish it (the incomplete story ended with the death of the dragon) and submit it for publication in 1937. Tolkien finished the story in late September 1936, and sent it to Allen & Unwin on 3 October. Stanley Unwin gave the manuscript to his ten-year-old son Raynor for review, for the standard fee of one shilling. Young Raynor liked the story, and a sentence from his review is worth noting: "He (Bilbo Baggins) had a very exciting time fighting goblins and wargs. At last they got to the lonely mountain; Smaug, the dragon who gawreds it is killed and after a terrific battle with the goblins he returned home—rich!"[5] Raynor thought the story was "good," did not need any illustrations, and thought it would be enjoyed by all children between the ages of five and nine.

Allen & Unwin's production department had some difficulties with the five maps planned for the book, and after discussion with Tolkien, they asked him to design them, with two eventually being used, Thror's Map and the Wilder land (Mirkwood) Map. After much discussion, many letters back and forth from Unwin and Tolkien, and several revisions, the British first edition of the *Hobbit* was published on 21 September 1937, with an initial printing of 1,500 copies, 150 of these review and sample copies. The book's complete title was the *Hobbit or There and Back Again Being the Record of a Years Journey Made by Bilbo Baggins of Hobbiton Compiled from his Memoirs*. It included "Thror's Map" (front endsheets), "Wilder land" (back endsheets), and ten additional illustrations by Tolkien: "The Hill: Hobbiton Across the Water," "The Trolls," "The Mountain-path," "The Misty Mountains Looking West from the Eyrie towards Goblin's Gate," "Beorn's Hall," "Mirkwood" (color), "The

---

[5] Wayne G. Hammond, *J. R. R. Tolkien: A Descriptive Bibliography* (New Castle DE: Oak Knoll Books, 1993) 8.

Elvenking's Gate," "Lake Town," "The Front Gate," and "The Hall at Bag-End, Residence of B. Baggins Esquire." Tolkien also designed the dust jacket (with several revisions) and drew the designs for the cover, which included dragons, mountains, moon, runes, and sun.

Tolkien wrote a descriptive blurb for the British edition, and part of it read, "If you care for journeys there and back, out of the comfortable Western world, over the edge of the Wild, and home again, and can take an interest in a humble hero (blessed with a little wisdom and a little courage and considerable good luck), here is the record of such a journey and such a traveler...you will learn by the way...much about trolls, goblins, dwarves, and elves, and get some glimpses into the history and politics of a neglected but important period."[6]

He received his advance copy of the book on 13 August 1937, it was published on 21 September, and the first printing was sold out by 15 December. A second printing of 2,300 copies was released on 25 January 1938 and sold out quickly, although over 400 copies of these (in sheets) were destroyed in warehouse by Hitler's bombs. The first US edition was published by Houghton Mifflin (Boston) on 1 March 1938, by June nearly 3,000 copies had been sold, and by the end of 1938 over 5,000 copies had been sold.

By 1947 the British edition was in its fourth impression, by 1991 it was reported that annual sales had reached 100,000 copies, and the 1992 centenary printing of 80,000 copies was sold out before publication. Since 1937, and after the success of the *Lord of the Rings*, the *Hobbit* has been reprinted scores of times by several publishers, in paperback, anniversary, children's, special, "gift," and even comic editions, and estimates of its sales to the present day have approached fifty million copies worldwide. It has been translated into over twenty-five languages, including Swedish (the

---

[6] Douglas A. Anderson, *The Annotated Hobbit* (Boston: Houghton Mifflin, 1988) 3.

first, 1947), Hebrew, French, Estonian, Bulgarian, Japanese, and Dutch.

After Tolkien submitted his *Hobbit* manuscript to Allen and Unwin, an editor there complained about his spelling of "dwarves," and pointed out that the *OED* spelled it "dwarfs." Tolkien's reply was: "I *wrote* the *Oxford English Dictionary!*"[7] This must not have helped, because the first British paperback edition (Puffin, 1961) contained several notable misprints, including "dwarves" and "elvish" being changed to "dwarfs" and "elfish."[8] Ballantine (a Houghton Mifflin imprint), which published the first US paperback edition (1965), did not include Tolkien's revisions or consult him about the design of the dust jacket.

Most of the early reviews were good, with many reviewers comparing the *Hobbit* to Lewis Carroll's *Alice in Wonderland* and *Through the Looking-Glass*. C. S. Lewis reviewed the book twice anonymously, in the 2 October 1937 issue of the *Times Literary Supplement*, and in the 8 October 1937 issue of the *Times*. In the first review, he wrote that the *Hobbit* "may well prove to be a classic," and in the second he said that Tolkien had united several things, including humor, an understanding of children, and "a happy fusion of the scholar's with the poet's grasp of mythology." In the United States, Anne Eaton reviewed the *Hobbit* for the *New York Times Book Review* and *Horn Book Magazine* and said the work was "written with a quiet humor and the logical detail in which children take delight." William R. Bent, writing for *Saturday Review of Literature*, called the *Hobbit* "a gorgeous

---

[7] Deborah Rogers quoted with approval an anecdote from Daniel Grotta-Kurska's usually unreliable biography (93). See Rogers, *Tolkien: A Critical Biography* (New York: Hippocrene Books, 1980) 20, 128. The 1933 edition of the *OED* (vol. 3, p. 732) defined *dwarf* as "one of a supposed race of diminutive beings, who figure in Teutonic and esp. Scandinavian mythology and folklore; often identified with the elves..."

[8] This would happen to Tolkien again, with the publication of the *Lord of the Rings*.

fancy." In May of 1938 the *New York Herald Tribune* awarded the book a $250 prize in an annual children's festival, calling it the best book published that spring for younger children. Sinclair Lewis's young son Michael (aged seven) called the *Hobbit* "an adorable story" (for an advertising blurb for Houghton Mifflin), and Tolkien provided a drawing of a hobbit for Houghton Mifflin's fall advertising push, which was printed in the Christmas edition of *Horn Book Magazine*.

Tolkien did not plan for the *Hobbit* to have a sequel. When the *Lord of the Rings* was nearing its completion in 1947, he understood that he would have to change the account of how Bilbo obtained the Ring, as in the original version the ring had magical powers but was not the Ring of Power, the One Ring. Tolkien then revised parts of chapter five of the *Hobbit* to show that Gollum planned to kill Bilbo from the beginning, and that his ring was the One Ring. This revised version was published in the second edition of the *Hobbit* in 1951, along with a note from Tolkien explaining that this version was "the true story" that Bilbo eventually told Gandalf.

Tolkien said several times that his inspiration for the story of Bilbo Baggins was derived from many sources, particularly the epics, myths, and fairy stories he had previously read, many of them in his childhood. Some of his sources included his own *Silmarillion, Beowulf,* the old Norse *Elder Edda, Sir Orfeo,* George MacDonald's *Princess and the Goblin* and *Princess and Curdie* (the "Victorian exceptions"), the fairy tales of the Brothers Grimm and Andrew Lang, and E. A. Wyke-Smith's the *Marvellous Land of Snergs*.[9] Tolkien's former student and friend

---

[9] See "On Fairy-Stories," *Essays Presented to Charles Williams,* ed. C. S. Lewis (London: Oxford University Press, 1947) footnote 15. The name "Middle-earth" came from the *Elder Edda*: "Odin fashioned Midgard or Middle Earth..." One also wonders how Tolkien would have used the Grimms' stories had he known that several modern works have debunked the tales as politically motivated, derived from educated middle-class French sources instead of peasants and other people of the land, and radically rewritten and passed off as

S. T. R. O. d'Ardenne wrote that Tolkien's own *Father Christmas Letters* were the origin of the *Hobbit*, along with his "great love of his own children that prompted him to invent and create the delightful hobbits and their mythology." The *Father Christmas Letters* might be discounted as a source for the *Hobbit*, since Miss d'Ardenne further mentioned the letters containing adventures of hobbits. There are elves, goblins, and a delightful polar bear in the *Father Christmas Letters*, but no hobbits.[10]

In January 1938, the *London Observer* published a letter asking Tolkien to tell his readers more about hobbits and suggesting that he might have been influenced by an article by Julian Huxley, which described "little furry men" seen in Africa by natives and "at least one scientist." The letter also mentioned an old (1904) fairy tale called "The Hobbit," and asked if the cup-stealing scene in Tolkien's tale was from *Beowulf*. Tolkien responded with a long letter, explaining that he had no recollection from his reading about "furry pigmies" in Africa, nor of the hobbit fairy tale. He protested that his hobbits did not live in Africa, had fur only on their feet, and that the two hobbits in the *Observer* were "accidental homophones" (a word having the same sound as another but meaning something quite different). Tolkien went on to say that he did not remember anything about the name and inception of Bilbo (the hero), and that he would leave the game of guessing the origins of hobbits to "future researchers."[11] Years later, he told an interviewer that the word *hobbit* might have been derived from Sinclair Lewis's *Babbitt* (1922). Tolkien had

---

genuine German folktales. See Kathryn Lindskoog, *Fakes, Frauds & Other Malarkey* (Grand Rapids MI: Zondervan, 1993) 85–86, and John Ellis, *One Fairy Story Too Many* (Chicago: University of Chicago Press, 1985).

[10] See S. T. R. O. d'Ardenne, "The Man and the Scholar," in *J. R. R. Tolkien, Scholar and Storyteller: Essays in Memoriam*, ed. Mary Salu and Robert T. Farrell (Ithaca NY: Cornell University Press, 1979) 34. Dr. d'Ardenne may have remembered hobbit stories being told during Christmas seasons after the Father Christmas letters arrived at the Tolkien home.

[11] See Carpenter, *Letters*, 30–32.

evidently read the novel, as he commented that "Babbitt has the same bourgeois smugness that hobbits do."[12]

There have been several other theories about the origin of hobbits. In British folklore there are several examples of certain wraiths and elves called *hobs*, *hobthrusts* (a good-natured goblin or "local spirit, famous for whimsical pranks"), and *hobyahs*, while *hob* is an old word for "rustic" or "clown," and a *hoball* or *hoblob* or *hobbil* or *hob-hald* is a "clown" or "fool."[13] Tom Shippey mentioned a collection of folklore tales called the *Denham Tracts* that describe supernatural creatures, written by Michael A. Denham and edited by Dr. James Hardy, which were published in two volumes in 1892 and 1895. In volume two, the word *hobbit* is mentioned as a "class of spirit."[14] Tolkien's hobbits were certainly not "spirits," and he could have known about them from the Denham book, but we will probably never know. In 1977, a Tolkien journal stated that the *London Times* reported (6 May 1977) that the word *hobbit* had been found in a 1586 catalogue of "hobgoblins, boggarts, and other fantastic creatures."[15]

Tolkien once told an interviewer that hobbits were "just rustic English people" that he made small in stature to reflect their (generally) small imaginations. Humphrey Carpenter wrote that hobbits were not small when it came to courage or "latent power," because they represented for Tolkien the combination of small imagination and courage he had seen and experienced in the trenches of World War I.[16] The creation of hobbits was perhaps

---

[12] See Anderson, *Annotated Hobbit*, 5.

[13] From the 1933 edition of the *Oxford English Dictionary*.

[14] See Shippey, *J. R. R. Tolkien: Author of the Century* (London: HarperCollins, 2000) 3.

[15] *Mythprint 15/5* (June 1977): 1. *Mythlore 16* (vol. 4, no. 4, June 1977) inside back page.

[16] Carpenter, *Biography*, 180. In Robert Foster's *The Complete Guide to Middle-Earth* (New York: Ballantine, 2001, 253) hobbits are described as "in times of danger courageous, skillful, and relatively undaunted by great terrors." Verlyn Flieger pointed out that "their (hobbits) stature as little people makes them the ideal embodiment of the common man...not consciously heroic, hobbits

one way Tolkien remembered and celebrated the courage of "quite small people" surviving and even flourishing against a huge and formidable enemy.

The *Hobbit* took place in the Third Age of Middle-earth, and chronologically precedes the *Lord of the Rings*. The peace-and food-loving Bilbo Baggins did not want to be a hero; all he wanted to do was stay at home. Bilbo's parents were Bungo Baggins and Belladonna Took—members of the Took family were known for their adventurous spirit. On a late April morning in 2941 of the Third Age, an old man named Gandalf arrived at Bilbo's home in the Shire, called Bag-End. Gandalf was a wizard (a lesser Valar), who had been sent to Middle-earth to help in the resistance against the evil Sauron. Bilbo invited Gandalf for tea the next week, and to his surprise, Gandalf returned, bringing with him thirteen dwarves, their leader being Thorin Oakenshield, heir to the dwarf kingdom of Erebor. Bilbo was stunned when he discovered that he had been recruited to help recover Thorin's treasure, which had been stolen and ravaged by the great winged dragon Smaug and was being hoarded at his lair, the Lonely Mountain east of Mirkwood, under which lay the abandoned kingdom of Erebor. Gandalf deceived Bilbo by scratching a message on his front door, advertising him as a burglar who was looking for a job that provided excitement.

The rest of the *Hobbit* detailed Bilbo's journey to the Lonely Mountain and his adventures with the dwarves, which in the early stage included a frightening incident with man-eating trolls. The party was ambushed by a band of orcs in a mountain pass, escaped by going underground into the Chamber of the Great Goblin, were rescued by Gandalf from the Goblin, and while being pursued by orcs were led by Gandalf into the mountain. In a battle with the orcs Bilbo hit his head on a rock, was accidently left behind, and after he awoke, followed a tunnel and accidently found the Great

---

do their jobs." See Flieger, *Splintered Light: Logos and Language in Tolkien's World* (Grand Rapids MI: Eerdmans, 1983) 134–35.

Ring, which he placed in his pocket. He continued following the tunnel, which led to an underground lake where Gollum ("a small, slimy creature") lived, and later escaped from Gollum when he slipped the Ring on his finger and became invisible. Bilbo then made his way out of the mountain underground to safety and rejoined his party.

Well on their way, the little party again encountered and battled orcs and was rescued by the Lord of the Eagles of Middle-earth, Gwaihir. Gandalf led the party to the home of Beorn, an amazing man who can change his body into the form of a bear. They then headed toward the perilous Mirkwood Forest, which they had to cross in order to reach the Lonely Mountain. When they reached the forest, Gandalf left to help fight Sauron at his fortress at Southern Mirkwood, and the party entered the forest alone. While traveling through the forest, they nearly drowned when crossing a river, and they saw visions of elves. Bilbo was captured by and fought a giant spider, rescued the dwarves from other spiders, and after all the chaos, discovered that Thorin was missing.

Thorin was captured by Wood-elves, and later the rest of the dwarves were captured and taken into dungeons. Bilbo escaped by placing the Ring on his finger, and eventually rescued his friends and sent them on barrel-rafts downstream on the Forest River toward Lake-town (Esgaroth), located on Long Lake. Thorin told the citizens of the town that he was the heir to the kingdom of Erebor, rallying the people around him. They helped prepare the little band for their assault on the Lonely Mountain, the home of Smaug. Once on the mountain, the party searched for its secret entrance (a distance away from the entrance of the dragon's lair), Bilbo placed the Ring on his finger, entered the cave alone, and found Smaug asleep on top of all the treasure. Bilbo took a huge two-handled cup, and fled back to his friends. Smaug woke, missed the cup flew into a rage, and went on an enraged search for the dwarves, who narrowly escaped into the tunnel. The next day Bilbo returned to Smaug's lair, and while in conversation (he wears the Ring and is still invisible) he mentioned that he is "the ringwinner and luckwearer and barrel-rider." This so infuriated Smaug that he flew off to destroy Lake-town, and though he set it on fire, an arrow from the bow of Bard the Bowman found the one vulnerable spot in his armor, and Smaug fell to his death in the lake.

After the dwarves celebrated and reclaimed their treasure, Wood-elves and Lake-men sent armies for their shares. Thorin refused to divide his wealth, and a major battle was averted when Gandalf came and warned them of an army of orcs headed their way. The battle between the orcs and the dwarves and elves lasted for hours (with Bilbo staying invisible most of the time), until the Eagles and Beorn (in his bear shape) intervened and defeated the orcs. Thorin was buried under the mountain, his warrior kinsman Dáin claimed and rebuilt Erebor, and Bard became king of Dale, the city-kingdom of Men. Bilbo returned to Hobbiton and to his home, Bag-End, on 22 June 2942. Later he gained a reputation as one of the Shire's wealthiest and most eccentric citizens, and kept the Ring.

Phillip Martin wrote that in the subtitle of the *Hobbit*, *There and Back Again*, Tolkien "knows that there and back again is the very heart of adventure. To journey through Middle-earth is not just a series of stops…It is a journey through a mythic place…To leave home is perilous…Fantasy is about going otherwhere. We journey afar and then return—tracing a circular path of discovery."[17] C. S. Lewis praised the *Hobbit* and rightly predicted it would become a classic, saying that only after many readings would adults (who had read it as children) "begin to realize what deft scholarship and profound reflection have gone to make everything in it so ripe, so friendly, and in its own way so true."[18] And a prophetic reader for Houghton Mifflin wrote this

---

[17] Martin, ed., *The Writer's Guide to Fantasy Literature* (Waukesha WI: The Writer Books, 2002) 115–16.

[18] C. S. Lewis, *Of This and Other Worlds*, ed. Walter Hooper (London: Fount, 1989) 111.

recommendation (16 March 1937) after the finished manuscript of the *Hobbit* arrived at the publisher's offices: "...This is an almost impossible book to describe adequately...I enjoyed it immensely...It is fine for reading out loud. The author has, I think, just the right touch...The success of this book in this country is a great gamble...but it might very easily go like wildfire. To publish."[19]

Farmer Giles of Ham

Tolkien first told this improvised "lighthearted tale" to his children sometime after early 1926, when the family took shelter under a bridge during a rainstorm that had interrupted a picnic. The first draft was handwritten (26 pages) in the late 1920s (with "Daddy" as the narrator and many nameless characters); a revised and slightly expanded second draft probably was written (the first typescript) in the early or mid-1930s, with "the family jester" taking "Daddy's" place.

In early 1937, after the *Hobbit* had been accepted, Allen & Unwin asked Tolkien to submit other children's stories he was writing. In August 1938 he sent them *Mr. Bliss*, *Farmer Giles*, and his story about the dog "Roverandom."[20] As with the *Hobbit*, eleven-year-old Raynor Unwin read *Farmer Giles* (in 1937) and called it "well written and amusing" and recommended that it be published in one volume with "Roverandom," adding that it needed illustrations. But due to the success of the *Hobbit*, Allen & Unwin wanted a sequel with more hobbits, or at best, *Farmer Giles* and more stories like it. In December 1937 Tolkien started

---

[19] Memo from Houghton Mifflin Co., 2 Park St, Boston MA. 02107, to Friends of J. R. R. Tolkien. See *The Tolkien Journal* 3/1 (1967): 22–23.

[20] It is interesting that Tolkien, in a letter to Allen & Unwin in 1947, wrote emphatically that *Farmer Giles* was *not* written *for* children (his emphasis), but this "would not prevent them from being amused by it." See Carpenter, *Letters*, 119.

work on the *Lord of the Rings* as the sequel, but could not finish in time for the 1938 Christmas season, as Unwin hoped. In July 1938 he wrote Unwin and told them about a third further revised draft he had written, which was 50 percent longer than the previous version.[21] He read this version (now called "The Legend of Worming Hall") to an undergraduate society at Worcester College in January 1938, and said the students were not bored and "generally conversed with mirth."

Tolkien had this revision retyped by an academic copying office and retitled it the *Lord of Tame, Dominus de Domito: A Legend of Worminghall*, but he abandoned this title and returned to the title *Farmer Giles of Ham*. In this version Tolkien enlivened the story with proper names, philological jokes, and allusions, and developed the characters more carefully, particularly the dog (now called Garm), the dragon Chrysophylax Dives ("rich goldkeeper"), and the blacksmith Fabricus Cunctator.

In August 1938, Tolkien submitted the new version of the story to Unwin, and after waiting months with no response wrote a sarcastic letter to Unwin, asking "Did *Farmer Giles* in the enlarged form meet with any sort of approval?...Is it worth anything?"[22] Little or nothing happened after that, although Tolkien continued to ask Unwin about the book through the end of 1939. His work on the *Lord of the Rings* consumed him during World War II, and the question of the publication of *Farmer Giles* was discussed little until July 1946, when he wrote Sir Stanley Unwin, who had inquired about the progress of the *Lord of the Rings*. Tolkien told Unwin that he was sending *Farmer Giles* to David Unwin (the author "David Severn"), and added that if he had more leisure time, he could possibly add some similar stories to *Farmer Giles*. Severn read the story and was delighted by it, although he

---

[21] At least one scholar believed there was another draft (now lost), between the second and third revisions. See Taum Santoski, "The Boundaries of the Little Kingdom," in *Selections from the Marquette J. R. R. Tolkien Collection* (Milwaukee WI: Marquette University Library, 1987) 11–15.

[22] Carpenter, *Letters*, 46.

and the firm thought it was still too short to publish by itself. Unwin finally decided to publish the book in 1947, and in July Tolkien revised the manuscript, adding corrections and changes "in both style and narrative." He also added a "mock foreword" (the earliest version from October 1946), in which he pretended to be the editor and translator of an ancient document; he would do this again in the first edition of the *Lord of the Rings* and the *Adventures of Tom Bombadil*.[23]

Some Tolkien scholars think that this "mock foreword" is a satire of his famous lecture, "Beowulf: The Monsters and the Critics" (1936). In that seminal talk, Tolkien criticized those who saw *Beowulf* only as a museum piece, not a work of literary art. In his foreword to *Farmer Giles*, Tolkien as "editor" is only interested in the history of the "Little Kingdom" (Britain) and the origins of some of its place names: "An excuse for presenting a translation of this curious tale…may be found in the glimpse it affords of life in a dark period of Britain, not to mention the light that it throws on the origin of some difficult place-names."[24] Tolkien may not have consciously intended satire here, but in this foreword and in the story he was having fun at the expense of several types of people and institutions. Katharyn Crabbe wrote that Tolkien created a king (August Bonifacius) whose name means "doer of good" but who does no good, parodied *Sir Gawain and the Green Knight* and *Beowulf*, and poked fun at linguists. Tolkien takes this even further when he parodies language and the *Oxford English Dictionary*. The "Four Wise Clerks of Oxenford" (the editors of the *OED*) add to their definition of "blunderbuss" (farmer Giles's weapon of choice) by writing that the weapon is "now superseded in civilized countries by other firearms." Tolkien

---

[23] See the fiftieth anniversary edition of *Farmer Giles*, ed. Christina Scull and Wayne G. Hammond (Boston: Houghton Mifflin, 1999) viii.

[24] Ibid., 7.

was amused by this, but also (probably) appalled at the idea that improved firearms was a mark of a "civilized" country.[25]

After Tolkien submitted his revised manuscript to Unwin in 1947, its publication was delayed for more than a year. Since he had drawn no pictures for the story, an artist his daughter Priscilla recommended was commissioned to draw them. Her work was slow and inadequate, and she was later replaced by Pauline Diana Baynes, whose work delighted Tolkien. He called it "beyond expectations" and said that when he showed Baynes's illustrations to his friends, they commented that the illustrations "reduced my text to a commentary on the drawings."[26] In 1976 Miss Baynes drew new cover art for the second edition of *Farmer Giles*, in 1980 drew new full-page illustrations for a reprint of the story in *Poems and Stories*, and in 1999 drew a map of the Little Kingdom for the fiftieth anniversary edition, giving her a half century of association with *Farmer Giles of Ham*.[27]

After Tolkien made a few more corrections and changes, *Farmer Giles of Ham* (subtitle: "The Rise and Wonderful Adventures of Farmer Giles, Lord of Tame, Count of Worminghall and King of the Little Kingdom") was finally published in October 1949 in England, and in America the next year. Although it never became a classic like the *Hobbit*, *Farmer Giles* has sold well through the years and has been popular with readers of all ages. The story is set in pre-Saxon England, specifically in the Thames valley east of Oxford. The towns of Ham(mo), Oakley, Worminghall, Farthingho(e), and Oxenford (now Oxford) are

---

[25] See Crabbe, *J. R. R. Tolkien* (New York: Continuum, 1988) 150–52.

[26] Carpenter, *Letters*, 133.

[27] Pauline Diana Baynes (1922–) is still considered a world-class artist and illustrator. Along with Tolkien, she also drew for such famous writers as Amabel Williams-Ellis, Allison Uttley, Rumer Godden, Mary Piers, and Mary Norton. She was the first illustrator for C. S. Lewis's *The Chronicles of Narnia*, and in 1968 won Britain's coveted Kate Greenaway Medal for her work for Grant Uden's *Dictionary of Chivalry*, which took over two years to complete.

mentioned, as well as Ot Moor (west of Oxford), and the Cherwell, Thames, and Windrush rivers.

One night a deaf, nearsighted giant came to the village of Ham and trampled Farmer Giles's (full name Ægidius Ahenobarbus Julius Agricola de Hammo) fields and animals, including his favorite cow. Giles's talking dog Garm (who could not talk dog-latin) warned Giles of the giant, and Giles became a nonheroic hero when he fired his ancient blunderbuss at the giant (who thought it was horseflies), forcing him to leave. Farmer Giles reveled in the attention he received after that, became the inadvertent Hero of the Countryside, and received a testimonial letter and a sword (called Tailbiter, once owned by a famous dragon-slayer) from St. Michael the King. Later, the giant (not named) told a dragon named Chrysophylax Dives about the rich kingdom, and he came to investigate and possibly plunder, because times were hard.

As the dragon came closer to the village, Giles (under pressure to be a dragon hunter and clad in a comical suit of armor) and Garm went off to find and slay him. Chrysophylax (who had just eaten the village parson) greeted Giles with "Good morning," and after seeing the sword, a battle ensued and Giles wounded the dragon's wing, making him unable to fly. He ran instead and Giles pursued him all the way to the village. The dragon gave up just outside the church and offered Giles a bargain. He would, if Giles would let him go home, pay for all the damage he had done (and for the funerals of those he killed), and return with treasure for all the inhabitants of Ham (plus gold collars for the dogs).

Giles agreed, and the dragon left for the far-off mountains, never intending to return. The rest of the story involved political maneuvering by the king, a tiring journey (Giles and the king's effete knights) to capture the dragon, the dragon's capture and the triumphal return to the village, the taming and humbling of the dragon, and the elevation of Giles to prince and then king. This very funny and entertaining story is a traditional fairy tale, and in some ways Giles was a traditional hero who had greatness thrust upon him. He was an ordinary person caught up in events, and as the narrator (Tolkien) implied, his most important virtues were luck and wits, which he utilized very well.

In August 1938, Tolkien wrote Unwin about a planned sequel to *Farmer Giles*, and in February 1938 wrote his publisher again, saying that the sequel would include "the adventures of Prince George (Giles's son), the fat boy Suovertaurilius (vulgarly Suet), and the Battle of Otmoor."[28] The sequel (probably a fragment) was discarded and never added to or published. *Farmer Giles* was published several times in foreign languages, including Polish (1965); Finnish (1978); Icelandic (1979); Malay (1980). The book is dedicated to Colonel C. H. Wilkinson, the English tutor at Worcester College who "egged" Tolkien to publish it.

Smith of Wootton Major

In a letter to Roger Lancelyn Green (December 1967), Tolkien wrote that *Smith of Wootton Major* "was not intended for children" and was "an old man's book, already weighted with the presage of 'bereavement.'"[29] In 1964, Pantheon Books of New York asked him to write the preface to a new edition of George MacDonald's story the *Golden Key*, probably because of the success of his Middle-earth stories and because Tolkien had mentioned *The Golden Key* in his just published "On Fairy-Stories."[30] He started

---

[28] Carpenter, *Letters*, 43.

[29] Ibid., 388–89. Though not written for children, *Smith* can be enjoyed by them (several have told the author they enjoyed it as a child), at least on a simple level. It is included in this section because it is currently in print and was published in tandem with *Farmer Giles of Ham*.

[30] Humphrey Carpenter wrote that Tolkien thought "The Golden Key" was a bad book [sic], and that it was "ill-written" and "incoherent," despite a "few memorable passages." See Carpenter, *Biography*, 244. But in a letter to the editor at Pantheon (7 September 1964), Tolkien wrote that he "thought well" of MacDonald's story. See Carpenter, *Letters*, 351. And in "On Fairy-Stories" he wrote that *The Golden Key* was a story of power and beauty. See "On Fairy-

work on the preface in January 1965, and intended to show the meaning of the word "fairy" through a short tale about a cook and cake. This piece was meant to be only a few paragraphs long, but Tolkien continued writing and an independent story emerged with an existence of its own. Its first title was "The Great Cake," but Tolkien soon changed it to *Smith of Wootton Major*, meant to "suggest" a short story by P. G. Wodehouse or a story in the *Boys' Own Paper*.[31] Tolkien's preface to "The Golden Key" was never finished, and the story was published in 1967 by Farrar, Straus, and Giroux, with an afterword by W. H. Auden (who quoted Tolkien) and pictures by Maurice Sendak. The second edition (1976) included an endorsement by Tolkien from his comments about MacDonald's story in "On Fairy-Stories."

Allen & Unwin thought that *Smith* was too short to be published, and Tolkien had nothing suitable in his unpublished papers to go with it—the next year his shorter works were published by Ballantine in the *Tolkien Reader*. He was astonished when over 800 people attended a reading of the story at the Blackfriars Refrectory in downtown Oxford, on 26 October 1966. Hoping for good publicity (and sales, particularly if Houghton Mifflin published the story in the United States), Unwin sold *Smith* in April 1967 to *Redbook* magazine for use in their Christmas issue. Tolkien hoped (and anticipated) that the demand for the story would persuade Unwin to publish it alone as a Christmas gift book with illustrations by Pauline Baynes, or

---

Stories" in Christopher Tolkien, ed., *The Monsters and the Critics and Other Essays* (Boston: Houghton Mifflin, 1984) 125.

[31] *The Boys' Own Paper* (*BOP*) was a British juvenile magazine published from 1879 to 1967. Created by a conservative religious society, its aim was to compete with the "cheap and sensational 'blood and thunder' magazines and novelettes" ("penny dreadfuls") then thought to be a corrupting influence on the young. Some of its writers included Jules Verne and Arthur Conan Doyle. See Victor Watson, ed., *The Cambridge Guide to Children's Books in English* (Cambridge: Cambridge University Press, 2001) 100.

perhaps as an addition to the next edition of *Tree and Leaf*.[32] He preferred the former, and by July 1967 Miss Baynes had completed ten black and white drawings.

After Tolkien corrected the page proofs and moved a few illustrations, *Smith of Wootton Major* was published by Unwin in October, the *Redbook* edition was published on 23 November (without Miss Baynes's drawings), and the Houghton Mifflin edition was published (30,000 copies) one day later. The first "combined" edition of *Smith* and *Farmer Giles of Ham* was published by Ballantine in 1969, by Unwin in 1975 with *Tree and Leaf* and "The Homecoming of Beorhtnoth Beorhthelm's Son," in *Poems and Stories* in 1980, and by Unwin with "Leaf By Niggle" in 1983. The first foreign translations of *Smith* were in Dutch and Afrikaans (1968), and it has also been published in Swedish, German, Polish, Spanish, Japanese, and several others, including Hebrew.

Smith of Wootton Major was the last story Tolkien wrote, and it was written with sad emotion. He was advancing in age, tired, near retirement, and knew that his imaginative gifts would soon be extinguished and he would no longer be able to visit "the land of faery" with his imagination and intellect. *Smith* is a compliment to "On Fairy-Stories" in that it narrates the relationship between the realm of faery and the human world. In the medieval village of Wootton Major, the setting for *Smith*, it is possible (as in Middle-earth) to come from and go into the faeryland as one pleases. A disguised elvin-king, Alf (modeled after the chef at Tolkien's Merton College; "Alf" is an old Norse form of "elf"), was an apprentice to Nokes ("fool"), the bungling Master Cook for the village. Once every twenty-four years the village celebrated the Feast of Good Children in the Great Hall, and only twenty-four especially good children were invited. The Master Cook baked a

---

[32] Unwin published *Tree and Leaf* in 1964, which included "On Fairy-Stories" and "Leaf By Niggle." A later Houghton Mifflin edition (1988) added "Mythopoeia."

special cake (very sweet and rich) for these celebrations, and in midwinter one year he found a small tarnished silver star to put on top of the cake. The star was a *fay* (from faery) that Alf smuggled in, and a little boy (Smith) accidentally ate it.

Later the fay-star fell out of Smith's mouth, and he placed it on his forehead, where it stayed for many years. The star gave young Smith access to faery and wonder, and he quickly became renowned in the village for his beautiful singing, and when he grew older, for great skill at ironwork. He and Alf became friends, and sometimes he would travel to faeryland, where he experienced visions (some frightening) and wonders that he could not have imagined. He learned that faeryland was a "perilous realm" of contrasts; it was both dangerous and peaceful, joyful and tragic, and playful and serious. As another Feast of Good Children neared, Smith reluctantly put the star back into the cake. Alf was now the Master Cook, to whom Smith gave the star, and he revealed himself as the King of Faery. The story ended with joy and sorrow when Alf and Smith decided to pass on the star to Tim, the grandson of Nokes, instead of to Smith's son, Ned. Smith never returned to faeryland, and went home for good.

Paul Kocher wrote that *Smith of Wootton Major* was Tolkien's "personal farewell to his art," and in having Smith never return to faeryland, he was saying that a man (himself) "can become too old for wanderings in Faery," and that his imaginative powers "of apprehending its (Faery) marvels and translating them into art decay with age."[33] Most other Tolkien scholars believe that *Smith* is allegorical in at least some respects, and that there are specific "meanings" behind the obvious patterns and strands of the story. Jane Chance wrote that *Smith*, while less Christian and allegorical than "Leaf By Niggle," still emphasized Christian themes and concepts and provided the Christian "the reward of

---

[33] See Kocher, *Master of Middle-earth: The Fiction of J. R. R. Tolkien* (Boston: Houghton Mifflin, 1972) 203.

grace for humility and suffering."[34] Clyde Kilby interpreted it as primarily about the creative process (and the figure of Nokes as representing George MacDonald), and Humphrey Carpenter saw it as a "creative vent" for Tolkien's anxieties about old age.[35] It is probable that the story is both allegorical, with various meanings, and autobiographical at the same time.[36] Tom Shippey called it an "autobiographical allegory" and wrote that the story is Tolkien's "Valedictory Address" in which he "defends the real-world utility of fantasy, insists that fantasy and faith are in harmony as visions of a higher world, and hopes for a revival of both."[37]

Professor Clyde Kilby of Wheaton College spent a summer with Tolkien in the sixties, and wrote that Tolkien often "fired verbal cannonades" at MacDonald, called him "terrible," and said that his aversion to MacDonald had been the "explosion" that started him writing his own story.[38] Nevertheless, it is worthy to note that Tolkien may have been influenced positively by "The Golden Key." In this beautiful story (considered one of MacDonald's greatest fantasies), a boy (Mossy) and a girl (Tangle) set out separately on journeys to Faeryland. Mossy finds a golden key at the foot of a rainbow and searches through Faeryland for the lock that it will fit. Mossy meets Tangle on the way, they experience a series of strange adventures, and at the end are united in the Other World, where their perceptions are heightened. MacDonald's biographer wrote that the story presents an "aspect

---

[34] Chance, *Tolkien's Art*, (Lexington KY: University of Kentucky Press, 2001, rev. ed.) 99.

[35] See Kilby, *Tolkien and the Silmarillion* (Wheaton IL: Harold Shaw, 1976) 36; Carpenter, *Biography*, 244.

[36] Verlyn Flieger overviewed the various interpretations of *Smith* in her *A Question of Time: J. R. R. Tolkien's Road to Faërie* (Kent OH: Kent State University Press, 1997) 227–53. In her study of an unpublished Tolkien manuscript, in which he "debated with himself" about the question of allegory and *Smith*, Professor Flieger concluded there was an "allegorical impulse" in the story (234).

[37] See Shippey, *Author of the Century*, 303.

[38] Kilby, *Tolkien and the Silmarillion*, 36–37.

of the soul's orientation to spiritual reality" and it is a "vision of the sweep of life from the time a person's spirit is awakened...until (it progresses) beyond what the human imagination can reach."[39] As Tolkien grew older, he realized that he was at last near to that spiritual reality that had been just beyond the reach of his amazing imagination. *Smith of Wootton Major* may have been his final, graceful attempt to make a declaration to all who would read his words that he was, at last, ready to go and live in that Other World.

The Father Christmas Letters

Tolkien was Reader (Instructor) in English Language, then Professor at Leeds University from 1920–1925. At the Leeds Christmas party in 1920 someone masqueraded as Father Christmas, and soon after that three-year-old John Tolkien received the first "Father Christmas letter" from his father. For over twenty years (till 1943), John, then Michael, Christopher, and Priscilla received these delightful and charming letters at Christmas. The children wrote letters to Father Christmas for weeks before Christmastime, and the letters always mysteriously disappeared. Every Christmas the children opened their presents like all children everywhere, and they always found an extra gift—a letter from Father Christmas himself, postmarked "the North Pole," and even including a "North Pole" stamp. The letters the children received were really stories, stories about the goings-on at the North Pole and stories about the escapades and adventures of Polar Bear (Karhu, Father Christmas's chief helper) plus assorted snow-elves, red gnomes, snow-men, cave-bears, and

---

[39] Rolland Hein, *George MacDonald: Victorian Mythmaker* (Nashville: Star Song Publishing, 1993) 187. Colin Duriez noted that Tolkien was preoccupied with "good death," a theme that permeates all of MacDonald's work. See Duriez, *Tolkien and The Lord of the Rings: A Guide to Middle-Earth* (Mahwah NJ: Hidden Spring, 2001) 20.

Polar Bear's nephews, Paksu and Valkotukka. Later, the children discovered that Father Christmas hired a secretary (an elf named Ilbereth), and that elves defended his home against goblin attacks.

Wayne Hammond and Christina Scull wrote that to make the letters seem more authentic, Tolkien would give each character who "wrote" a distinctive script. Father Christmas (over 1000 years old) had a shaky handwriting; Polar Bear, with his thick paw, wrote at first in thick letters; and Ilbereth the elf had a "secretarial" handwriting.[40] The various envelopes were addressed with different colored inks and pencils, and they all came with carefully drawn "stamps," make-believe postcards, and instructions (usually) urging fast delivery, as the letter for 1932 implored: "By *gnome carrier* *. Immediate haste!" And sometimes Tolkien would write on the envelope an apology for the lateness of a letter, as in this from 1931: "I am so sorry I forgot to post this: Love Karhu" "*Urgent*—By flying messenger—*please*." In addition, he included many amusing figures, action scenes, and bright colors, which always appealed to his children.

In the first edition of *Father Christmas,* the second letter is dated 1925, and afterwards one per year was sent through 1938; the last letter is not dated. In the 1995 revised edition several more previously unpublished letters and drawings were added, with the letters going through 1943. The *Hobbit* was published in 1936, and the years from 1930–1933 contain the longest and possibly most interesting letters from Father Christmas. Although the letters were written purely for the enjoyment of his children, and Tolkien did not consciously include aspects of his mythology, there are some similar and corresponding details and characters. Among these include the elf Ilbereth, fireworks, bad goblins, good elves, and the "dwarvish" sound of Polar Bear's name Karhu. Also, Karhu invents an alphabet, in some ways acts and looks like Gandalf, has a temper that conceals his overall good nature and

---

[40] See Hammond and Scull, *J. R. R. Tolkien: Artist & Illustrator* (Boston: Houghton Mifflin, 1995) 69.

joy, and loves firecrackers. And in some ways he is like a hobbit. He is accident-prone, always gets into humorous trouble (especially when he floods Father Christmas's house with bathwater), and has two mischievous nephews who are reminiscent of Merry and Pippin. Hammond and Scull pointed out that in the 1933 letter, the enormous Polar Bear pictured may have been inspired by an account in the *Hobbit* that had been written by this time, Beorn's appearance as a huge bear in the Battle of Five Armies.[41]

The last letter to Priscilla (1943) was dark and pessimistic with a reference to the war: "people call it 'grim' this year; I think they mean miserable, and so it is, I fear, in very many places where I was specially fond of going."[42] All the letters and pictures were kept in a large brown envelope on Tolkien's desk in his study, and after his death they were edited by Christopher's wife Baillie and published by Allen & Unwin and Houghton Mifflin in 1976. In 1994, HarperCollins published three miniature volumes, each thirty-two pages, with the letters for 1931–1936 and 1938 and later omitted. In 1995, HarperCollins and Houghton Mifflin published two works based on the *Father Christmas Letters*, both called *Letters From Father Christmas*. The pocket version included facsimiles of five complete pull-out letters with transcriptions, and parts of five others, with two of these abridged and rewritten. Revised full-size editions published in 1999 included previously unpublished letters, pictures, and illustrations from 1939–1943.

The *Father Christmas Letters* are a delight and are wonderful to read aloud to children, especially at Christmas. The letters are fun and interesting for adults, who can not only laugh at and enjoy the adventures and simple fantasies, but also marvel at and

---

[41] Ibid., 76.
[42] Baillie Tolkien, ed. *Letters From Father Christmas* (Boston: Houghton Mifflin, 1976) 154.

appreciate Tolkien's often overlooked creative gifts as an artist and illustrator.

Mr. Bliss

Mr. Bliss was Tolkien's first children's story. It was told to his children and probably composed around the summer of 1928 (based on a diary kept by Michael Tolkien) and was written in the early 1930s, probably between 1932–1937.[43] According to Mrs. Michael Tolkien, the story was inspired by Christopher Tolkien's toy car and the three teddy bears owned by Tolkien's three sons.[44] It is a slapstick story about a man, a car, three bears, and a talking "girabbit," a cross between a giraffe and rabbit. The setting is a Cotswold village in the early 1900s (when cars were a recent invention), and the eccentric Mr. Bliss, who wore tall hats, decided to buy a bright yellow car (with red wheels) and show it to his friends. On his first excursion he knocked over two people (who were not harmed), was hijacked by three bears named Archie, Teddy, and Bruno, and had other mishaps and comic adventures. At the end of the tale, Mr. Bliss grew to dislike motor-cars, gave his away, and drove a donkey-cart.

Hobbit-like names appear in the story, including Sergeant Boffin and Gaffer Gamgee, and several anticipations of Middle-earth are evident, including Mr. Day and Mrs. Knight (reverse gender from Sun and Moon in Middle-earth), and the bears live in a Beorn-like Great Hall in the wood. Mr. Bliss, like Bilbo Baggins, live alone as a well-to-do bachelor at the top of the hill, away from the rest of the villagers. And there are several Middle-

---

[43] In his notes to the *Mr. Bliss* manuscript held at Marquette University, Professor Jared Lobdell suggested that it was written 1928–1932. See Wayne G. Hammond, *Descriptive Bibliography*, 240.

[44] Humphrey Carpenter was in error when he wrote that the story was inspired by the Tolkien family car and Tolkien's misadventures in it. See Carpenter, *Biography*, 165.

earth-like trees in Tolkien's drawings, particularly in the Dorkinses' kitchen-garden and in Three Bears Wood.

Tolkien submitted his color-illustrated manuscript of the story to Allen & Unwin in late 1936. Production manager C. A. Furth compared the story to *Alice's Adventures in Wonderland*, but eventually rejected it because of the prohibitive (war-time) costs for color printing. Tolkien worked on making the illustrations easier to reproduce and submitted the manuscript again in November 1937, together with the *Silmarillion* and others. It was rejected again, and Unwin asked for more revised illustrations, suggesting that Tolkien redraw a little larger and in three colors and black. Tolkien objected and asked for more colors, particularly green (essential), and brown (for the bears). Unwin agreed to publish the story in color half-tones, but without glossy paper (probably due to the cost), which was essential. The story languished with Tolkien till August 1938, when he submitted it again after Unwin had considered it to be the successor to the *Hobbit*. Tolkien promoted his story again in February 1939, but by this time he was deep into the writing of the *Lord of the Rings*, and this and his normal heavy college work load, together with Unwin's continued resistance over costs, caused him to abandon the promotion of the story.

In 1957, he sold the manuscript of *Mr. Bliss* to Marquette University in Milwaukee, Wisconsin.[45] Professor Clyde Kilby of Wheaton College, Illinois, corresponded with Tolkien (probably late 1964) about the possible publication of the story, and Tolkien told him that its publication "would not enhance his reputation."[46] He came to dislike the story and considered it a "private joke," and decided that it would be better if *Mr. Bliss* was published posthumously. After several American publishers inquired, the story was finally published first in 1982 by Allen & Unwin and a

---

[45] Marquette also purchased the manuscripts of the *Hobbit*, *Farmer Giles of Ham*, and the *Lord of the Rings*.

[46] Kilby, *Tolkien and the Silmarillion*, 15.

London book club, then by Houghton Mifflin in 1983, nearly fifty years after its conception.

Regardless of Tolkien's dislike for *Mr. Bliss*, which he did not mention in his collected letters after 1939, the story is a treasure and does not damage his reputation. It is probably more suited for ten-year-olds and under, but can be read with enjoyment by anyone of any age, even by childlike adults. It is very much a children's picture book in the tradition of Beatrix Potter, and it was written in dramatic, exuberant style that is just right for reading aloud to children.

Roverandom

In the summer of 1925, Tolkien took his family on holiday to the Yorkshire coast town of Filey to celebrate his appointment as Rawlinson and Bosworth Professor of Anglo-Saxon at Oxford. His son Michael lost his miniature lead dog on the beach after a storm and was heartbroken. This event inspired Tolkien to write a story that explained Michael's loss, a story that was to become *Roverandum*. The 25,000-word story is about a real little white dog (with black ears) named Rover, who is turned into a tiny toy dog by the wizard Artaxerxes. After meeting the sand-magician (Psamathos Psamathides, chief of the Psamathists, and the "P" was never silent), he was dropped on the beach by a little boy, then transported to the moon by way of a moonpath, carried on the back of Mew the seagull, who was the Man in the Moon's postal carrier. The Man in the Moon renamed him Roverandum[47] and gave him wings, and on the moon he met and became friends with moondog. Roverandum and moondog had many escapades, including encounters with dragons, spiders, and dragon-moths.

---

[47] Tolkien perhaps called the dog "Roverandom" to distinguish him from the moondog, also called Rover, but also for the randomness of his travels. Later in the story Roverandom meets, becomes friends with, and has many adventures with a seadog also called Rover.

From the moon he returned to the real world, where Psamathos allowed him to ride Uin the giant whale and visit the Kingdom of the Sea. By then Artaxerxes was the resident Magician of the Ocean (PAM: Pacific Atlantic Magician), and Roverandom wanted to apologize for biting him, hoping then he would be turned back into a real dog.

Roverandom is filled with Tolkien's famous linguistic wit, including word play, literary references and allusions, personal asides, hints of Middle-earth, and even references to his feelings about pollution, when he expressed disgust about litter on the beach. In the earliest manuscript the wizard is called a *Psammead* and was borrowed from the "sandfairy" of E. Nesbit's *Five Children and It* (1902) and the *Story of the Amulet* (1906). The idea that toys come alive late at night is a convention found in many children's stories, such as "The Steadfast Tin Soldier" by Hans Christian Andersen (1846).[48] There are also allusions to the *Tales of the Arabian Nights* (The Old Man of the Sea is a character in this tale), *Peter Pan*, and Lewis Carroll's *Sylvie and Bruno*, to nursery rhymes such as "Old Mother Hubbard," and to Greek, Celtic, and Norse mythology. The wizard Artaxerxes wears a blue feather in his hat, as does Tom Bombadil in the *Lord of the Rings*. The moon dragon resembles Smaug from the *Hobbit*, and the whale Uin carries Roverandom across the ocean to the edge of Faeryland, where he sees the Mountains of Elvenhome, the geography described by Tolkien in his earliest Silmarillion tales, from the *Book of Lost Tales*.

The story also has many linguistic delights, and as a whole contains some of Tolkien's most enjoyable writing, particularly

---

[48] Another story of this type is "The Wax Doll" (1869) by Edward H. Knatchbull-Hugessen (1829–1893). His short fairy story "Puss Cat Meow" (1869) was a childhood favorite of Tolkien, and includes an ogre who disguises himself as a tree, which may have partly inspired Tolkien's Ents, tree creatures in the *Lord of the Rings*. See Humphrey Carpenter and Mari Prichard, eds., *The Oxford Companion to Children's Literature* (Oxford: Oxford University Press, 1991) 297–98.

the lyrical descriptions of the moon and seascapes, and the children's party on the moon, where they visit in their dreams. An early passage, after Rover has been turned into a toy, is a good example: "That morning, when they woke and pulled up the blind, they saw the sun jumping out of the sea, all fiery-red with clouds about his head, as if he had a cold bath and was drying himself with towels."[49] There is also a listing of scholarly adjectives applied to sea serpents, and most of these are authentic marine fauna: sea-worms, sea-cats, sea-cows, sea-tigers, cephalopods, manatees, and five others. Some of the vocabulary is high for a children's story, and Tolkien included such words as *paraphernalia, phosphorescent, primordial, rigmarole, subterranean, prodigious, arcana,* and *mottled.* Tolkien the teacher is evident here, and he contended that children learn new words by reading ones they do not already know. In a 1959 letter he advised that in writing children's stories an author should not "write down to Children or to anybody," and that children can acquire a good vocabulary by reading books "above one."[50]

There are four versions of the text of *Roverandom* among the Tolkien papers in the Bodleian Library, Oxford, and the shortest of these (nine pages) was the manuscript Tolkien prepared for submission to Allen & Unwin for publication at the end of 1936. In January 1937, Raynor Unwin called the story "well-written and amusing," but it was not accepted. By October 1937, the *Hobbit* was so successful that Unwin wanted a sequel about hobbits, and Tolkien began his work on the *Lord of the Rings. Roverandum* was put aside and not mentioned by Tolkien in his collected letters or by his biographers. Thanks to editors Christina Scull and Wayne Hammond, the story was rescued from obscurity and published by Houghton Mifflin in 1998. Their superb, very well written fourteen-page introduction is a model of scholarly insight and

---

[49] Christina Scull and Wayne G. Hammond, eds., *Roverandom by J. R. R. Tolkien* (Boston: Houghton Mifflin, 1998) 9.

[50] Carpenter, *Letters*, 298–99.

thorough research. They included five of Tolkien's illustrations for the story, with the "Lunar Landscape's" inscription almost certainly being an early form of his Elvish script *tengwar*, and the watercolor "House Where 'Rover' Began His Adventures as a Toy" perhaps the most memorable.

Tolkien obviously enjoyed writing *Roverandom*, and the "adult" words and literary references do not obscure the wonder and fun of the story. It is not on a level with the *Hobbit*, but in regards to (especially) wit and fun, it will entertain and amuse children of all ages. And *Roverandom* demonstrates once again that Tolkien was a visual storyteller, and that his invented worlds and characters "come alive" in the imaginations of anyone who loves good storytelling.

The Lord of the Rings

What is the *Lord of the Rings*? Various critics and interpreters have called it a fairy-story, traditional epic, romance, novel, collection of novels, political satire, moral exhortation, saga, fantasy, glorified science fiction, myth, contemporary mythology, sequel to the *Hobbit*, trilogy, an allegory, and probably others. In a letter to a magazine editor in early 1956, Tolkien said it was a "fairy-story for adults" that was "written to *amuse* (in the highest sense) and to be readable." He also wrote that in the *Lord of the Rings* "there is *no* 'allegory,' moral, political, or contemporary in the work at all."[1] Though in the 1950s Tolkien called his story a novel (see below), in a draft of a 1971 letter he emphatically wrote that his work was "*not* a 'novel,' but an heroic romance a much older and quite different variety of literature."[2] In other letters, Tolkien wrote that the *Lord of the Rings* was an aesthetic or essay that grew out of his love and study of linguistics,[3] and that its main idea was not a product of World War II.[4]

---

[1] Humphrey Carpenter, *The Letters of J. R. R. Tolkien* (London: Allen & Unwin, 1981) 232–33. Tolkien mentioned in seven other letters that the *Lord of the Rings* was not an allegory. See *Letters*, 41, 121, 212, 220, 239, 246, 262.

[2] Ibid., 414, letter dated October 1971.

[3] Ibid., 220; 264–65.

[4] Ibid., 216.

The *Lord of the Rings* is not and never was intended to be a "trilogy." In a letter to Houghton Mifflin, circa 1966, Tolkien wrote: "The book *is not* of course a 'trilogy.' That and the titles of the volumes was a fudge thought necessary for publication, owing to length and cost...The story was written and conceived as a whole..."[5] The *Lord of the Rings* was divided into three volumes for ease of publication, and each volume contained two books (or sections), with appendices. It is not generally known that the six books were originally titled by Tolkien; later these were discarded by his publisher. Volume one, *The Fellowship of the Ring*, included "The First Journey" (Book One, twelve chapters) and "The Journey of the Nine Companions" (Book Two, ten chapters). Volume two, *The Two Towers*, included "The Treason of Isengard" (Book Three, eleven chapters) and "The Journey of the Ring-bearers" (Book Four, ten chapters). Volume three, *The Return of the King*, included "The War of the Ring" (Book Five, ten chapters) and "The End of the Third Age" (Book Six, nine chapters). Tolkien wrote to a doctoral student, probably in the 1950s, about the divisions, saying, "Of course, the present division into volumes, mere practical necessity of publication, is a falsification. As is shown by the unsatisfactory titles of the last two volumes. The work is in no legitimate literary sense a 'trilogy.' It is a three-decker novel. The only units of any structural significance are the 'books.' Personally I should have preferred...the volumes designated merely by numbers."[6]

The *Hobbit* was a huge success immediately after its publication in 1937, and Allen & Unwin told Tolkien that "a large

---

[5] Ibid., 221.

[6] Richard C. West, "Progress Report on the Variorum Tolkien," *Orcrist* 4 [also *Tolkien Journal*, 4, No. 3, Whole No. 13] (1969–1970): 6–7. The title of the second volume was unsatisfactory to Tolkien because there are five towers in the story instead of three, and he suggested the third volume be titled *The War of the Ring*, as that title gave away less. This article concerns research on the Tolkien papers at Marquette University, which houses the manuscripts, typescripts, and galley proofs for the *Lord of the Rings* and others, including the *Hobbit*.

public" would be "clamouring" to hear more about hobbits. In an October 1937 letter to Sir Stanley Unwin, Tolkien wrote that he could not think of anything more to say about hobbits, but that he would start "the process of thought, and try to get some idea of a theme from this material in a similar style and for a similar audience—possibly including actual hobbits."[7] But he wanted to return to his Silmarillion mythology instead ("the Silmarils are in my heart"), and in November he submitted the *Silmarillion* and other related manuscripts to Unwin. Unwin rejected the manuscripts (which included "The Lay of Leithian"), and pushed Tolkien for the sequel, primarily for ease of publication and because it would help increase sales of the *Hobbit* at Christmas.

He began writing the *Lord of the Rings* in December 1937 and worked steadily until the spring of 1938, when Christopher became ill.[8] Later, his work was further delayed at various times by ill health, the Second World War, his university and familial duties at Oxford, work on other writing projects, "many hours of failed inspiration," and because he often underestimated the book's final size and wrongly predicted the date(s) of its completion. He stopped writing in late 1939 or early 1940, probably due to anxiety over his son Michael's military service and because bombs were falling over London. He resumed work in late 1941 and continued more or less steadily until the summer of 1943, when he was "stuck." Lewis persuaded him to start again in spring 1944, and he wrote hard and long until October. He did not write for nearly two more years, while he contemplated and tried to finish "The Lost Road." At Unwin's insistence, he reluctantly resumed working in the summer of 1946, and by 1948 the *Lord of the Rings* was completed, in a manner of speaking.

---

[7] Carpenter, *Letters*, 23–24.
[8] The history of the writing of the *Lord of the Rings* was detailed by Christopher Tolkien in volumes 6–9 of the *History of Middle-Earth*: *The Return of the Shadow*, *The Treason of Isengard*, *The War of the Ring*, and *Sauron Defeated*.

Although at times the story seemed to write itself, Tolkien wrote very slowly, with a great emphasis on detail, "considering every word." In a retrospective letter, he said that he wrote the story for himself (at different levels), that it was an "experiment in the arts of long narrative, and of inducing 'Secondary Belief,'" and that it finally emerged as a "Frameless Picture: a searchlight...on a brief episode in History, and on a small part of our Middle-earth, surrounded by a glimmer of limitless extensions in time and space." He went on to explain that the story "felt like history," and that he felt that it had been used [by God?] to pour down "forgotten sunlight" over the dark world.[9]

Michael Stanton wrote that the unfolding of the book for Tolkien was "not as if he were planning it, much less writing it, but as though it were happening to him."[10] In a letter to W. H. Auden, Tolkien explained that "the essential Quest started at once. But I met a lot of things on the way that astonished me." He went on to say that he already knew Tom Bombadil, Gollum, and Sam, among others, but that he "had never been to Bree," and Strider, the Forest of Fanghorn, Saruman, and other events, places, and characters were new to him, although he "recognized" some of them.[11] He started writing the story with the aid of maps, and made the story fit into it, taking great care with the distances and geography. Later, when it became more complex, he constantly rewrote and used a calendar to tie the story together, in order to

---

[9] Carpenter, *Letters*, 412–13. Humphrey Carpenter wrote that Tolkien, in writing his Silmarillion mythology, believed that in a sense he was writing "an embodiment of profound truth," and that in his other writings Tolkien suggests that a person may be given by God the gift of discerning "underlying reality or truth." Tolkien was not just "inventing" stories, he was recording what was already "there," put into his creative imagination and mind by God. This same discernment was true for Tolkien in the writing of the *Lord of the Rings*. See Carpenter, *J. R. R. Tolkien: A Biography* (Boston: Houghton Mifflin, 2000) 99–100.

[10] Stanton, *Hobbits, Elves, and Wizards* (New York: St. Martin's Press, 2001) 9.

[11] Carpenter, *Letters*, 216–17.

work backward to coordinate dates and determine where and when the primary characters and groups were on a particular day and what they were doing.

Tolkien received much encouragement from his family and friends while writing the *Lord of the Rings*, and in particular the Inklings and C. S. Lewis. He, and later Christopher, read passages from "the new Hobbit" at Inklings meetings, and although praise for the work often was generous (especially from Lewis and his brother Warren),[12] he received less than flattering comments from others. Hugo Dyson never liked the story and often irritated Tolkien and Christopher with his rants against it. He voiced his impatience so often with the *Lord of the Rings* (and all readings on Tuesday nights), that he was allowed a veto, and on more than one occasion he walked in late when Tolkien or Christopher was reading, and voiced his displeasure, often loudly.[13]

As Tolkien continued to work, the *Lord of the Rings* "grew darker" until it was not just another hobbit story, but the "continuation and completion" of the *Silmarillion*. In a letter to Unwin (1950), he asked that the two books be published together or concurrently, but Unwin could not publish because of rising costs, nor could Collins Publishing, with whom Tolkien dealt from 1949–1952. He finished the book in 1952, and during this time he was often ill and discouraged. In a penitent letter to Raynor Unwin (who had joined the firm and remained friendly with Tolkien) in

---

[12] Warren Lewis recorded in his diary on 12 November 1949 that he had read the *Lord of the Rings* in manuscript: "Golly, what a book! The inexhaustible fertility of the man's imagination amazes me...Sam Gamgee and the dwarf Gimli are I think the two best characters." He wrote further that Tolkien "would be wise to prepare himself for a good deal of misunderstanding and many critics" who would call the work a political satire. See Clyde S. Kilby and Marjorie Lamp Mead, eds., *Brothers and Friends: The Diaries of Major Warren Hamilton Lewis* (San Francisco: Harper & Row, 1982) 231.

[13] H. V. D. "Hugo" Dyson (1896–1975), was Fellow and Tutor at Merton College, Oxford, from 1945 till his retirement in 1963. After his retirement he spoke often on the BBC, and in 1966 appeared in John Schlesinger's film *Darling*, which starred Julie Christie and Dirk Bogarde.

June, he wrote that he would "gladly consider the publication of any part of this stuff," and asked Unwin if anything could be done about that (publishing the *Lord of the Rings*) "to unlock gates I have slammed myself?"[14] Unwin replied positively, requested the manuscript, and also asked for the *Silmarillion* when Tolkien "was able." On 19 September 1952 Raynor Unwin visited Oxford and received the manuscript from Tolkien.

Late in 1952, Allen & Unwin determined that the book would have to be published in three volumes to save on costs (and to receive three reviews), finally deciding that it was a work of genius and that "another and bigger book on hobbits" would not be a disaster. The firm minimized its potential for risk by contracting with Tolkien to withdraw legally if the first volume failed, and also signed a rather uncommon profit-sharing plan with him. Instead of the author receiving the usual 10 or 15 percent royalties on every book sold, Unwin and Tolkien agreed on a "half and half" plan. Tolkien would receive no payment from sales of the first volume until Unwin's production costs had been met (about £1,000); thereafter he would share all profits equally. This agreement turned out to be very beneficial for both.

The first edition of the *Fellowship of the Ring* was published by Unwin on 29 July 1954 at a cost of 21s.—3,000 copies were printed. The *Two Towers* followed on 11 November (3,250 copies), and 7,000 copies of the *Return of the King* were distributed on 20 October 1955. Wayne Hammond noted that a team of scholars would be needed to compile the textual history of the *Lord of the Rings* (before and after publication), as errors and inconsistencies, especially in spelling and punctuation, "abound in the various editions," and these are partly the fault of Tolkien himself. He not only had an enormous manuscript to deal with, but he also changed his mind frequently, constantly rewrote, and was

---

[14] Carpenter, *Letters*, 163.

often maddeningly late with corrections.¹⁵ Some of the inconsistencies were the fault of the publisher and proofreaders, who misinterpreted some of Tolkien's spellings and variants, such as when he used *Orcs* as well as *orcs*. The printers also "corrected" some of his seemingly esoteric spellings in the first proofs, changing *dwarves* to *dwarfs*, *elvish* to *elfish*, *further* to *farther*, and worst of all to Tolkien, *elvin* to *elfin*.¹⁶

The rest of the history of the reception of the *Lord of the Rings* has been well documented. The reviews were mixed although mostly favorable, and the books sold modestly well in England. Two of the most positive reviews were written by C. S. Lewis, who also wrote a publisher's blurb for the *Fellowship of the Ring*.¹⁷ In his now famous review of the book in *Time & Tide* (August 1954, published as "The Gods Return to Earth"), he wrote that the book was like "lightning from a clear sky," that nothing quite like it had been written before, that the hobbits were not allegories of the English, and that it was not "escapism." In another review for *Time and Tide* (October 1955), Lewis reviewed the completed book ("The Dethronement of Power") and called it "too original and too opulent for any final judgement," and added that it "has done things to us" and that it would soon be considered indispensable.¹⁸ Tolkien's worst critic was probably himself. In

---

[15] Tolkien once told an interviewer that he loved revision, and was a "natural niggler," fascinated by detail.

[16] Mr. Hammond wrote a non-exhaustive but excellent and detailed survey and chronology of the publishing history and production problems with the *Lord of the Rings*. See his *J. R. R. Tolkien: A Descriptive Bibliography* (New Castle DE: Oak Knoll Books, 1993) 82–176.

[17] Lewis wanted to help Tolkien all he could, but before he sent his blurb to Unwin, he warned Tolkien: "Even if he and you approve my words, think twice before using them: I am certainly a much, and perhaps an increasingly, hated man whose name might do you more harm than good." Some of the reviewers of Tolkien's book used their reviews, in part, to vent their hostilities toward Lewis. See Carpenter, *Biography*, 222.

[18] Both of Lewis's reviews were published under the title "Tolkien's *Lord of the Rings*," in *C. S. Lewis—Of This and Other Worlds*, ed. Walter Hooper

the foreword to the second edition of the *Fellowship of the Ring* he called himself "the most critical reader of all," and his letters were filled with tough, often detailed analysis and second thoughts, always with the idea of improving what he wrote.

Sales of the *Lord of the Rings* gradually increased in England and were helped by a radio dramatization, which was not approved by Tolkien. But he had tax worries, and in 1957 sold the manuscripts of the *Lord of the Rings*, the *Hobbit*, *Farmer Giles of Ham*, and the still unpublished *Mr. Bliss* to Marquette University, a Catholic school in Milwaukee, Wisconsin, for the sum of £1,250, then the equivalent of $5,000. Also in 1957 Tolkien received an offer from three American businessmen to make an animated film of the *Lord of the Rings*. He quickly rejected their story line, which contained misspellings, removed all walking from the story, had the Company of the Ring transported everywhere on the backs of eagles, and described elvish waybread as a "food concentrate."[19]

The book continued to win approval and sold well (but not overwhelmingly) in hardcover in England and the United States until 1965, when Ace Books of New York published, without Tolkien's approval, three paperback editions of the individual volumes. When the *Lord of the Rings* was published in hardcover in 1954–1955, Allen & Unwin declared it to be under an international copyright (the Berne Convention), but made no effort

---

(London: Fount, 1989) 112–21. In his preface, editor Hooper wrote that Tolkien told him that Lewis, who encouraged him to write the book, "had to have a story," and that the *Lord of the Rings* "was written to keep him quiet" (22). This is open to wide conjecture.

[19] The *Louisville Courier Journal* reported (1 April 2002) that in the sixties Tolkien was approached about (and turned down) a proposed movie version of the *Lord of the Rings* that would have featured the Beatles. John Lennon wanted to portray Gollum; Paul McCartney was to play Frodo; George Harrison would have starred as Gandalf; and Ringo Starr would have been cast as Sam Gamgee. In 1978 Ralph Bakshi produced an animated version of the first half of the *Lord of the Rings* for United Artists that was not received positively by critics or Tolkien fans.

to obtain an American copyright.[20] The book's American publisher, Houghton Mifflin, imported unbound sheets from Unwin and published the work in the US, making no copyright claim. When the *Fellowship of the Ring* was released by Houghton Mifflin in 1954, Ace immediately recognized that the book had no American copyright, and usually a paperback publisher would abide by the conventions of international copyright law and pay royalties in good faith.

Ace announced its plans to publish the *Lord of the Rings* in three volumes without honoring such accepted (unstated) rules, which was not illegal. At almost the same time, Houghton Mifflin announced an arrangement with Ballantine (their imprint) to publish the "authorized edition," with full royalties going to Houghton Mifflin, Allen & Unwin, and Tolkien. Tolkien issued an appeal to Ballantine's readers to buy only that edition, and Ace eventually was forced to withdraw its books and agreed to pay full royalties to Tolkien.

The court battles, claims, counterclaims, and threatened lawsuits in this controversy made national headlines in the United States. Articles were written about the furor in Tolkien journals and newsletters, letters were written complaining about "moral piracy," news items were released shouting "exploitation," Tolkien specialists and non-specialists were interviewed, and editorials appeared in various literary periodicals, fanzines, and newspapers. In autumn 1965 Ballantine, in agreement with Houghton Mifflin, published the "authorized" paperback editions of the *Lord of the Rings*, without revisions. The interest and publicity generated by the controversy, added to word of mouth recommendations, caused sales of the book to skyrocket. In the first ten months after the Ballantine edition was released, 250,000

---

[20] The two major international copyright treaties are the Berne Convention for the Protection of Literary and Artistic Works and the Universal Copyright Convention. The United States has been a member of the UCC since 1955, and joined the Berne Convention in 1989.

copies were sold.[21] Tolkien lost no royalties, and several of his other books were published and sold well during this time, including *Tree and Leaf*, *Smith of Wootton Major*, and the *Road Goes Ever On: A Song Cycle*.

After sales soared, and coinciding with "the turbulent sixties," Tolkien became a cult figure in the United States. "Frodo Lives!," "Gandalf is God," and other slogan buttons, lapel badges, bumper stickers ("Bilbo loves books"), signs, and graffiti ("J. R. R. Tolkien is Hobbit-forming") were seen everywhere, Tolkien societies were formed, and calendars, maps, and posters were produced yearly. Fan clubs held "hobbit picnics" in which they dressed up as hobbits and other characters from the stories, conferences were held all over the US, Canada, England, and Europe, and Tolkien figures, figurines, pottery, belt buckles, chess sets, dolls, and countless other "memorabilia" were mass produced. Tolkien became a household word all over the world, and was even studied and written about in some academic circles. Books of "Middle-earth criticism" appeared in bookstores, and in the fifties and sixties several doctoral dissertations were written about Tolkien's mythology; today the total number is up to nearly 200.[22]

He was often bothered by fans, who would call him from America late at night (forgetting the time change) and ask to speak to "the man who wrote about hobbits." Often people would visit his home without appointment and ask for autographs, or even

---

[21] For a comprehensive summary/review of the Ace Books controversy, see Richard E. Blackwelder, "The Great Copyright Controversy," *Beyond Bree* (September 1995). This article can be ordered for a nominal cost from Mrs. Nancy Martsch, PO Box 55372, Sherman Oaks CA 91413. There was a repeat of this duel between Ace and Ballantine over the rights to publish the works of Edgar Rice Burroughs, both the Tarzan novels and the science fiction featuring John Carter. See Kenneth C. Davis, *Two-Bit Culture: The Paperbacking of America* (Boston: Houghton Mifflin, 1984) 327–30.

[22] Humphrey Carpenter reported that one of these was titled "A Parametric Analysis of Antithetical Conflict and Irony in J. R. R. Tolkien's *The Lord of the Rings*." See Carpenter, *Biography*, 233.

worse, would take photos through his windows, sometimes at night. In the late sixties his correspondence was enormous, and because the *Lord of the Rings* and the *Hobbit* had been published in several languages, strangers from all over the world wrote and sent him gifts: photos of people dressed as characters from the books, food, drink, tobacco, paintings and drawings "based" on the stories, and more. He accepted Unwin's offer to assist in answering his fan mail, and in 1968 he decided to move to Bournemouth on the south coast, removed his address and phone number from directories, and instructed Unwin not to inform inquirers of his actual new address.

The story told in the *Lord of the Rings* has been reviewed, discussed, dissected, and "interpreted" hundreds, perhaps thousands of times, and is familiar to most (if not all) readers who know anything at all about Tolkien. Nevertheless, a brief synopsis of the events leading up to the tale is called for here. Tolkien's secondary world was called Middle-earth, his name for a part of the world (about the size of western Europe) that existed thousands of years before our recorded history. The events in the *Lord of the Rings* took place about seventy years after the ending of the *Hobbit* and detailed a year's journey that happened near the end of the Third Age—every place mentioned in the story is where something happened many years ago.

In the First Age, ("Elder Days," "the Silmarillion proper"), most of the history of Middle-earth was not known, because the races did not keep journals and records. It was known that in the beginning God (Ilúvatar, "the One") created the Valar (archangels) to rule over Middle-earth, and that one of them (Melkor, later Morgoth) rebelled, following his own evil impulses. Morgoth stole the three great illuminating jewels (Silmarilli), and seduced a follower, Sauron ("abominable") to carry out his evil deeds. The First Age was the great period of the elves, and most of the time Middle-earth was a peaceful and happy land, and evil did not exist. The hobbits lived a simple life in the Shire, eating several meals a day, gardening, and (mostly) keeping to themselves. After many years, Middle-earth fell on evil times, and the First Age came to an end with the Great Battle (War of Wrath) and the defeat of Morgoth, the "Black Enemy," Tolkien's equivalent to the biblical Satan. These events happened over 6,000 years before the story told in the *Lord of the Rings*.

This led to what became known as the Second Age. Middle-earth again fell on dark times, and Sauron attempted to control the world. After a deep sleep of 500 years he awoke, and 500 years later he established a fortress called Mordor, which became a stronghold of evil. He commanded the noble elf Celebrimbor ("silverfist") to forge the three Magic Rings of Power for the elves, the Seven Rings for the dwarves, and the Nine Rings for humans. The holders of the Great Rings would have special powers, and any mortal possessing one would not die. After ten years- Sauron treacherously forged the "One Ring" that would give him control over all other rings and their holders. The One Ring could extend the life of its holder and make him or her invisible, but also could control and change the holder physically and emotionally, devouring the mind and soul and causing the holder and anyone else who desired after it to be filled with hate, jealousy, greed, and fear. When the elves learned about the One Ring, they became Sauron's major opponents, but he had gained so much power that they were always on the defensive—he ruled Middle-earth with an iron fist for nearly 2,000 years. Late in the Second Age, Sauron was defeated and captured by the warriors from Númenor, a great island in western waters. After fifty years, Sauron deceived the Númenorians into worshipping Melkor, and Ilúvatar destroyed the island in a flood, similar to the story of Atlantis. A few of the good Númenorians escaped, and one of them, Elendil, with his sons Isildur and Anárion, formed the good Kingdom of Gondor in Middle-earth. Isildur and Anárion became joint kings, and later Aragorn ("Strider") was heir to the kingdom.

On the One Ring Sauron inscribed: "One Ring to rule them all. One Ring to find them / One Ring to bring them all and in the darkness bind them." Celebrimbor saw Sauron's treachery and hid the Three Rings for the elves; he was later killed when his kingdom, Eregion, was destroyed in 1697 during the War of the Elves and Sauron. The Three Rings remained hidden, and Sauron lost the One Ring (which was now completely evil) during a final battle, when Isildur cut off his finger. After two years, Isildur was ambushed by Orcs at Gladden Fields, and the One Ring slipped off his finger and fell into the Anduin River.

During the Third Age, the Three Rings were kept safe, but evil reappeared again after 1,000 years. Sauron returned in 2460, and wars emerged all over the land between the forces of good and evil. Sauron began gathering all the Rings and was obsessed in finding the One Ring. Déagol the Stoor (hobbit) found the Ring while fishing in the Anduin with his cousin Sméagol (Gollum), and was murdered by him. The Ring soon consumed Gollum (his "precious") and he became repulsive to his family. Gollum hid in the Misty Mountains and lost the Ring in 2941. The hobbit Bilbo Baggins, of Bag End, Hobbiton, found it while on an adventure with Gandalf the Wizard (Gandalf the Grey), told in the story the *Hobbit*—by 2944 Gollum began to look for the "thief" of the Ring. In 3001 Bilbo celebrated his 111th birthday by giving a huge party for himself ("the Farewell Feast"), and then said farewell to the Shire. Before he left, he gave the One Ring to his hobbit nephew, Frodo Baggins. Later, Gandalf suspected that Frodo now had the One Ring and challenged him to destroy it. This is the beginning of the *Lord of the Rings*, which culminated in the War of the Ring and the beginning of the Fourth Age.

Thanks in part to the recent movie the *Lord of the Rings: The Fellowship of the Ring*, many know now at least the basic plot of the first third of the story. The whole story (and also the *Hobbit*) is primarily concerned with the never-ending struggle between good and evil, and is also an investigation into the sources and nature of evil. Tolkien was a veteran of World War I, had been shot at and shelled, and several of his closest friends were killed. He also lived through the bombings of England in World War II and the unknowing terror of anticipated invasion. He knew firsthand about the horrors of war, and in the *Lord of the Rings* he gave his response to the problem of evil. Tolkien also knew about the subtleness of evil, which he saw in the impersonal, mechanized society of the Western world. He associated machinery (particularly labor-saving devices) as a desire for power and control (domination), and once said that "mechanism" was the modern equivalent of the "evil spirit" or "Enemy." Although Tolkien disliked much of the modern world and longed for quieter, simpler days, he did not resent the world he lived in. And in the *Lord of the Rings*, he represented the battle between good and evil with a variety of original characters who were timeless. He created some who were completely good, some completely evil, and some who wavered, despaired, and were completely fallible. He showed that anyone can give in to the enticement of evil, and even a good person (Boromir, Frodo, Sam) can have evil forced into their lives.

There are many other "themes" that can be found in the *Lord of the Rings*, including death and immortality (which Tolkien said was the major theme),[23] the quest, heroism, freedom, peace, "ordinary life," the Ring as a symbol of the "will to mere power," the relation of Creation to sub-creation and "making," and many others. Good in the story is pictured by Tolkien as always positive and natural, while evil is always negative, destructive, and selfish. Some characters are always good, such as Galadriel, and some are always evil, such as Sauron. The most pervasive evil characteristic is the desire for power, to dominate and control others. Some of Tolkien's "ordinary (good) virtues" are perseverance, mercy, kindness, enduring friendship, wonder, and humility. In some characters, evil eventually "wins" and controls, such as with Gollum and Saruman, and others succumb to despair and

---

[23] In a November 1957 letter Tolkien wrote there was "*no* symbolism or conscious allegory" in the *Lord of the Rings*, that it was "not really" about power and dominion but these did "set the wheels going," and it was about "Death and the desire for deathlessness." See Carpenter, *Letters*, 203.

eventually "break down," such as when Denethor kills himself, possibly because of grief over the death of his wife.

The Ring made its wearer invisible, but also made him or her more visible to Sauron and the Black Riders. The Ring also symbolized evil power; it controlled its wearer by infecting his or her worldview and making it dark, pessimistic, and paranoid. The Ring also infused its wearer with a sense of possessiveness and a desire for power and control, such as in Boromir, who fell under the Spell of the Ring and tried to kill Frodo. Even Sam, although he was essentially good and kind, was tempted by the Ring after Frodo was poisoned by Shelob and taken prisoner. Only the noblest characters, such as Gandalf and Aragorn, used power well and wisely, although they were tempted by it. Frodo was an "ordinary" hobbit, yet he became heroic by constantly denying his ambitions and desire for power.

The *Lord of the Rings* chronicles two major and parallel quests, and also demonstrates Tolkien's view that all of life is a quest. One is Frodo's and his friends' journey from "ordinary innocence" to hard-won wisdom, and the other is Aragorn's quest to become king and restore the rule and honor of his ancestors. Aragorn was Sauron's opposite in that his intentions were noble. The quests these characters take are often lonely, exhausting, and depressing, but true to the nature of the heroic quest in classical literature, they continue "keeping on keeping on," and some gain maturity at the end of their journeys, particularly Frodo and Pippin. Mark Smith wrote that the courage exhibited by Tolkien's heroic characters seemed to be made up of equal parts of "pity, wonder, love and faithfulness, occasionally mixed in with a liberal dollop of wrath."[24] In other words, they were human, and in their heroic human quests, Tolkien reinvented heroism, but only made it half-sized. Katharyn Crabbe noted that (using a paradigm developed from Joseph Campbell's the *Hero with a Thousand*

---

[24] Mark Smith, *Tolkien's Ordinary Virtues* (Downers Grove IL: InterVarsity Press, 2002) 112.

Faces) "there is one heroic life, and quest stories differ only as to how they make use of different parts of it."[25]

The *Lord of the Rings* and all of Tolkien's Middle-earth works grew out of his love for and study of languages and words. It is well known that he spent much of his life learning, creating, and studying languages, and that the central core of his vocational life was linguistics, or philology. As a young man, his mother introduced him to Latin, French, and German, and while at college he taught himself or was taught Greek, Middle-English, Anglo-Saxon (Old English), Icelandic (Old Norse), Gothic, medieval and modern Welsh, Finnish, Spanish, and Italian. He also had a good working knowledge of Swedish, Danish, Norwegian, Dutch, Russian, and Lombardic (a dialect of Northern Italy).

In one of his most-quoted comments, Tolkien wrote, "What...I think a primary 'fact' about my work, [is] that it is all of a piece, and *fundamentally linguistic* in inspiration...The invention of languages is the foundation. The 'stories' were made rather to provide a world for the languages than the reverse. To me a name comes first and the story follows."[26] The vernacular of Middle-earth was called "Westron," and "Hobbitish" was its rustic form. There are few genuine examples of Westron in the story, as Tolkien translated most names into the equivalent English forms. There are many examples of his use of linguistic interpretation in the *Lord of the Rings*, and Michael Stanton noted that these show the importance of language to Tolkien, in his use of proper names. For instance, *Saruman* was derived from the Old English or Anglo-Saxon root word that meant "treachery" or "cunning." The word *Sauron* was taken from an old Norse or Icelandic stem that meant "filth," or "dung," or "uncleanness," and Gollum's name before he stole the Ring was *Sméagol*, taken from the Old English root *smeagan*, which meant "to ponder" or "to inquire"; related words gave a sense of "creeping" or "craftiness." The giant female

---

[25] Crabbe, *J. R. R. Tolkien* (New York: Continuum, 1988) 69.
[26] Carpenter, *Letters*, 219.

spider *Shelob* was derived from an Old English word, *lobbe*, which meant "spider," and *ent* in Old English once meant "giant."[27]

Tolkien's attitude toward words and language was very different than most writers and critics of his time, or even our time. He believed that his own art (or pastime) of "linguistic invention" was rare (although he admitted it was for his own pleasure), and that few in his day understood or took the time to try to understand what he was trying to do with words. In his view, words and language stood on their own merits and ordered their own functions. As Tom Shippey wrote, "(modern) critics think that man is master: that poets and artists use words originally, individually, for their own inner purposes. Tolkien feels that words have a life of their own, which continues irrespective of rough treatment from time and careless speakers."[28]

In a letter to his friend Fr. Robert Murray, Tolkien said that the *Lord of the Rings* was "fundamentally a religious and Catholic work," and that he did not put in, or later cut out "practically all references to anything like 'religion,' to cults and practices, in the imaginary world." He added that the "religious element is absorbed into the story and the symbolism," and that he was grateful to have been "brought up into a Faith that has nourished me and taught me all the little that I know."[29] And in 1965 W. H. Auden wrote to Tolkien and asked him if the creation of orcs, "an entire race that was irredeemably wicked," was not heretical. Tolkien replied that he "did not feel under any obligation to make my story fit with formalized Christian theology, though I actually intended it to be consonant with Christian thought and belief…"[30]

---

[27] Stanton, *Hobbits, Elves, and Wizards*, 19–20.

[28] See Shippey, "Creation from Philology in *The Lord of the Rings*," in *J. R. R. Tolkien, Scholar and Storyteller: Essays in Memoriam*, ed. Mary Salu and Robert T. Farrell (Ithaca NY: Cornell University Press, 1979) 301.

[29] Carpenter, *Letters*, 172.

[30] Ibid., 355.

Although the *Lord of the Rings* is permeated with the spirit of Christianity and Christian ideals, there is no mention of the Christian God or other gods, no mention of Jesus, no mention of organized religion or its rituals and customs, and no mention of Christianity proper. There are no chapels or churches in Middle-earth, no formal prayers, and no theological writings or pronouncements. Hobbits do get married, but there is no mention of who marries them or where. Tolkien did not tell us where hobbits are buried, and no tombstones or named graveyards are mentioned. Tom Shippey noted that on the Rohan border there is a mountain called Halifirien, which is from an Old English word meaning "Holy Mountain," but "we never find out who or what it was once holy to."[31]

But there many hints and allusions to Christian belief in the *Lord of the Rings*. Frodo is considered by many to be a Christ-like figure, who carried his "cross," the Ring, to its ultimate destiny. Gandalf often inferred that he believed in a divine providence or power, as when he said that Bilbo was *meant* to find the Ring, and that this was not a "strange chance." There are veiled references to immortality in the mention of Aragorn never returning to Cerin Amroth as a "living man" and when Théoden said (the *Return of the King*) as he was dying, "I go to my fathers."[32] And there are many others. One author wrote that "(in Tolkien's story) one can find the themes of justice and mercy, the economy of grace, the persistence of evil, and the demand for hope...any transference of Tolkien's stories to another medium should take into account his Christian intentions...one cannot separate his Christian message from his stories."[33]

---

[31] Shippey, *J. R. R. Tolkien: Author of the Century* (London: HarperCollins, 2000) 175.

[32] See Shippey, "Creation from Philology," in Salu and Farrell, *Scholar and Storyteller*, 309–10.

[33] Bradley J. Bizer, "The Christian Gifts of J. R. R. Tolkien," *New Oxford Review* (November 2001): 25–29.

The *Lord of the Rings* is, as Tolkien said, "fundamentally" Christian and Catholic. A Christian foundation of the work is not visible at first glance, but is dispersed through the story, rarely in any particular detail. Jesus never visited Middle-earth, and there are no direct connections to him, but Tolkien did not attempt to write a Christian apologetic or a story of "concealed evangelism," as C. S. Lewis did. Tolkien, as an essentially private Christian, did not create an obvious religious or Christian element in the *Lord of the Rings* because he believed (contrary to Lewis) that it might overwhelm his story, and because he also believed that in his sub-created fairy tale, God would be fully in place. The *Lord of the Rings*, set in a "pre-Christian age" thousands of years before the advent of the great religions of humankind (including Christianity), does dramatize Tolkien's own Christian sensibilities, and his moral outlook was revealed by the virtues of his characters, which also can rightly be called Christian. His great story, while not explicitly religious, nevertheless is grounded in what Tolkien called a "monotheistic world of natural theology." His creation of a secondary world of Middle-earth in the Third Age was his way of escaping a war-torn, urbanized, and mechanized world and offering something better to his readers, and perhaps to himself.[34]

One explicit Christian reference in the *Lord of the Rings* deserves notice here. Professor Mike Foster (Illinois Central College, East Peoria, Illinois) studied the Tolkien manuscripts at Marquette University and found a handwritten note by Tolkien at

---

[34] In *The Road Goes Ever On–A Song Cycle* (Boston: Houghton Mifflin, 1967) 65, Tolkien mentioned that Elbereth (Middle-earth for Varda, the power who created the stars in *The Silmarillion*) could be said to be "looking afar from heaven," was a "divine" or "angelic" person, that the elves sang hymns to her, and that elves and men "invoke her" (pray) "in peril or grief," as do the hobbits Sam and Frodo. Tolkien also stated that "these and other references to religion in *The Lord of the Rings* are frequently overlooked." And later (p. 66), he mentioned the Valar (similar to angels) and their love for the "Children of God," perhaps his first (published) use of the word "God" in connection with *The Lord of the Rings*. See Clyde S. Kilby, "Mythic and Christian Elements in Tolkien," 142.

the bottom of one manuscript page. The note said that Frodo and the other eight members of the Fellowship *must* set off on their quest from Rivendell on Christmas Day. In Tolkien's calendar, the quest ended on March 25, a date that English medieval tradition held was the original Good Friday, and the day in which the Catholic Church celebrates as the Annunciation of the Angel Gabriel to Mary that she will conceive the savior.[35] Many readers, including scholars, missed this "hidden" reference that displayed Tolkien's Christian sensitivities, but it is just one example from many in the *Lord of the Rings*.

The tributes to the *Lord of the Rings* have been numerous, from all over the world. It is obvious that the story touches people on many different levels, in many different ways. One of the most moving accolades came from a perhaps unexpected place. An American fanzine writer recently interviewed a twenty-seven-year-old Russian lady, who had first read the *Fellowship of the Ring* in 1988. It moved her to tears, and a few years later she read the rest of the story in two borrowed volumes. She had to read and remember the characters and events in four days, and could not photocopy the book, as copiers were scarce in Russia during that time—thankfully she had a photographic memory and could call up any page and recite it to her friends. Later, she reflected on the enormous impact the book had on her. She told the interviewer, "Soviet people were raised as atheists, and Tolkien's books offered me hope for our world, the hope that Tolkien's elves call *estel*. Tolkien does not mention God in the *Lord of the Rings* at all, but you can feel something really wonderful when you read it. Later I recognized it as faith."[36]

---

[35] Tom Heinen, "Tolkien's 'Rings' teems with spiritual undertones," *Houston Chronicle*, 29 December 2001, 4E.

[36] Erik Davis, "The Fellowship of the Ring," *Wired* (October 2001): 124.

The Silmarillion

Tolkien considered the *Silmarillion* ("The Book of the Silmarils") his most important work, "the work of his heart," and he labored on it for most of his adult life, finally leaving it incomplete for his son Christopher to finish. His reading of the story of Kullervo, one of the tales in the *Kalevala* ("Land of Heroes," the mythology of Finland), around 1911–1912 stimulated his desire to write a national epic or mythology for England, and he was "intoxicated" by both the story and its language.[1] This story and the reading of C. N. E. Eliot's *A Finnish Grammar* led him to develop his own Finnish-like language, the High-elven "Quenya," which became the "original germ" of the *Silmarillion*.

Several scholars think the actual writing of the book began in September 1914, when Tolkien wrote the poem "The Voyage of Eärendil, the Evening Star," when he was on holiday in

---

[1] In a letter to Christopher during World War II, Tolkien called the Finnish language "the germ of the Silmarillion." See Humphrey Carpenter, *The Letters of J. R. R. Tolkien* (London: Allen & Unwin, 1981) 87. The *Kalevela* ("the songs of Kaleva," based on collections of ancient poems and ballads), the national epic of Finland, was first published in 1835–1836 and revised in 1849 by Elias Lonnrot (1802–1884), a physician, philologist, and scholar. It compares with the *Iliad* and *Odyssey* and begins with the creation of the world and the birth of a semi-divine hero, and closes with the departure of the hero and the advent of Christianity.

Nottinghamshire, visiting his Aunt Jane Neave.² He had been entranced by his reading of the Old English Christian poem *Crist* ("Christ"), by the eighth-century poet Cynewulf, and particularly by the second part of the poem, which deals with the ascension of Christ. He read the opening lines of the poem, "Hail Earendel, angel brightest / over middle-earth unto men sent," and knew that "Eärendel" meant "shining light" in Anglo-Saxon and referred to the planet Venus. Tolkien "felt a curious thrill" on the reading of these words, "as if something had stirred in me, wakened from sleep. There was something very remote and strange and beautiful behind those words..."³

Tolkien found the evening star again in his Old Norse studies at Exeter College, when he read the saga of Aurvandil (the Norse equivalent of Eärendil), and probably when he read of the star again in the medieval Icelandic (*Prose Edda*) story of Orentil. "Orentil" is the Icelandic equivalent of Eärendil, a great hero, a mariner who is shipwrecked and later marries a beautiful woman.⁴ As early as 1914 Tolkien wrote a new story about the mariner ("Lay of Eärendil"), which became the foundation for his story of Eärendil in the *Silmarillion*. Here the mariner's beautiful wife becomes a star.

He was also influenced by the imaginative works of William Morris (1834–1896), among these the *House of the Wolfings* (a prose and verse romance published in 1888), a translation of the Icelandic epic the *Völsung Saga*, and particularly the long

---

² Tom Shippey wrote that Tolkien worked on a story that became a "seed" of a section in the *Silmarillion* as early as 1913, when he wrote his own "Story of Kullervo," a never-published "prose and verse romance" which is similar to the story of Túrin in chapter 21. See *J. R. R. Tolkien: Author of the Century* (London: HarperCollins, 2000) 227. In a letter to Katherine Farrer (15 June 1948?), Tolkien mentioned "about 1914" as when he first started work on the *Silmarillion*.

³ Carpenter, *J. R. R. Tolkien: A Biography* (Boston: Houghton Mifflin, 2000) 72.

⁴ See Randel Helms, *Tolkien and the Silmarils* (Boston: Houghton Mifflin, 1981) 2.

narrative poem (three volumes) the *Earthly Paradise*.[5] The latter, which tells about mariners who search for a far-off land that will give them immortality, inspired Tolkien, particularly its telling of the mythological story called "The Land East of the Sun and West of the Moon." Around 1915 he wrote a poem, "The Shores of Faëry," which begins with the words "West of the Moon, East of the Sun / There Stands a lonely hill."[6] From the *House of the Wolfings* Tolkien found the great forest Mirkwood, which he later incorporated into the *Hobbit*. Morris's careful descriptions of his imagined lands and locales impressed Tolkien, and this accuracy carried over into his own works, starting with what became the *Silmarillion*.

By 1915, Tolkien, through his reading of the great national sagas and poems and his own poems and scattered writings, had managed to create his own ideas about a secondary (invented) world, a world which much later was to become incorporated into the *Silmarillion* as Valinor, visited by the mariner Eärendil.[7] His letters reveal that during the First War (1915–1917) he worked on the stories that eventually became part of the *Silmarillion* as often

---

[5] Tolkien's first working title for the *Silmarillion* was "The Book of Lost Tales," and early on he wanted to model it, structurally, after Morris's the *Earthly Paradise*. The purpose of *Earthly Paradise* was to "provide an escape from the unsettled present into a secure, slow-changing past, which would make reality easier to bear." See Paul Thompson, *The Work of William Morris* (New York: Viking, 1967) 171.

[6] Charles E. Noad has noted that "The Shores of Faëry" was Tolkien's first writing that reflected a coherent mythology. See Noad, "On the Construction of 'The Silmarillion,'" in *Tolkien's Legendarium: Essays on the History of Middle-earth*, ed. Verlyn Flieger and Carl F. Hostetter (Westport CT: Greenwood Press, 2000) 36.

[7] Other stories, sagas, poetry, and songs that Tolkien read and was influenced by include the Icelandic *Poetic Edda*, the Old Norse *The Saga of King Heidrek the Wise* and *Popular Tales from the Norse*, the fairy-tale collections of the Brothers Grimm, J. F. Campbell's *Popular Tales of the Western Highlands*, L. C. Wimberly's *Folklore in the English and Scottish Ballads*, Axel Orlick's (ed.) *A Book of Danish Ballads*, and others. See Tom Shippey, *The Road to Middle-Earth* (London: George Allen & Unwin, 1982) appendix A, 296–302.

as he could, in army huts, dugouts, "grimy canteens," and when on sick leave and in the hospital. The war had a profound effect on him and increased his desire to write fantasy and create a secondary world. Years later he wrote: "A real taste for fairy-stories was wakened by philology on the threshold of manhood, and quickened to full life by War."[8]

He wrote the first complete story of his imagined world in the hospital (recuperating from trench fever in 1917), the original version of "The Fall of Gondolin," which in its later version appeared near the end of the *Silmarillion*. This story about a lost battle was perhaps his way of coping imaginatively with the lost battle of the Somme from which he had just come.[9] He was later to read "The Fall of Gondolin" to the Exeter College Essay Club on 10 March 1920. Two members of the club who heard him that day were Nevill Coghill and Hugo Dyson, later friends and members of the Inklings.

Another tale Tolkien created during this time, and one he perhaps loved most of his own stories, was the first version of "Of Beren and Lúthien," which became chapter 19 of the *Silmarillion*. This celebrated tale was the first of many Tolkien created that has at its center the theme of love, when a man meets and falls in love with a fair female elf. There are five of these stories in Tolkien's works (in one the story is reversed when a male elf meets and falls in love with a female), but the Beren and Lúthien tale was obviously his favorite, and it at least partly grew out of his own life, when he met and fell in love with his future wife, Edith.

---

[8] See "On Fairy-Stories" in *Tree and Leaf* (Boston: Houghton Mifflin, 1965) 42.

[9] Gondolin is a beautiful Elven city, the most famous in Middle-earth. It was invaded by evil forces and fell in 511. See Robert Foster, *The Complete Guide to Middle-Earth* (New York: Ballantine, 2001) 214–15, and Dianne Purkiss, *At the Bottom of the Garden: A Dark History of Fairies, Hobgoblins, and Other Troublesome Things* (Washington Square NY: New York University Press, 2001) 282–83. Purkiss speculated that Gondolin was an imaginary refuge for Tolkien "from the dreadful memory of the Somme," but that it "is invaded and captured by the forces of darkness."

Tolkien thought this "heroic fairy-romance" beautiful and powerful, and in it Beren succeeds in capturing one of the Silmarilii from the Iron Crown (when all the armies and warriors have failed), primarily because of the help of the "mere maiden" Lúthien. It is reasonable to assume that Edith, always his helper and confidant, was Tolkien's model for Lúthien in the finished versions of the story. He also worked on a poetic version of this story between 1925 and 1931 called "The Lay of Leithian" (also called "The Geste of Beren and Lúthien"), which was read and commented on by C. S. Lewis.

Tolkien continued working on the various parts of the *Silmarillion* in between and around his university work at Leeds and Oxford. He had completed a major portion of his elvish tales by 1920, later to be published in the early 1980s as the two-volume *Book of Lost Tales*. In the early 1920s (while at Leeds), he completed the poetic version of the tale of Beren and Lúthien, published after his death as the *Lays of Beleriand* in 1987. In the mid-twenties he completed a "Sketch of the Mythology," which later became "The Earliest Silmarillion" in the *Shaping of Middle-earth*, published in 1986. A revised version of this (titled "The Quenta Silmarillion") was published in the *Lost Road* in 1987.

In the 1920s, Tolkien, though he had finished some of the stories of the *Silmarillion* and had written outlines and sketches of others, failed to finish the work and bring it to a satisfactory conclusion. He began revising and rewriting, almost, as Humphrey Carpenter wrote, "as if he did not want to finish it."[10] Carpenter and other scholars reasoned that he either didn't think it would be accepted by a publisher, or his overly-perfectionistic nature prevented him from "finishing anything easily," or perhaps the demands of his university work interfered with his attempts at regular, sustained writing. His longtime T.C.B.S. friend Christopher Wiseman ventured the idea that Tolkien did not want to finish his great work because "sub-creating" was the essence of

---

[10] Carpenter, *Biography*, 113.

his very life, and he could not bear the thought of not creating: "Why these creatures live to you is because you are still creating them. When you have finished creating them they will be dead to you as the atoms that make our living food."[11]

He continued reworking, polishing, shaping, and revising his mythology into the thirties, and read aloud much of what he wrote to Lewis, who in a letter to Arthur Greeves called Tolkien an author of "voluminous unpublished metrical romances."[12] Tolkien appreciated Lewis for his "sheer encouragement" and because Lewis saw the work as more than Tolkien's "private hobby" and urged him to see the book through and try to have it published. Many believe that Tolkien's friends, particularly the Inklings, had no real influence on him and that he would have written his Middle-earth stories had he never met them. But Diana L. Pavlac suggested that Tolkien indeed did rely on the encouragement of others and followed specific suggestions from friends. For Tolkien, "the debt of sheer encouragement" he owed to Lewis was a broad and persuasive type of influence, and without it he might not have written as much of the *Silmarillion* as he did, especially when he grew older and his energy waned.[13]

After the *Hobbit* was published in the autumn of 1937, it quickly became so popular that Allen & Unwin told Tolkien that

---

[11] Ibid., 114. Another Tolkien scholar, Randel Helms, says almost the same thing, that Tolkien did not hurry to finish the book because of an "unwillingness to say farewell to Faërie." See Helms, *Tolkien's World* (Boston: Houghton Mifflin, 1974) 148.

[12] Walter Hooper, ed., *They Stand Together: The Letters of C. S. Lewis to Arthur Greeves (1914–1963)* (London: Collins, 1979) 341. Lewis sent Tolkien fourteen pages of criticism on "The Lay of Leithian" which he incorporated into the poem before leaving it in the early 1930s.

[13] See Pavlac, "More than a Bandersnatch: Tolkien as a Collaborative Writer," in *Proceedings of the J. R. R. Tolkien Centenary Conference*, ed. Patricia Reynolds and Glen H. GoodKnight (Altadena CA: The Mythopoeic Press, 1995) 367–74. Charles Noad's "The Construction of 'The Silmarillion,'" in Flieger and Hostetter, *Tolkien's Legendarium*, is the most lucid and detailed study of the making of the *Silmarillion* available to date.

the public would want another book about hobbits. Tolkien had no more to write about hobbits, but agreed to "start the process of thought" about another work that would be "similar in style" and for a "similar audience." On 15 November 1937, he met with publisher Stanley Unwin[14] in London and gave him the manuscripts of *Farmer Giles of Ham*, *Mr. Bliss*, the *Lost Road*, "The Ambarkanta" (later in the *Shaping of Middle-Earth*), "The Lay of Leithian," and three from the *Silmarillion*: the prose "Quenta Silmarillion," "The Ainulindalë," and "The Akallabêth." Unwin dismissed "The Lay of Leithian" as a "long poem," and called the Silmarillion and Ambarkanta manuscripts "gnomes material," probably because they were too long, difficult, and so unlike the *Hobbit*. Unwin enjoyed the children's stories but rejected them because they had no hobbits, and the *Lost Road* was obviously not for younger readers. Mr. Unwin gave "The Lay of Leithian" to a reader, who did not know what to do with it and thought there would not be a market for "a long, involved, romantic verse-tale of Celtic elves and mortals."[15]

Unwin returned the *Silmarillion* manuscript to Tolkien on 15 December, and obviously trying to keep from hurting Tolkien's feelings, sent a letter praising the work as containing "much wonderful material." Tolkien wrote back the next day, expressing joy that his life's work had not been "rejected with scorn," mentioning that some of the work, being "rough material," had "grave defects," and expressing the hope that it could be published someday. He mentioned also that "the construction of elaborate and consistent mythology (and two languages) rather occupies the [my] mind, and the Silmarils are in my heart. So that goodness knows what will happen...And what more can hobbits do?...Do you think Tom Bombadil, the spirit of the (vanishing) Oxford and

---

[14] Tolkien thought Mr. Unwin, "small, bright-eyed, and bearded," looked "exactly like one of my dwarves." See Carpenter, *Biography*, 187.

[15] Ibid., 217. Carpenter mentions that Tolkien also gave Unwin the *Roverandom* manuscript; Hammond, in *J. R. R. Tolkien: A Descriptive Bibliography* (New Castle DE: Oak Knoll Books, 1993), does not mention it.

The Silmarillion

Berkshire countryside, could be made into the hero of a story?"[16] He immediately started work on a new book about hobbits, the magisterial heroic romance that became the *Lord of the Rings*.

In 1949, when he was finishing work on the *Lord of the Rings*, Tolkien met Milton Waldman, an editor at Collins Publishing in London. Waldman was interested in both the *Lord of the Rings* and the *Silmarillion*, and Tolkien considered leaving Allen & Unwin for a publisher with more money and resources, and who initially was more open to publishing his "saga of the Jewels and the Rings." Out of loyalty to the Unwin family, and probably also because he liked them personally, Tolkien wrote to Mr. Unwin on 24 February 1950, saying that the *Silmarillion* had "infiltrated" everything "even remotely Faery" that he had written (he kept it out of *Farmer Giles of Ham* "with effort"), that it had "captured" the *Lord of the Rings*, and that he wanted to publish both the *Silmarillion* and the *Lord of the Rings* "in conjunction or in connexion." Unwin wrote back with a suggestion that the two books be divided into three or four volumes, but Tolkien was in no mood to compromise. He wrote Tolkien again on 3 April, saying that his son Raynor had suggested that "really relevant material" could be taken from the *Silmarillion* and incorporated into the *Lord of the Rings*, and that if this could (or would not) be done, the *Lord of the Rings* would be published and the *Silmarillion* would not. Tolkien quickly wrote back a polite (but angry) letter asking for a decision. Unwin answered "No," not having seen a final manuscript and considering the great cost of publishing such a large book.

Tolkien now turned to Collins, but had unexpected bad results. Editor Waldman was in ill health, living in Italy most of the time (except for occasional visits to London), and no one at Collins was familiar with Tolkien or his work. Problems arose when Waldman irritated Tolkien by suggesting he cut substantial amounts of material from the *Lord of the Rings*, and because of

---

[16] Carpenter, *Letters*, 26.

Tolkien's overestimated projected large length of *Silmarillion*, the cost of which worried Waldman. Late in 1951 Tolkien wrote Waldman (at his suggestion) a long, ten-thousand-word letter, explaining the book and why it and the *Lord of the Rings* were "interdependent and indivisible." This amazing nineteen-page letter (in the paperback edition of Tolkien's collected letters), is as good a starting place as any to learn about his passion for his invented mythologies, the "whys and wherefores" of who he was as a writer and creative artist.[17]

But Waldman wavered, and by March 1952 Tolkien still did not have a contract with Collins. Tolkien angrily demanded that Collins publish the *Lord of the Rings* immediately, but Waldman would not, due to the length of the book and the rising cost of paper. Meanwhile Allen & Unwin had kept *Farmer Giles of Ham* in print, had published a second edition of the *Hobbit*, and in the summer of 1952 Raynor Unwin resumed friendly relations with Tolkien. Allen & Unwin agreed to publish the *Lord of the Rings* by itself, and the work was published in three volumes in 1954–1955. Immediately afterwards, Unwin encouraged Tolkien to finish the *Silmarillion*, but he never did.

What followed was almost twenty years of encouragement, some writing, Tolkien's apologies, more writing, more encouragement, and more apologies, with Tolkien often complaining about "professional concerns." This saga became, as Wayne Hammond noted, "a tale of hope and frustration."[18] But Tolkien's apologies were legitimate; he was getting older and was often very tired. There were many demands on his time, both familial and professional, and he often just did not have enough sustained time and energy for prolonged work on the *Silmarillion*. The book was often in a "confused" state because of its complexity and enormous amount of names, places, and events, and Tolkien was often discouraged because he believed it would

---

[17] Carpenter, *Letters*, 143–61.
[18] Hammond, *Descriptive Bibliography*, 219.

never have the appeal of the *Lord of the Rings*. In a letter to Anne Barrett of Houghton Mifflin in 1956 he wrote: "...I do not think it would have the appeal of L.R.—no hobbits! Full of mythology and elvishness, and all that 'heigh stile' (as Chaucer might say), which has been so little to the taste of many reviewers. But I am not allowed to get at it. I am not only submerged (sans secretary) under business of the L.R., but also under professional business..."[19]

As mentioned, some think that Tolkien could not finish the *Silmarillion* because it was so much a living part of who he was, a man who had to create. This is probably true in some degree, but less tenable is the idea that he would not finish because he knew that the book's projected income would bring large death taxes on his estate, as his later secretary Joy Hill suggested. So he asked his son Christopher to complete the work after his death. Tolkien trusted and loved Christopher, and he was the one person who knew almost as much about the *Silmarillion* as Tolkien did himself.

For some, the *Silmarillion* is not an easy book to read or understand. Tom Shippey wrote that it "can never be anything other than hard to read," that it was unlikely that the book would have been published at all except for the success of the *Lord of the Rings*, that a modern audience could not relate to its lack of hobbits, and that it scorned "novelistic convention" with so much detail and so many characters.[20] Others agreed with Shippey and noted that the work is difficult to enjoy and is sometimes

---

[19] Carpenter, *Letters*, 238. Richard Matthews noted that the style of the *Silmarillion* is "unique in twentieth century English literature" and affirmed the opinion of another scholar, who wrote that "high style" was natural for Tolkien, and he adopted a "lower style" in his other fictional works to make them more marketable. See Matthews, *Lightning from a Clear Sky: Tolkien, The Trilogy, and The Silmarillion* (San Bernadino CA: Borgo Press, 1978) 56.

[20] See Shippey, *Author of the Century*, 261. When J. E. A. Tyler revised his *Tolkien Companion* dictionary to include the *Silmarillion*, he had to add over 1,800 entries.

unreadable, primarily because of its lack of narrative continuity (it does not "tell a story" in a conventional manner), its elevated and sometimes stilted rhetoric, its lack of a primary hero, its lack of celebration of the ordinary, and (again) the enormous amount of names of people, individuals, and places (often unpronounceable) that confuse the reader, in spite of Christopher Tolkien's helps and aids to the reader at the end of the book. But the *Silmarillion* was an immediate bestseller, and has sold extremely well all over the world since its publication. Allen & Unwin released 600,000 copies in 1977, making the book, according to a reviewer, "the biggest hardback fiction first edition in British publishing history."[21]

The completed *Silmarillion* (particularly "Quenta Silmarillion") is Tolkien's saga of the First Age of his invented world, "the ancient drama" in which several characters of the *Lord of the Rings* look back on and took part in, such as Galadriel and Elrond. The three Silmarils were majestic jewels, and the Quenta Silmarillion is largely the story of their creation by the Noldorin prince Fëanor, their subsequent loss to the evil Morgoth (originally Melkor), their recapture, and doom. The book is, as a whole, the "Bible" for the elves, and it is an ancient history textbook for the peoples of Middle-earth.

The *Silmarillion* is divided into five parts, including genealogical tables, notes on pronunciation, a name index, and an appendix detailing elements in the two languages of the book, Quenya and Sindarin. The first section is "The Ainulindalë," Tolkien's "Genesis" essay describing the music sung by the Ainur (angelic spirits created by the thought of God) which created the world (Arda).[22] The second part, "Valaquenta," details the history

---

[21] John Ezard, "Tolkien's Paradise Lost," *The Guardian* (15 September 1977), in Meredith Veldman, *Fantasy, the Bomb, and the Greening of Britain* (Cambridge: Cambridge University Press, 1994) 98–99.

[22] Tolkien wrote several versions of the creation of the world, including "The Music of the Ainur" in *The Book of Lost Tales, I*, "The Ambarkanta" in *The Shaping of Middle-Earth*, and "The Ainulindalë" in *The Lost Road*. Earlier versions of *The Silmarillion* include both books of *The Lost Tales* (the beginning

of the Valar, the powers (angelic beings) who were created by God (Eru, the One, or Ilúvatar) and entered the world (Middle-earth, the Undying Lands) at its creation. The third section, "Quenta Silmarillion," the history of the Silmarils ("the Silmarillion proper"), is the primary and largest section and consists of twenty-four sections totaling more than 200 pages. The elves make their appearance here in chapters 3–8, 11, and also the Silmarils, which are majestic jewels that contain the light of the Two Tress of Valinor, the trees that illuminated the world before the creation of the sun and moon. The fourth section, "Akallabéth," is the story of the downfall of Númenor at the end of the Second Age, Akallabéth being the name given to Númenor after its destruction. The fifth and final section, "Of the Rings of Power and the Third Age," is a retelling of the history of the *Lord of the Rings*.

In his foreword to the *Book of Lost Tales*, Christopher Tolkien wrote that "to read the *Silmarillion* one must place oneself imaginatively at the time of the ending of the Third Age—within Middle-earth, looking back: at the temporal point of Sam Gamgee's 'I like that!'—adding, 'I should like to know more about it.'" Christopher added that due to the compendious form of the *Silmarillion*, "with its ages of poetry and 'lore' behind it," the book strongly evokes a sense of "untold tales," in which "distance is never lost."[23] The *Silmarillion* invokes surprise, curiosity, and awe, and its reading can be a wonderful experience if the patient reader is prepared to look back at a world where beauty and terror coexisted, and where Old Testament values of right and wrong were taken as absolutes. It is not as easy to read as the *Lord of the Rings*, but the *Silmarillion* has had for many a great fascination.

---

of the stories), "The Earliest 'Silmarillion'" and "The Quenta" in *The Shaping of Middle-Earth*, and "The Quenta Silmarillion" in *The Lost Road*.

[23] *The Book of Lost Tales, Part I* (Boston: Houghton Mifflin, 1984) 4.

Poetry

Tolkien scholars are divided on his merits as a poet, and many think that he was a better prose writer. His poetry was pre-twentieth century in style, often repetitious and simplistic (with many references to "wind in the trees"), and sometimes lapsed into slack diction. He preferred old-fashioned techniques of rhyme and a strict meter blended with alliteration, and did not care for modern free verse or techniques and "personal poetry."[1] However, the many poems of Middle-earth, representing different styles and formats, often represented songs, and modern techniques would have been inappropriate, even anachronistic, in Tolkien's tales of fantasy and the fantastic. In a letter to his son Michael (August 1967), Tolkien wrote that the verses in the *Lord of the Rings* were not "personal" and "soul searching" but dramatic, "fitted in style and contents to the *characters* in the story that sing or recite them, and to the situations in it..."[2] And Tom Shippey observed that Tolkien's poems gave his work a mythic

---

[1] Alliteration is the repetition of consonant or vowel sounds in poetry, which enhances the musical qualities of language. It is used to achieve a strong texture of sound, either dissonance or harmony, depending on the patterning of consonants. *Beowulf* is a prime example of a narrative poem that has powerful alliterative patterns.

[2] Humphrey Carpenter, *The Letters of J. R. R. Tolkien* (London: Allen & Unwin, 1981) 396.

Poetry 89

and imaginative dimension that has never been duplicated, especially among fantasy writers.[3]

Tolkien's Middle-earth poems are often dramatic, and at the same time many of them are concise, charming, funny, and imaginative, particularly in the *Hobbit*, the *Lord of the Rings* (over sixty poems and songs, counting repetitions and variants), the *Book of Lost Tales*, and the *Lays of Beleriand*. They add immensely to the dramatic presentations of his stories and make them more of a pleasure to read.[4]

Tolkien's poems can be loosely categorized as "hobbit poetry" ("simple and occasional," nineteen in the *Lord of the Rings*), "Tom Bombadil's songs" (merry, lighthearted nonsense with an added serious dimension), "Elvish poetry" (the most consistently musical, ten in the *Lord of the Rings*), "Ent poetry" (primarily dealing with Tolkien's tree-creatures like Treebeard, six in the *Lord of the Rings*), "the poetry of Aragorn and the men of Rohan" (the men who inhabit Middle-earth, eight in Old English in the *Lord of the Rings*), and "miscellaneous" (such as by Gandalf the wizard and Gimli the dwarf). There are several verse forms in the *Lord of the Rings*, including rhymed couplets in different meters, tetrameter quatrains (three of them variants of "The Road Goes Ever On and On"), Old English prosody, ballad stanza, and several nonce-forms (for one occasion) of stanza, rhythm, or rhyme. Most of the poems in the *Lord of the Rings* (over thirty) are really song lyrics that were meant to be sung, chanted, or recited. One is an epitaph (Snowmane's epitaph—Snowmane was the

---

[3] Tom Shippey, "Tolkien and Me," Internet essay, 21 June 2001, Borders.com (http://go.borders.com/features/shippey.xcv).

[4] Of the seventy-five or so poems in the *History of Middle-Earth*, forty had been previously published. One of them (circa 1915), "*Kôr*: In a City Lost and Dead" (*Book of Lost Tales*), is a sonnet, which Tolkien would not be expected to write, a sonnet not being a Teutonic or medieval English verse form. See Joe R. Christopher, "Tolkien's Lyric Poetry," in *Tolkien's Legendarium: Essays on the History of Middle-earth*, ed. Verlyn Flieger and Carl Hostetter (Westport CT: Greenwood Press, 2000) 143–60.

horse of King Théoden, killed in the battle of Pelennor Fields in the *Two Towers*), which was meant only to be read. One Tolkien scholar wrote that these verses "are used to expand, to emphasize, to rarefy the prose" of Middle-earth, "are natural and appropriate to the context," and "reinforce the remoteness and unreality of his work"[5], while another said that Tolkien's success as a mythmaker was "enhanced by the poetry that readers so often praise as the 'icing on the cake' of his thrilling narratives."[6]

Tolkien's poetry and songs received little praise in his lifetime, even from his friends and admirers.[7] But he never abandoned his pre-twentieth-century poetic style, and even after his Middle-earth stories and poems became world-famous, he was modest about his poetry. In a letter to his illustrator Pauline Baynes, he mentioned that his verses were "small things...which are lighthearted...but not very profound in intention."[8] Tolkien's poems and songs were the expressions of his spirit, and this section will introduce some of his Middle-earth "small things" and others, both well-known and obscure.

---

[5] Maria Q. Kelly, "The Poetry of Fantasy: Verse in *The Lord of the Rings*," in *Tolkien and the Critics*, ed. Neil D. Isaacs and Rose A. Zimbardo (Notre Dame IN: University of Notre Dame Press, 1968) 170, 172. See also Diane Marchesani, "Tolkien's Lore: The Songs of Middle-Earth," in *Mythlore 23* (March 1990): 3–5, and Melanie A. Rawls, "The Verse of J. R. R. Tolkien," *Mythlore 71* (Winter 1993): 6.

[6] Steven M. Deyo, "Niggle's Leaves: *The Red Book of Westmarch* and Related Minor Poetry of J. R. R. Tolkien," *Proceedings of the Sixteenth Annual Convention of the Mythopoeic Society, Mythlore 27* (July 1985): 48.

[7] Tolkien's friends were sometimes wildly divergent in their views about his poetry. In a blurb for the *Lord of the Rings* George Sayer called Tolkien the "greatest living poet," but C. S. Lewis called his poetry on the whole "poor, regrettable, and out of place." See Carpenter, *Letters*, 168–69.

[8] Ibid., 312.

"Goblin Feet"

"Goblin Feet" was Tolkien's third published poem, and he wrote it in early April 1915 when he was twenty-three years old. It was written for his future wife Edith, who liked "spring and flowers and trees, and little elfin people." Much later, Tolkien wished that this thirty-four-line poem ("the unhappy little thing"), with its leprechauns, pretty flitter-mice, coney-rabbits, and glow-worms, "could be buried forever."[9] He wrote the poem as an undergraduate, and his ideas about goblins as "tiny elfin creatures" had radically changed since then. Perhaps another reason was that he knew the poem (early as it was), was not very good stylistically, especially when one line is past tense, and all the others are present. But Tom Shippey noted that it does have "hints of hope," especially when Tolkien characterizes "the road" as "a slender band of grey" and "the crooked fairy lane" as a harbinger of one of his enduring images, "the road which goes ever on."[10] This image is used often in the *Hobbit* and the *Lord of the Rings*, the often "hard and unforeseen" road one chooses that leads to quests and perils and adventures.

"Goblin Feet" was Tolkien's first real success, and has since been reprinted several times, partly because of its charm, but most likely because it is part of Tolkien's canon of "juvenile writings." It was published in a famous annual Oxford poetry series (*Oxford Poetry 1914–1916*), the *Book of Fairy Poetry* (1920), the Basil Blackwell anthology *Fifty New Poems for Children* (1924, which included such notable writers as Edith Sitwell and Robert Graves), and most recently in the *Annotated Hobbit* (2002).

---

[9] J. R. R. Tolkien, *The Book of Lost Tales, Part I*, ed. Christopher Tolkien (London: Allen & Unwin, 1983) 32.

[10] Shippey, *The Road to Middle-Earth* (London: Allen & Unwin, 1982) 28.

"Songs for the Philologists"

While at Leeds in the early 1920s, Tolkien and colleague E. V. Gordon helped form the Viking club for English Department undergraduates, which would meet regularly to drink beer, sing comic songs, and read stories. The songs were written mostly by Tolkien and Gordon, and consisted primarily of nonsense verse (one was sung to the tune of "Twinkle, Twinkle, Little Star"), but also included modern and traditional songs in Old and Modern English, Gothic, Icelandic, and Latin. Thirty of the songs were typed by Gordon (thirteen were written by Tolkien) and given to students, and in 1935 or 1936, a former student, then teaching at University College, London, distributed a few copies to his students. Most of the copies were destroyed by fire, but two copies were sent to Tolkien in 1940–1941, which he annotated with corrections and changes.

According to Tom Shippey, although most of Tolkien's poems in this collection were either satirical or "remarkable only for their linguistic dexterity," four had "something more personal to say."[11] Two, "Flower of the Trees" and "Good Luck to You," celebrate the birch tree and its strength, which represents disciplined learning. "Elf-Fair Lady" and "Across the Broad Ocean" show a mortal trapped by an immortal; in both there are elements of despair and loneliness.

"The Homecoming of Beorhtnoths Beorhthelm's Son"

"Beorhtnoth" is an alliterative verse drama first published for a popular audience in the *Tolkien Reader* (1966), and reissued in *Poems and Stories* in 1980. It is a sequel to the famous Anglo-Saxon poem the *Battle of Maldon*, which is second in fame among

---

[11] Ibid., 303.

early English poems only to *Beowulf*, and is considered by many the greatest battle poem in the English language. Maldon was a battle fought in AD 991 between the English and a Viking fleet that plundered the coast of Kent, sacked the town of Ipswich, and established a base near Maldon ("cross on a hill") a few miles northeast of London.[12] Tolkien's drama tells of an imaginary episode after the battle when two servants of Duke Beorhtnoth (commander of the English army) come in the darkness of night to retrieve their master's corpse from the battlefield.

The drama consists of three parts. Part one tells of the death of Beorhtnoth, and this episode is an introduction to part two, the "homecoming" of the two servants, young Torhthelm and old Tidwald, to search for and retrieve their master's body, found headless. Part three, "Ofermod," was published first in *Essays and Studies of the English Association* (1953), and was Tolkien's critical survey of the Old English poem, in which he comments on the overconfident "heroic excess" that became Beorhtnoth's undoing.[13] Here he went against much of the scholarly thinking of his day that saw the poem primarily as a celebration of heroism, and instead maintained that, although the poem does celebrate "the heroism of obedience and love," the poet's main intention was to censure an "overmastering pride" and a lust for fame. Beorhtnoth first offered the Vikings money ("rings and bracelets") in return

---

[12] A definitive text of the poem, with excellent introductory notes, was edited by Tolkien's colleague E. V. Gordon, *The Battle of Maldon* (London: Methuen, 1937). Tolkien helped Gordon with the manuscript. An essay that supports and expands on Tolkien's view of the heroic in this drama is by Fred C. Robinson, "God, Death, and Loyalty in *The Battle of Maldon*," in *J. R. R. Tolkien, Scholar and Storyteller: Essays in Memoriam*, ed. Mary Salu and Robert T. Farrell (Ithaca NY: Cornell University Press, 1979) 76–98.

[13] The Old English word *ofermod* is translated "great, high courage," while the Flemish word *overmoed* is translated "recklessness" or "overboldness." The Flemish meaning sheds light on the Old English word, and the meanings of the two words overlap. See R. M. Wilson, "Old English," in vol. 34 of *The Year's Work in English Studies*, ed. F. S. Boas and B. White (London: Oxford University Press, 1955) 50.

for their "protection." When he was "chivalric" and allowed the Vikings to cross a ford and thus "have a fair fight," this was seen as a non-heroic act that proved fatal to Beorhtnoth and his soldiers.

Tolkien, in his character Tidwald, tells the reader that war should never be idealized, but never suggests that a fight with an enemy is to be avoided. Paul Kocher wrote that "Tolkien's deep hatred of waste and death would make him insist that they (wars) be plainly necessary to the defense of freedom at home."[14] This poetic drama, in verse dialogue, was Tolkien's way of at least partly examining the traditional English view of courage and heroism in war, and asking that it be rethought and reevaluated.

The Adventures of Tom Bombadil and Other Verses from the Red Book

Tom Bombadil (the name is based on a Dutch doll that belonged to Tolkien's son Michael) is a collection of lighthearted and sometimes frivolous verse from "The Red Book of Westmarch," supposedly written by Bilbo Baggins, Sam Gamgee, and other hobbits. In his explanatory note to the collection Tolkien tells the reader that the verses are mostly concerned with "legends and jests of the Shire at the end of the Third Age." Tolkien also mentioned that the hobbit verses are "fond of strange words, and of rhyming and metrical tricks." And Tolkien's hobbit verses in *Tom Bombadil* are very "hobbitlike": often very neat, comic, simple, sometimes simplistic, entertaining, descriptive (especially of food), and easy to memorize.

The title poem was published by *Oxford Magazine* in 1935, and in 1937 Tolkien wrote to his publisher Stanley Unwin and asked if Tom Bombadil ("the spirit of the vanishing Oxford and

---

[14] Kocher, *Master of Middle-earth: The Fiction of J. R. R. Tolkien* (Boston: Houghton Mifflin, 1972) 194.

Berkshire countryside") could be the hero of a new story, perhaps a successor to the *Hobbit*. Unwin gave the question to his son Raynor, who said that the story was good, but could be only a continuation of the *Hobbit*. Tolkien never wrote a prose version of "Tom Bombadil," but did introduce the highly enigmatic character of Tom into the *Lord of the Rings*, and he has been one of the most discussed and analyzed of all of Tolkien's creations.[15]

In 1961, Tolkien's aunt Jane Neave asked him to write a small book "with Tom Bombadil at the heart of it." Tolkien liked the idea, especially if his illustrator for *Farmer Giles of Ham*, Pauline Baynes, would illustrate it. He wrote to his publisher, suggesting the book as an "interim amusement" between the *Lord of the Rings* and the unfinished *Silmarillion*. The original poem ran only 127 lines, so Tolkien enlarged the book with revisions of several previously published poems, including "Errantry," "The Man in the Moon Came Down Too Soon," and "The Sea-Bell," considered by W. H. Auden to be his finest poem (Tolkien regarded it as poor and did not want to include it in this collection). He added and revised more poems later, including three from the *Lord of the Rings*: "The Man in the Moon Stayed Up Too Late" (sung by Frodo at the inn in Bree), "The Stone Troll" (sung by Sam to cheer up his friends and originally "The Root of the Boot" in *Songs for the Philologists*; a later and less sophisticated version appears in the *Fellowship of the Ring*, chapter 12), and "Oliphaunt" (a nursery rhyme recited by Sam at the battle in the Vale of Ithlien in the *Two Towers*).[16] "Bombadil

---

[15] Robert Foster in *The Complete Guide to Middle-Earth* (New York: Ballentine, 1978) described Tom as a "being" and possibly a "Maia (angel) gone native" (492). Other Tolkien scholars have called him a "nature spirit" or god in various forms, and one conjectured that he was Aulë, the god-like master craftsman who made the raw materials of which Arda (Earth) was composed. See Gene Hargrove, "Who Was Tom Bombadil?" at Internet site "The Grey Havens: The Ultimate J. R. R. Tolkien Home Page," 3 January 2002 (http://www.cas.unt.edu/~hargrove/bombadil).

[16] The poem "Oliphaunt" was published separately by Eden Press of Toronto in 1984 and has been reprinted several times.

Goes Boating" was added to further blend the character of Tom into the *Lord of the Rings*. Other poems in the collection include "Princess Mee," "Cat" (which Tolkien wrote to amuse his granddaughter), "Perry-the-Winkle," "The Mewlips," "Fastitocalon" (a whale), "Shadow Bride," "The Hoard," and "The Last Ship."

The total collection was sixteen poems, and they were published later in the *Tolkien Reader* and *Poems and Stories*, and with *Farmer Giles of Ham*. Tolkien commented on the initial reviews of the poems in a letter to Unwin, saying that he had seen two reviews and "was agreeably surprised: I expected remarks far more snooty and patronizing." He was also pleased that the reviewers had begun "not wanting to be amused, but had failed to maintain their Victorian dignity intact."[17] *Tom Bombadil* was a commercial success, at first largely due to Tolkien's popular literary reputation. It sold nearly 8,000 copies before publication, prompting him to remark gleefully: "...that, even on a minute initial royalty, means more than is at all usual for anyone but Betjeman to make on verse!"[18]

One author wrote that "the hobbit verse" in *Tom Bombadil* is "very much in keeping with Tolkien's characterization of hobbits...easy, comic, simple, sometimes simpleminded, meant to entertain, easy to memorize, and much given to descriptions of food and other creature comforts."[19] But two Tolkien scholars have pointed out that the last four poems in the book "shift to a serious tone."[20] "Shadow Bride" is an enigmatic tale of a bewitched man without a shadow except once a year, when a mysterious lady visits and "wraps her shadow around him." "The Hoard" is a short discourse on the corruptive power of greed, and "The Sea-Bell" is a dreamlike quest journey where nothing goes

---

[17] Carpenter, *Letters*, 322.
[18] Ibid., 322.
[19] Melanie A. Rawls, "The Verse of J. R. R. Tolkien," *Mythlore 71* (Winter 1993): 6.
[20] Ivor Rogers and Deborah Rogers, *J. R. R. Tolkien: A Critical Biography* (New York: Hippocrene Books, 1980) 52.

right and loneliness is pervasive: "I have lost myself, and I know not the way...." Verlyn Flieger called it "a story of 'There and Back Again.' It is about the uncommunicable experience of Faërie, about what it is like to find it and what it is like to give it up and go on."[21] "The Last Ship" is a haunting poem in which the fair mortal Firiel must continue her mundane existence and not travel to Elvenhome, where she would always be beautiful.

In one of the later editions of *Tom Bombadil*, the publisher added this introduction: *"The Adventures of Tom Bombadil* tells us of Tom's encounters with Goldberry, the River-woman's beautiful daughter; with Old Man Willow, who tries to trap Tom inside his trunk; with the Badger-folk; with the ghostly Barrow-wight, who dwells in the ancient mound on the hilltop. In other verses we meet a princess lovely as an elvensong, The Man in the Moon, Trolls, Dwarves, and legendary beasts...here is a delightful volume of songs, rhymes, and poems..."[22] This is a delightful volume, but the publisher perhaps should have mentioned that its reader must be prepared, especially when reading the last four poems, to think about serious subjects.

The Road Goes Ever On – A Song Cycle

The well-known British composer Donald Swann (born in Wales, 1923–1994), was a great admirer of Tolkien's work, and in 1965 he set to music six of the poems in the *Lord of the Rings*. Swann met with Tolkien in May 1965 and played for him five poems from the *Fellowship of the Ring*: "The Road Goes Ever On" (sung by Bilbo as he departs the Shire for the last time), "Upon the Hearth the Fire is Red" (a "walking song" hummed by Frodo, Sam, and Pippin), "In Western Lands" (sung by Sam), "Namárië"

---

[21] Flieger, *A Question of Time: J. R. R. Tolkien's Road to Faërie* (Kent OH: Kent State University Press, 1997) 229.

[22] J. R. R. Tolkien, *The Adventures of Tom Bombadil*, illustrated by Roger Garland (Boston: Houghton Mifflin, 1991) inside jacket cover.

("Farewell," the song of Lady Galadriel), and "I Sit beside the Fire" (sung by Bilbo to Frodo), and one song from the *Two Towers*, "In the Willow-meads of Tasarinan" (hummed and chanted by Treebeard). Swann also played a new song, a setting for "Namárië," which Tolkien did not approve.

Swann became friends with Tolkien and later performed and published his settings for Tolkien's poetry, with Tolkien's enthusiastic permission. Allen & Unwin's Joy Hill introduced Swann to a music student friend of hers, William Elven (Tolkien thought his name a "good omen"), and supported Swann in his efforts to produce a long-playing record of the poems, with Elven singing. In March 1966, Elven and Swann performed the Song Cycle for Tolkien and his wife and guests at Merton College, Oxford, at the celebration of the Tolkiens' golden wedding anniversary. In May 1966 Swann performed "I Sit Beside the Fire" on the BBC radio "Today" program, and he and Elven performed all of the poems a few days later at the Lakeland Theatre at Rosehill, Cumberland, in a program titled "The Lyric Songs of Donald Swann," which included songs from the works of Byron, Shakespeare, and John Betjeman.

Later in 1966, Swann and his partner Michael Flanders took their two-man musical show *At the Drop of Another Hat* to America, in which they included a rendition of "I Sit Beside the Fire." A Houghton Mifflin representative in the audience met with Swann and Flanders afterwards and suggested Caedmon Records of New York as a publisher for the record. The record was recorded on 15 June 1967, with the original songs performed by Swann and Elven and Tolkien's "Errantry" (from *Tom Bombadil*) added, and Tolkien himself reading five poems from *Tom Bombadil* and (in Elvish) "A Elbereth Gilthoniel," from the *Fellowship of the Ring*. The published record was a commercial success and included liner notes by W. H. Auden.

In 1967, the book version of the songs was published by Houghton Mifflin, and included a foreword by Swann and Tolkien's linguistic notes and translations for "Namárië" and "A

Elbereth Gilthoniel," the two Elvish poems. The front cover of the book jacket was decorated by Tolkien's Tengwar (a middle-earth writing system) text of "Namárië," and the back cover pictured the Elvish refrain from "I Sit Beside the Fire." The second edition of the book (Allen & Unwin, 1978), added "Bilbo's Last Song" (see below) to Tolkien's and Swann's original renditions. Another song, "Luthien Tinuviel" (written for Tolkien's wife, Edith, whom he called "Luthien"), written in 1978, was not published in either of the first two editions of the *Road Goes Ever On*. A noncommercial recording of all nine songs was made by Swann in 1993 and is now deposited in both the Donald Swann Archive in England and the Marion E. Wade Center at Wheaton College, near Chicago.

In his foreword to the 1993 German edition of the *Road Goes Ever On*, Swann wrote: "The Road Goes Ever On…is certainly as much Tolkien as Swann, and its very genesis depended on Tolkien's enthusiasm for the music, also that of his wife Edith."[23]

"Mythopoeia"

On Saturday night, 19 September 1931, C. S. Lewis (then thirty-three years old) invited Tolkien and Professor H. V. D. ("Hugo") Dyson to dine at Magdalen College. After dinner, the three friends walked around Addison's Walk and talked for hours about "metaphor and myth" and the Christian faith. It was a *very* long walk and talk, for Tolkien went home at 3:00 A.M. and Dyson stayed till about six. By this time in his spiritual journey, Lewis was a believer in God (theist), but had not yet come to committed belief in Jesus as the Christ. He had long loved reading and thinking about literature and myth, but did not believe it as truth in

---

[23] William Phemister, "Fantasy Set to Music: Donald Swann, C. S. Lewis and J. R. R. Tolkien," in vol. 13 of *SEVEN: An Anglo-American Literary Review* (1996): 71.

the formal sense, particularly the "Christian myth" contained in the gospels and in the story of Jesus. Lewis told Tolkien and Dyson that he believed that myths were "lies and therefore worthless, even though breathed through silver." They countered Lewis by convincing him that God works through myth and story, and that the "Christ myth" was really true and based on historical fact; the incarnation of Jesus was the historical realization of the "dying and resurrecting gods" stories of ancient cultures.

So due in large part to this long talk with his friends, Lewis came to realize that the Christ myth in the Gospels made a truth claim that was both distinctive and demanded a personal response. Lewis also came to believe that the Christian myth communicated a reality about what truth is; Christ was a "true myth" because the Word became human in the fact of the historical Jesus. Furthermore, Tolkien and Dyson convinced Lewis that Christianity "works" and that a believer can become a "new person." This "long night walk and talk" was a pivotal event in Lewis's life and was instrumental in his conversion to authentic Christian faith in Jesus as Christ and to a committed life of piety and discipleship.

This was the occasion that led to Tolkien's writing of "Mythopoeia" ("the making of fables"). There are seven versions of the poem, and according to Christopher Tolkien's notes it probably was written sometime before 1935.[24] The title of the earliest version was "*Nisomythos: a long answer to short nonsense.*" None of the versions have addressees, and all have been changed and edited. On the fifth version of the poem, Tolkien wrote "J. R. R. T. for C. S. L.," and also on the sixth, adding "Philomythus Mismytho" ("lover of myth hater of myth").

"Mythopoeia" was written in rhyming couplets and contained five primary ideas, which, in a brief compass, expressed Tolkien's creed of sub-creation and myth. One, God created and controls

---

[24] See the introduction by Christopher Tolkien in *J. R. R. Tolkien, Tree and Leaf* (Boston: Houghton Mifflin, 1989) footnotes 1, 7.

nature, something he and Lewis already agreed on. Two, language allows humans to name and thus know and experience the world. Three, humans, though "long estranged" and "dis-graced," are not "wholly lost" and can "draw some wisdom from the only Wise." Fourth, humans can and should be "subcreators" of truth through myths and stories.[25] And fifth, the assertion that fantasy and myth and "godlike" ideas about beauty are nothing more than "wish fulfillment" (here Tolkien is taking a jibe at one of the prevalent Freudian ideas of his day) is missing the whole point.[26] Tolkien also in this poem expressed his awareness of evil in the world ("...and of Evil this/alone is deadly certain: Evil is"), and that God alone is the "answer" to it.

Joseph Pearce wrote that the final lines of "Mythopoeia" are "Tolkien's highest achievement in verse," and picture a vision of Heaven similar to Dante's *Paradiso*.[27]

"Bilbo's Last Song at the Grey Havens"

"Bilbo's Last Song" was not the last poem Tolkien wrote, nor do we know exactly when he wrote it. It is not mentioned in his letters, nor does Humphrey Carpenter mention it in his authorized biography. After his Middle-earth stories became internationally popular, Tolkien was deluged by fan mail, and Joy Hill of Allen &

---

[25] Although there is no evidence that Dorothy L. Sayers knew or met Tolkien, the main point of her *Mind of the Maker* (1941) is very similar to his idea of sub-creation, that God is the "Master Maker" (Creator) and that in the craft of creative writing we have a close example of how God works. Sayers admired the *Fellowship of the Ring* (the only work by Tolkien mentioned in her collected letters), but Tolkien despised her mystery stories, particularly *Gaudy Night* and *Busman's Honeymoon*.

[26] For insightful discussions of the themes in "Mythopoeia," see Verlyn Flieger, *Splintered Light: Logos and Language in Tolkien's World* (Grand Rapids MI: Eerdmans, 1983) 43–52, and Charles Moseley, *J. R. R. Tolkien* (Plymouth UK: Northcote House, 1977) 21–23.

[27] Pearce, *Tolkien: Man and Myth* (San Francisco: Ignatius Press, 1998) 176–77.

Unwin was hired as his secretary to help him answer it. She became a close friend and visited him regularly in Oxford and Bournemouth in his later years. Joy found "Bilbo's Last Song" in an exercise book while helping Tolkien put his library in order before he moved to Bournemouth.[28] Tolkien later gave her the poem and its copyright as gifts in early September 1970. It was published for the first time in 1974 by Houghton Mifflin on a poster (105,000 copies printed), in book form by Houghton Mifflin the same year, and in the second edition of the *Road Goes Ever On—A Song Cycle* in 1978. Albert House Press of London published *Bilbo's Last Song* in 1992, the first separate edition of Donald Swann's setting of the poem, written out in calligraphy—fifty copies signed by Swann.

As every reader of the *Hobbit* knows, Bilbo Baggins is its congenial, courageous hero, the riddle-and map-loving, smoke-ring-blowing adventurer who stole the One Ring, defied dragons and goblins, and finally passed on the Ring to Frodo, the new ring-bearer. His Last Song was composed just before he returned to the West, and it interweaves his regret of saying goodbye to Middle-earth and his friends with the call of the sea and his yearning to travel the great voyage to the Uttermost West beyond the sunset. Bilbo sails from Grey Havens, a town and harbor founded by the shipbuilder Cirdan (among the wisest of the Elves), after the destruction of Beleriand, in the later ages the name of all the land that was overwhelmed by the sea in the north of Middle-earth.

In book form (beautifully illustrated by Pauline Baynes, the Houghton Mifflin reprints of 1990), "Bilbo's Last Song" shows Bilbo's journey to Grey Havens (accompanied by Frodo, Sam, Elrond, Galadriel, and Gildor), and the start of the last voyage. Miss Baynes added pictures of scenes from the *Lord of the Rings* (larger pictures, on the right-hand pages) and the *Hobbit* (smaller pictures, running at the bottom of both pages), and the book,

---

[28] See Wayne G. Hammond, *J. R. R. Tolkien: A Descriptive Bibliography* (New Castle DE: Oak Knoll Books, 1993) 207.

thirty-two pages, ends with the poem "Bilbo's Last Song" (three octaves) and two pages of explanatory notes.

Joy Hill died in December 1991, and her extensive collection of Tolkien books (many signed), letters, and memorabilia was auctioned at Sotheby's, London, in December 1992. The typescript of "Bilbo's Last Song," with two minor autograph corrections and a signed autograph note giving the poem and its copyright to Joy, and two autographed letters to Joy, giving further details of the gift and marked "Private and Confidential," with an envelope (dated 28 October 1971) were included in the auction, and the asking price was £1,000–1,500.[29]

---

[29] Christina Scull, ed., *J. R. R. Tolkien Collecting and Bibliography Special Interest Group Magazine*, no. 1, n.d. (probably 1992): 11.

Works of Scholarship

The Oxford English Dictionary (OED)

Tolkien was an assistant lexicographer for the *OED* from November 1918 till Spring 1920, where he worked under the supervision of Dr. Henry Bradley. Each weekday he walked the few blocks from his home on St. Johns Street to downtown Oxford to Broad Street and the Old Ashmolean Building (now the Museum of the History of Science), where the greatest dictionary of the English language was being assembled.[1] Work on the dictionary began in 1858, and the historical method used involved tracing over 400,000 words from their earliest appearances and giving (by completion in 1928) nearly two million quotations as examples of their use; these quotations were collected by over 800 voluntary contributors. By Tolkien's time, "U to Z" had not been completed due to delays caused by the First War.

---

[1] At its conception the dictionary was called *A New English Dictionary on Historical Principles*; by 1895 and after the *OED*, although *NED* is still frequently used. For a while it was called *The Historical English Dictionary* (*HED*; never attained general popularity), and at various times it has been called "Murray's" (after Dr. James A. H. Murray, its first editor), and the Oxford Philological Society by tradition called it "the Society's Dictionary."

Tolkien worked on words beginning with *W*, and researched the words *wain* (wagon), *waggle, waist, waistband, waist-cloth, waistcoat, waistcoated, waistcoateer, waist-rail, waist-tree, waisted, waister, waistless, wait-a-bit, waiter, waitership, waiting, waiting-maid, waiting-man, waiting-room, waiting-woman, waitress, wake, wake-robin, wake-wort, waldend, wallop, walloper, walloping, walm, walming, walnut, walrus, wampum, wan, wander, wanderable, wandered, wandering, wanderment, wander-year, wandreth, wane, want, want-louse, wariangle, warlock, warlockry, warm, weald, wealden, wealding, wield, wild, wold*, and possibly *wampumpeag, wasp, water, wick,* and *winter.* An example of Tolkien's etymological skill is shown by his entry for the word *wasp*, which cites comparable forms of the word in Old Saxon, Middle Dutch, Modern Dutch, Old High German, Russian, Latin, and several others, while listing quotes using the word in its various forms from circa 725 through 1887, by authors and works as diverse as H. G. Wells, the *Taming of the Shrew*, Sir Walter Scott, John Ruskin, *Gulliver's Travels*, and over sixty others. Tolkien regarded his time at *OED* as one of the most educational of his life, and he enjoyed the working environment and his colleagues, especially Professor C. T. Onions, who later became editor, and Professor Kenneth Sisam, his tutor at Exeter.

Dr. Bradley, who was a no-nonsense but fair supervisor, praised Tolkien by saying that he had no equal, and that his work gave "evidence of an unusually thorough mastery of Anglo-Saxon and of the facts and principles of the comparative grammar of the Germanic languages."[2] Later, Tolkien reviewed one of the volumes of *OED* for the *Year's Work in English Studies* (1926), and spoke about it at least once (January 1922) at a meeting of the Yorkshire Dialect Society and the English Association. Tolkien did not agree with all of the *OED*'s definitions. In *Farmer Giles of Ham,* he makes fun of how the word "blunderbuss" is defined in

---

[2] Humphrey Carpenter, *J. R. R. Tolkien: A Biography* (Boston: Houghton Mifflin, 2000) 108.

the *OED* by "the Four Wise Clerks of Oxenford," who are editors Murray, Bradley, Craigie, and Onions. And in "On Fairy-Stories," he wrote that the *OED*'s definition of "fairy" was less respectable than it should have been.[3]

Tolkien's former student Robert Burchfield became the editor of the three-volume *OED Supplement* in 1957, and in 1970 wrote Tolkien, asking him to provide a definition for the word "hobbit" for the second, revised supplement. Tolkien's reply was never sent, but has been published in his collected letters.[4]

A Middle English Vocabulary

A Middle English Vocabulary was published in 1922 and was Tolkien's first book. The initial printing was 2,000 copies, some of which were bound separately and some with Tolkien's former tutor Kenneth Sisam's *Fourteenth Century Verse and Prose*. The 168-page *Vocabulary* was added as a glossary and included an index of names. Tolkien had been appointed as Reader in English Language at Leeds University in 1920, was married, and by 1923 had two children, John and Michael. In February 1923, he wrote to Mrs. Joseph Wright, the wife of his respected teacher, saying that he had "lavished an amount of time" on his glossary, "which is terrible to recall, and long delayed the Reader bringing curses on my head; but it was instructive."[5]

---

[3] See Tom Shippey, "Creation from Philology in *The Lord of the Rings*" in *J. R. R. Tolkien, Scholar and Storyteller: Essays in Memoriam*, ed. Mary Salu and Robert T. Farrell (Ithaca NY: Cornell University Press, 1979) 286–316.

[4] See Humphrey Carpenter, *The Letters of J. R. R. Tolkien* (London: Allen & Unwin, 1981) 30–32, 404, for his thoughts on the origin of the word "hobbit." For a perceptive essay on Tolkien's work at the *OED*, see Peter M. Gilliver, "At the Wordface: J. R. R. Tolkien's Work on the *Oxford English Dictionary*," in *Proceedings of the J. R. R. Tolkien Centenary Conference*, ed. Patricia Reynolds and Glen H. GoodKnight (Altadena CA: The Mythopoeic Press, 1995) 173–86.

[5] Carpenter, *Letters*, 11.

The glossary, along with his next work, a translation of *Sir Gawain and the Green Knight* (below) helped establish Tolkien's reputation as a philologist and Anglo-Saxon scholar and secured his promotion to Professor of English Language at Leeds, at age thirty the youngest person ever elected to a professorship there.

Tolkien mentioned in his introductory note that his glossary "does not aim at completeness, and it is not a glossary of rare or 'hard' words. A good working knowledge of Middle English depends less on the possession of an abstruse vocabulary than on familiarity with the ordinary machinery of expression..."[6] The fact that his glossary has been reprinted over twenty times, and is still in print today and used in graduate English literature courses, is a testimony to Tolkien's skill at producing a glossary that has aided students and scholars for years in understanding the Middle English "ordinary machinery of expression."

Sir Gawain and the Green Knight, Pearl, Sir Orfeo

Sir Gawain and the Green Knight is considered one of the greatest early alliterative narrative poems in the English language. The author is unknown and is thought to have written sometime after 1350. He was a contemporary of Chaucer and was probably a native of the West Midlands of England. From the many studies of the Gawain-poet, it has been learned that he was religious, serious, had a sense of humor, had an interest in theology, and knew Latin and French. The earliest text of *Sir Gawain* is preserved in the British Museum in a late fourteenth-century manuscript with three other poems—*Pearl, Purity* (sometimes translated *Cleanness*), and *Patience*; *Sir Gawain* is the longest with 2,530 lines. Most scholars now believe that all four were written by the same

---

[6] J. R. R. Tolkien, *A Middle English Vocabulary*, in *Fourteenth Century Verse & Prose*, ed. Kenneth Sisam (Oxford: The Clarendon Press, 1962) 3.

unknown author, and that their language, style, and dialect (the Northwest Midlands) combining Old and Chaucerian Middle English came from Irish-Welsh folklore.

Sir Gawain is an Arthurian romance, a fairy tale for adults, and tells the story of how Sir Gawain, the bravest of the Knights of the Round Table, accepts the giant Green Knight's challenge to uphold the honor of Arthur's court and sets out on a quest that is essentially a test of his virtue. The Gawain-poet employs two well-known medieval literary motifs—the beheading story and the temptation story—and in the final scene, Gawain reveals his courage and human fallibility. The poet also develops other well-known literary themes, all developed with high cultural sensitivity, including the journey or quest and the "rite of passage." There has been an enormous amount of scholarly interest in this extraordinary poem, which attests to its high standing as a supremely interesting and exciting narrative. One author has expressed the view of many: "No other alliterative poet can match the Gawain-poet in his ability to meet the demands of both story and theme, sacrificing neither intellectual lucidity nor narrative richness."[7]

Tolkien's interest in *Sir Gawain* and its anonymous author lasted more than fifty years. He and his colleague at Leeds, E. V. Gordon, began work on a Middle-English translation of *Sir Gawain* sometime in early 1922, and the book was published in Oxford in 1925. It was successful immediately and became a seminal work in English medieval studies. As late as the early 1990s it was still the standard edition, as revised in 1967 by Tolkien's student Norman Davis. Its success led to the suggestion that Gordon and Tolkien publish a translation of *Pearl* from the same manuscript. But Tolkien left for Oxford, while Gordon stayed on and took Tolkien's professorship at Leeds. The two men

---

[7] J. A. Burrow, "Old and Middle English (c. 700–1485)," in *The Oxford Illustrated History of English Literature*, ed. Pat Rogers (Oxford: Oxford University Press, 1990) 34.

never collaborated on the translation, as Tolkien worked on other projects and Gordon died in 1938. *Pearl* appeared early in 1953, and though Gordon's name was on the title page, it had really been edited by his widow Ida L. Gordon, a well-known medieval scholar. In her preface to the work, Mrs. Gordon mentioned that *Pearl* initially was a joint project, that Tolkien withdrew from the project when he was "unable to give sufficient time to it," and that Tolkien, who held the original typescript, had added "valuable notes and corrections."

On Wednesday, 15 April 1953, Tolkien gave the W. P. Ker Memorial Lecture at the University of Glasgow on *Sir Gawain and the Green Knight*. In his talk, he gave particular attention to Gawain's temptation to commit adultery with the Lady and his confession in the chapel before meeting the Green Knight, and read aloud the temptation scenes in translation. The translation was broadcast on the BBC's Third Programme in December 1953, and was repeated in September 1954 with an introduction and afterward by Tolkien. He also gave a talk on Third Programme (January 1954) about *Sir Gawain* and its meaning and place in Chaucerian literature. Tolkien's introduction to the poem was later included in the modern English translation, published in 1975 with *Pearl* and *Sir Orfeo* (see below).

Humphrey Carpenter noted that Tolkien's interest in the Gawain poet went beyond the scholarly, because as a boy Tolkien was drawn to *Sir Gawain* (and *Pearl*) because they were written in the West Midland dialect of his mother's ancestors.[8] Another Tolkien scholar noted and described a number of "resemblances" between *Sir Gawain* and the *Lord of the Rings*, including similarities of plot and incident: both are heroic quests, both contain carefully constructed secondary worlds, both make "the unreal seem real," both have thematic stresses on youth and

---

[8] Carpenter, *Biography*, 43.

childhood, and both show moral development as resulting from physical and spiritual trials.[9]

In 1975 UK Tolkien Society founder Mrs. Vera Chapman wrote a story called the *Green Knight* (published by Rex Collings in England and in 1978 by Avon in the US), a "metrical romance" inspired by the story of Sir Gawain. In her book the esteemed Mrs. Chapman mentioned Tolkien's Gawain studies in an introductory note.

Tolkien's interest in and work on *Pearl* started even before *Sir Gawain*. His translation of the alliterative dream/vision poem (1,212 lines) began at Leeds in the 1920s and was in a finished form by 1926. Tolkien was challenged by the poem's complex metrical and verbal structure, and while in Leeds (1924), he wrote "The Nameless Land" in the metrical form of *Pearl*. This poem, his "preliminary work" on *Pearl*, was published in *Realities*, an anthology of verse (edited by G. S. Tancred), in 1927, and in two revised versions in the *Lost Road and Other Writings* (1987) as "The Song of Ælfwine."

Publisher J. M. Dent did not want to publish *Pearl*, but did arrange for part of it to be broadcast on radio in August 1936. In the early 1940s, Basil Blackwell offered to publish the poem, but by early 1945 the proofs still needed to be corrected, and Tolkien had not written an introduction. The project stalled due to Tolkien's absorption in other writing projects, and by 1959 it was abandoned by Blackwell. It was not until 1975 that Allen & Unwin published *Pearl* in translation, with *Sir Gawain* and *Sir Orfeo*.

The first three parts (of six) of the introduction are by Tolkien. Part I, on the authorship of *Sir Gawain* and *Pearl*, was

---

[9] Miriam Y. Miller, "The Lord of the Rings and Sir Gawain and the Green Knight," in vol. 3 of *Studies in Medievalism* (Winter, Spring 1991): 345–65. For another excellent essay on Tolkien and how he used the "theories, eccentricities, and linguistics" of the Gawain-poet, see Tom Shippey, "Tolkien and the *Gawain*-poet," in *Proceedings of the J. R. R. Tolkien Centenary Conference—Keble College, Oxford, 1992*, 213–19.

Works of Scholarship 111

drawn by Christopher Tolkien from his father's notes; Part II, on *Sir Gawain*, is a "slightly reduced" version of Tolkien's BBC radio talk; Part III, on *Pearl*, is a reprint of Tolkien's contribution to the introduction of E. V. Gordon's edition, and Christopher Tolkien added notes on *Sir Orfeo*, on the latest editions of the three poems, the text of the translations, and a glossary. "Gawain's Leave-taking," a poem added as an appendix, was Tolkien's translation of another medieval English poem.

Pearl was the narrator's daughter and only child, and she died before reaching two years of age. As her father wandered in sorrow and misery ("my hands I wrung dismayed") in the garden where she was buried, he fell asleep and had a dream vision of a river, beyond which is Heaven. He saw a "gentle maid of courtly grace" whom he recognized as his daughter. She rebuked him for his excessive grief, then told him how happy she is in Heaven. He then argued with her about the justice that made her a queen of Heaven when she died so young, and when she convinced him otherwise, he dove into the river in an attempt to join her. The father then awoke and was comforted and reassured of his faith in God. *Pearl* is primarily concerned with salvation and asks the much-discussed question, "What heavenly rewards are enjoyed by infants who die after baptism?"

The form and language of *Pearl* is considered brilliant, and the dialogue between the maid and the narrator is rich in sentiment and even comedy. The poem is "original" in the sense that the author constructs his own story rather than deriving it from old books, as was often the case in his time. *Pearl* has been studied by generations of students and scholars, and it has influenced poets such as Boccaccio (*Olympia*), Dante (*Purgatorio*), and many others. It has much in common with Dante's work in that the maid, similar to Beatrice in the *Divine Comedy*, details and explains the mysteries of Paradise.

Tolkien probably translated *Sir Orfeo* sometime during 1943, when he prepared a version of the poem in Middle English for use by an English class for naval cadets, which he organized in early

1943 and directed through March 1944. Christopher Tolkien has stated he could not find anything about the poem in his father's writings after his death, and it is not mentioned by Tolkien in his published letters.

Sir Orfeo was composed in the late thirteenth or early fourteenth century by an unknown author. A metrical romance of about 600 lines, it is a Celtic reinterpretation made into a folktale of the classical story of Orpheus and Eurydice. Queen Heurodys is carried off to "the Other World" (the land of fairies) by Eurydice and is pursued by her husband King Orfeo, whose melodious harp playing succeeds in bringing her back to the world of men. The poem is much admired as one of the most charming and interesting of Middle English romances and was interpreted by such classical writers as Ovid (*Metamorphoses*), Virgil (*Georgics*), and Boethius (the *Consolation of Philosophy*). The author of *Sir Orfeo* captured the world of Celtic folk-beliefs perhaps better than any other, and his tale of the mysterious powers of the fairies and their eerie kingdom is at once beautiful and terrifying.

Tolkien was much influenced by this story, and Tom Shippey speculated that *Sir Orfeo* is the "master text" for Tolkien's portrayal of the wood-elves in the *Hobbit*, in his description of the hunting king. Shippey further noted that Tolkien's acknowledgment to ancient stories such as *Sir Orfeo* was due, at least in part, to his feeling that "underneath" these stories lay a consistency, a sense, an "impression of depth" that he could find nowhere else.[10]

---

[10] Shippey, *The Road to Middle Earth* (London: Allen & Unwin, 1982) 57, 59, 203.

"Beowulf: The Monsters and the Critics"

Tolkien gave the Sir Israel Gollancz Memorial Lecture on *Beowulf* to the British Academy on 25 November 1936, and it was published the following year. It has been reprinted and anthologized many times and was included in the *Monsters and the Critics and Other Essays* (1984). This landmark lecture (in print form fifty pages, with notes) is the most highly acclaimed of all of Tolkien's works of scholarship and a significant key to understanding his work. One scholar noted that it "completely altered the course of *Beowulf* studies,"[11] while another wrote that the lecture deserves "our loudest notes of praise" and "...that *Beowulf* is now viewed rather more as a poem and rather less as a museum for the antiquarian...is due in large measure to Professor Tolkien's famous British Academy Lecture..."[12]

Praise of Tolkien's essay continues to the present day. In the introduction to his new translation of *Beowulf*, Irish poet and Nobel Laureate Seamus Heaney wrote: "...when it comes to considering *Beowulf* as a work of literature, there is one publication that stands out. In 1936, the Oxford scholar and teacher J. R. R. Tolkien published an epoch-making paper titled "Beowulf: The Monsters and the Critics" which took for granted the poem's integrity and distinction as a work of art...He assumed...that the *Beowulf* poet was an imaginative writer rather than some kind of back-formation derived from nineteenth-century folklore and philology. Tolkien's brilliant literary treatment

---

[11] Donald K. Frye, ed., *The Beowulf Poet: A Collection of Critical Essays* (New York, Prentice Hall, 1968), as quoted by Rand Kuhl, "Lore of Logres," *Mythlore* 3 (July 1969): 34. See also Joseph F. Tusso, *Beowulf* (New York: Norton, 1975) xi.

[12] Bruce Mitchell, "J. R. R. Tolkien and Old English Studies: An Appreciation," in *Proceedings of the J. R. R. Tolkien Centenary Conference*, 209.

changed the way the poem was valued and initiated a new era—and new terms—of appreciation."[13]

Before Tolkien, many commentators suggested that *Beowulf* was a muddle of literary traditions, a source for archaeological information, Anglo-Saxon history, folklore, and mythology, and that it was useful for literary research but not literary criticism—it had no merits as a literary work of art, and certainly none as a carefully crafted poem. Tolkien went against the grain and asserted that *Beowulf* was interesting, significant, and powerful poetry, and only by considering it in this light could it be appreciated in the best way. The eminent Oxford literary critic W. P. Ker wrote in his renowned *Epic and Romance* (1897) that *Beowulf*'s style was "grand" but as a complete story it was weak, and the monster narratives in the poem were insignificant and weakened it. Tolkien countered this by maintaining that the superhuman opposition of the monsters elevated the poem to a heroic level: "a dragon is no idle fancy." He compared Greek and Roman (southern) with northern mythologies and concluded that it was necessary to have monsters at the center of *Beowulf*: "Northern mythology is better because it deals with the defeat of man in Time by the hostile world, and its use in poetry can revive a spirit of doom and finality even in our day."

Tolkien saw *Beowulf* not as an "epic" but as a heroic-elegaic poem, with strong historical roots and written by a learned man about a long, past history. *Beowulf* is the earliest surviving alliterative poem in a major European vernacular language, and one of the very few specimens of Germanic heroic poetry known. The earliest manuscript (3,182 lines) dates from the eleventh century and tells of two major events in Beowulf's life. As a young man he wrestles with and kills Grendel (who is immune to metal weapons; Beowulf kills him by tearing his arm off at the shoulder), a water monster who has been attacking Heorot, the

---

[13] Seamus Heaney, *Beowulf: A New Verse Translation* (New York: Norton, 2000) xi.

feasting hall of the Danish king Hrothgar, then kills Grendel's mother who comes to avenge her son by kidnapping a Danish noble.

Fifty years later, Beowulf, who has become King of Geatland, fights a dragon (with the help of a young nobleman, Wiglaf) who has attacked his people. Tolkien's account of the fight with the gold-hoarding dragon Smaug in the climactic episode of the *Hobbit* is modeled after the fight between Beowulf and the dragon.[14] In the battle, both Beowulf and the dragon are mortally wounded; as he dies, Beowulf anoints Wiglaf as his successor. His body is burnt on a great funeral pyre and the dragon's treasure is buried with his ashes; twelve of his followers ride around the funeral mound proclaiming his greatness: "They extolled his heroic nature and exploits and gave thanks for his greatness; which was the proper thing...They said of all the kings upon the earth he was the man most gracious and fair-minded, kindest to his people and keenest to win fame."[15]

For Tolkien, the monsters in *Beowulf* were central to the theme of human struggles against an evil and hostile world. He knew that the *Beowulf* poet who created them had a wide knowledge of Christian poetry and the Bible (specifically the book of Genesis), demonstrated when the minstrel at Heorot sings of the "Creation of the earth and the lights of Heaven" and when Cain is called the ancestor to "the giants" and to Grendel.[16] In this lecture, Tolkien affirmed how a (probable) Christian writer could create a story that was essentially true to Christian moral ideals and virtues

---

[14] Tolkien wrote in a letter to the writer Naomi Mitchison (18 December 1949) that the idea of "Smaug and his conversation" came from the story of the dragon Fáfnir in the Norse epic *Saga of the Volsungs*. See Carpenter, *Letters*, 134.

[15] Heaney, *Beowulf*, 213.

[16] Tom Shippey pointed out that there are about seventy references to God, Hell, Doomsday, Cain, and the Flood in *Beowulf*, "enough to make it obvious, both from their number and their type, that the poet was as firm a Christian and Catholic as Tolkien himself." See Shippey, "Creation from Philology in *The Lord of the Rings*," in *Essays in Memoriam*, ed. Salu and Farrell, 310.

without specifically mentioning Jesus and Christian dogma, something he did himself in the *Lord of the Rings*. Some of the poem's critics had complained that the poet had merely confounded the Bible with Northern fairy-tale monsters, perhaps out of ignorance, but Tolkien disagreed, calling this a strength of the book rather than a weakness, and a product of deep emotion and much thought.

After Tolkien's lecture, some *Beowulf* scholars disagreed with his views, including Kenneth Sisam, in his the *Structure of Beowulf*, published in 1965. But even he acknowledged that Tolkien's fresh ideas, "fineness of perception," and "elegance of expression" elevated his insights about *Beowulf* above those of most others and was "rare in the field." He also mentioned that Tolkien's lecture should be read very carefully and that he had no criticism of what the poem meant to Tolkien personally, or how, as a storyteller, he treated the plot. Professor Sisam further affirmed Tolkien's general interpretation of the poem as an "original variant"of the struggle between good and evil and agreed with Tolkien's conclusions that the monsters in the poem symbolize evil, and that its unifying theme is "man at war with the hostile world and his inevitable overthrow in Time." Sisam did disagree with and elaborate on some of Tolkien's points within his general interpretation.[17]

In 1940 Tolkien wrote prefatory remarks, with extracts from his Modern English verse translation of *Beowulf*, to a new edition of C. L. Wrenn's *Beowulf and the Finnesburg Fragment*, translated by John R. Clark Hall; his comments were later published as "On Translating Beowulf" in the *Monsters and the Critics and Other Essays*. Some of his remarks revealed his frustration with uninformed criticism and the tendency by many who relied on translations rather than primary sources. Tom

---

[17] Tolkien had great respect and affection for Sisam (1887–1971) and credits him for teaching him not only to read texts but to study used book catalogues for help in building his library. See Carpenter, *Letters*, 406.

Shippey wrote that Tolkien was making the point that words mean more than their dictionary entries and protesting the translating of *Beowulf* "only into polite modern English."[18] Tolkien added to this when he said, "Too many people are willing to form, and even to print, opinions of this greatest of the surviving works of English poetic art after reading such a translation, or indeed after reading only a bare 'argument,' such as appears in the present book...one famous critic informed his public that *Beowulf* was 'only small beer.' Yet if beer at all, it is a drink dark and bitter: a solemn funeral-ale with the taste of death...The proper purpose of a prose translation is to provide an aid to study...No translation that aims at being readable in itself can, without elaborate annotation, proper to an edition of the original, indicate all the possibilities or hints afforded by the text."[19]

In 1996, an interesting discovery was made concerning Tolkien's work on *Beowulf*. The American scholar Michael Drout, while completing his doctoral dissertation on Anglo-Saxon texts, visited the Bodleian Library in Oxford to examine Tolkien's notes for "The Monsters and the Critics." To his surprise, he found about 200 pages of unpublished material and notes on *Beowulf* at the bottom of a box containing Tolkien's writings. He discovered that Christopher Tolkien had donated the material in 1986 and that it was unknown to scholars. On a close reading of the pages, Drout learned that the material contained two manuscripts, both longer than the original essay; the longer manuscript (107 folio pages) is a revision of the first (71 folio pages) but very different; and the original essay is different from both. Drout also noticed that in the discovered manuscripts, Tolkien is more frank. He flatly states that *Beowulf* was written in 750, and he is more critical of other *Beowulf* scholars. With the blessing of the Tolkien estate, Drout plans to edit and publish the manuscripts, with an introduction and

---

[18] Shippey, *Road to Middle-Earth*, 41, 42.
[19] John R. Clark Hall, trans., *Beowulf and the Finnesburg Fragment: A Translation into Modern English Prose* (London: Allen & Unwin, 1967) ix, x.

his and Tolkien's annotations, sometime in 2002. The book will be titled *Beowulf and the Critics*.[20]

"On Fairy-Stories"

Many scholars think that "On Fairy-Stories" is Tolkien's most important and influential work of nonfiction.[21] Originally presented as the Andrew Lang Lecture at the University of St. Andrews, Scotland (8 March 1939), it was revised and published in *Essays Presented to Charles Williams* (edited by C. S. Lewis) in 1947, *Tree and Leaf* in 1964 (further revised), and the *Monsters and the Critics and Other Essays* in 1983. Two manuscript sentences deleted by Tolkien were published in *Amon Hen*, the bulletin of The Tolkien Society (England) in 1992. It is interesting to note that in Tolkien's unpublished notes for the essay (in the Bodleian Library), he mentioned his love for an old children's classic, almost forgotten today: "I should like to record my own love and my children's love of Wyke-Smith's *Marvellous Land of Snergs*, at any rate of the snerg-element in that tale, and of Gorbo the gem of dunderheads, jewel of a companion in an escapade."[22]

Tolkien started reading fairy tales when he was about four years old,[23] and this talk was a vigorous defense of fairy tales for adults, which many in his time thought were suitable just for

---

[20] For the Internet essay containing this information, see Jason Clarke, "The Fingerprint of the Master—Beowulf and the Critics," *Tolkien Online: The One Ring*, 9 March 2001 (http://www.tolkienonline.com/docs/2164).

[21] In November 1956 C. S. Lewis published a corresponding essay, "Sometime Fairy Stories May Say Best What's to be Said," in the *New York Times Book Review, Children's Book Section*; later it appeared in *Of Other Worlds: Essays and Stories* (London: Geoffrey Bles, 1956).

[22] See the introduction by Douglas Anderson in E. A. Wyke-Smith, *The Marvellous Land of Snergs* (reprint, Baltimore: Old Earth Books, 1996) I, ii. *Snergs* was originally published in 1927, by Ernest Benn of London, and Wyke-Smith (1871–1935) wrote seven other novels, three for children and four for adults. Tolkien's second son Michael particularly loved this story.

[23] See Carpenter, *Letters*, 30.

children, or "relegated to the nursery." Tolkien wrote: "If a fairy story as a kind is worth reading at all it is worthy to be written for and read by adults." He also said that to regard fairy tales as trivial or unimportant was unfair both to children and the fairy tale. Originally promised to an undergraduate society, "On Fairy-Stories" was particularly suitable for the lecture in that Andrew Lang (1844–1912) was a famous Scottish folklorist, poet, and man of letters whose works were extremely popular in England, particularly the *Gold of Fairnilee* (1888), the *Blue Fairy Book* (1889), and the *Lilac Fairy Book* (1910).[24] Tolkien's former colleague George Gordon gave the first Lang lecture in 1927, and Lang's the *Red Fairy Book* (1890, a modern rendition of an old Norse story about a dragon) had been one of his early introductions to myth and legend. Tolkien mentioned Lang several times in his talk, saying his fairy-tale collections were "largely a by-product of his adult study of mythology and folklore."

"On Fairy-Stories" is divided into five sections, with a brief introduction, epilogue, and notes: "Fairy Story," "Origins," "Children," "Fantasy," and "Recovery, Escape, Consolation." Tolkien believed that the fairy story's central concern was "fairie," a secondary world or "Perilous Realm" where fairies "have their being" and where magic satisfies basic human desires, both psychological and spiritual. These desires include the wish for exploration of time and space, the wish for communication with God and other humans, and the wish for escape from death, "the oldest and deepest desire." Furthermore, Tolkien emphasized that fairy tales were fantasy ("a higher form of Art") and they allowed their reader to "survey the depths of time and space." The successful fairy tale creates a "secondary world" in which any reader can enter, especially if they "enter with the heart of child." By this

---

[24] For an excellent overview of Lang's life and works, see Humphrey Carpenter and Mari Prichard, *The Oxford Companion to Children's Literature* (Oxford: Oxford University Press, 1991) 302–303, and Roger Lancelyn Green, *Andrew Lang: A Critical Biography* (Leicester England: Edmund Ward, 1946).

Tolkien did not mean the reader should have "an uncritical wonder or tenderness," but rather openness, humility, and innocence.

Perhaps the most interesting aspect of this talk (and commented on most by scholars) is "Recovery, Escape, Consolation." By "recovery" Tolkien meant "a regaining of a clear view," or "recovering" the power to see the world magically, with wonder, and helping one "see" with a fresh perspective and outlook. He read an anecdote in one of G. K. Chesterton's essays, in which Charles Dickens had a strange feeling when he saw the letters MOOREEFFOC written on the glass door of a coffee room, then realized he was looking at it from the inside. Chesterton used this anecdote to illustrate the "queerness of things that have become trite, when they are seen suddenly from a new angle."[25] Tolkien believed fairy tales and creative fantasy help us look behind familiar, ordinary things and events, keep us from taking them for granted, and "make new" our old perceptions—this he called recovery.

Tolkien saw one of the main functions of fairy tales as "escape," and he said that tales of this sort were some of "the most obvious forms of escapist literature," comparing them with romances and works "out of or about the past." One work on Tolkien defined his view of "escape" as "a mental vacation away from hard and ugly places and times,"[26] while another Tolkien scholar wrote: "the good fairy story offers escape from one's narrow distorted view of reality and meaning. This is the escape of the prisoner rather than the flight of the deserter."[27] The former

---

[25] C. S. Lewis mentioned a similar approach to "seeing" the familiar in a new way, which he called "quiddity," in *Surprised By Joy*. Quiddity is a "love of everything which has its own strong flavour." For a discussion of "quiddity," see Walter Hooper, *C. S. Lewis: Companion & Guide* (San Francisco: HarperSanFrancisco, 1996) 599.

[26] Ivor and Deborah Rogers, *J. R. R. Tolkien: A Critical Biography* (New York: Hippocrene Books, 1980) 48.

[27] Colin Duriez, *The J. R. R. Tolkien Handbook* (Grand Rapids MI: Baker, 1992) 197.

definition is probably closer to Tolkien's meaning, as he elaborated on his age as being an age of "improved means to deteriorated ends" that produced the desire to escape "from our present time," with its "evil and ugliness" and "noise, stench, ruthlessness, and extravagance of the internal combustion engine."

After Tolkien declared that fairy tales offer an imaginative satisfaction for our "oldest and deepest desire," the "great escape" or escape from death, he mentioned "the human stories of the elves that are doubtless full of the Escape from Deathlessness." Here he was talking about his own stories of Middle-earth and the *Silmarillion*, which contain many references to death. Tolkien may have been preoccupied with death, and escape from it, as most of his old friends from World War I were dead, he was an orphan, and he had never really known his father. England at the time of his lecture was becoming embroiled in a world war, and the idea of death was on everyone's mind, including Tolkien's. When he recommended fairy stories as an imaginative escape from death (or the thought of it), Tolkien was perhaps providing one for himself.[28]

For Tolkien, fairy tales give their reader the "consolation" of the joy of a happy ending, or "the sudden joyous turn." He called this ending "eucatastrophe" (a good catastrophe), and it is the true form of the fairy tale, and its highest function. Eucatastrophe is not "escapist" but in a fairy-tale setting it is a "sudden and miraculous grace," which often does not reoccur. Katharyn Crabbe has pointed out that this type of ending to a fairy tale "is for Tolkien a repudiation of the possibility of a universal, final defeat," and from this repudiation comes, in the best fairy tales, "a stab of joy as poignant and moving as sorrow."[29] In a letter to Christopher (7–8 November 1944), Tolkien explained that fairy-tale eucatastrophe

---

[28] Tolkien wrote in 1956 that the "real theme" of the *Lord of the Rings* was death and immortality. See Carpenter, *Letters*, 246.

[29] Crabbe, *J. R. R. Tolkien*, revised and expanded edition (New York: Continuum, 1988) 156.

brings this type of joy "because it is a sudden glimpse of Truth...it perceives that this is indeed how things really do work in the Great World for which our nature is made."[30]

It was this insight that led Tolkien to the Epilogue of his lecture, and here he gave one of his most personal (and one of his very few public) statements concerning his Christian beliefs. Good fairy tales for him pointed to the greatest fairy-tale story of all, the Christian story, and particularly the resurrection. He believed the resurrection was the eucatastrophe of Jesus' incarnation, was the "greatest eucatastrophe possible," and the fairy tale of the gospel story, which is the word of God, represents God himself. There is no story that human beings would rather find *is* true, and none other that so many who are skeptical have accepted on its own merits.

Tolkien thought that the Christian who experiences joy and consolation after reading and taking to heart the fairy tale of the gospels hopes for the same "happy ending" to his or her life that Jesus did: ultimate reconciliation with God. The Christian is still human, and still has to live, work, suffer, and die, but with the real hope of redemption that God promised to those who believe in and follow the Jesus of the Christian story. The eucatastrophe of the gospel story is a world of deeper knowledge and clearer vision (the "Secondary World"); when we look into it, we, as sons and daughters of God, are guided by his Spirit.[31]

"English and Welsh"

"English and Welsh" was the title of an O'Donnell Lecture given by Tolkien at Oxford on 21 October 1955, the day after the publication of the *Return of the King*. The prestigious lectures,

---

[30] Carpenter, *Letters*, 100.

[31] For an excellent brief discussion of Tolkien and "eucatastrophe," see John Navone, *Seeking God in Story* (Collegeville MN: The Liturgical Press, 1990) 250.

established by Oxford, Edinburgh, and Wales Universities, focused on British and Celtic elements of the English language, and Tolkien's lecture was the first in a series at Oxford. "English and Welsh" was first published in 1963 in *Angles and Britons: O'Donnell Lectures* (University of Wales Press), and later in the *Monsters and the Critics and Other Essays*. It was turned down for inclusion in the *Tolkien Reader*.

In a 1962 letter to his aunt Jane Neave (then ninety-one, who had read a proof copy of the text), Tolkien complained that his lecture was "rather dull except to dons," "was not learned," and that his task in the talk was to "thread together items of common (professional) knowledge in an attempt to interest English people." He wrote further that the only original things in it were "the autobiographical bits, the reference to 'beauty' in language, and the theory that one's 'native language' is not the same as one's 'cradle-tongue.'"[32] It is interesting that for a talk that was not "learned," Christopher Tolkien included after it thirty-four notes on three pages in the *Monsters and the Critics*.

In his lecture, Tolkien said he was "a philologist in the Anglo-Saxon and Germanic field," and acknowledged his "great en-courager," the Yorkshireman Joseph Wright. Wright was a professor of comparative philology at Exeter College, whose *Primer of the Gothic Language* Tolkien read as a teenager. Wright's enthusiasm for philology remained with Tolkien his entire life, and his advice to "Go in for Celtic, lad" was characteristic of this occasionally eccentric but always interesting and fascinating man.[33]

Later in his talk Tolkien discussed the value of Celtic (particularly Welsh) philology, how in his view the English Tudor monarchy in the fifteenth century had tried to "destroy Welsh on earth as well as in Heaven" by the publication of a dictionary of

---

[32] Carpenter, *Letters*, 319.

[33] See Carpenter, *Biography*, 63–64 for a humorous and insightful look at Wright.

English and Welsh, with its avowed purpose to teach the "literate Welsh" (English). He further stated how the English and Welsh languages "coinhabited" Britain (with linguistic and etymological comparisons and how "Anglicized" words derived from the original Welsh), and how many British place names were actually derived from fragments of "long-forgotten Neolithic or Bronze Age tongues, celticized, romanized, anglicized, ground down by the wear of time."[34]

Tolkien concluded his lecture by discussing at length the Celtic language in Britain, "some of the points in which this study may offer special attraction to the speakers of English." These points included the antiquity of the Celtic language in Britain, the history of varieties and changes in the language (with much emphasis on Latin influence), "the interests and uses of Welsh and its philology to students of English," and two illustrations for the "student of English as a Germanic tongue," dealing with Old English/Germanic verb parallels and phonetic developments.

Perhaps the most interesting aspect of this talk was an "autobiographical bit" that sheds a great deal of light on Tolkien and his love of philology, the study of the history of language. Toward the end of the lecture he mentioned that language is "related to our total psycho-physical makeup," is "a product of our individuality," "we each have a native language" that is not our "cradle-tongue," and this language, "though it may be buried, it is never extinguished."[35] A Tolkien scholar pointed out that these words show that for Tolkien, language was "the repository and conveyance of myth through time. He had an almost mystical belief in the relationship of language to human consciousness... This is not a scholar speaking about an academic interest, but a person expressing a deeply held belief. The phrase 'psycho-physical' implies that language...can be inherited rather than

---

[34] *The Monsters and the Critics and Other Essays*, ed. Christopher Tolkien (Boston: Houghton Mifflin, 1984) 171.

[35] Ibid., 190.

learned. Such a concept carried Tolkien's philological interest beyond the academic into the psychological, and beyond that into the frankly psychic."[36]

This interest was reinforced in a June 1955 letter to W. H. Auden when Tolkien wrote: "I am a West-Midlander by blood (and took to early west-midland Middle English as a known tongue as soon as I set eyes on it)...I daresay such linguistic tastes...are as good or better a test of ancestry as blood-groups."[37] For Tolkien, inherited "native language" came out of his "home roots" and personal experiences, and language was a memory and guide for nearly all he wrote.

The Ancrene Wisse

This work ("the Guide or Rule for Anchoresses") was an allegorical devotional manual composed sometime around 1230. It has been admired for many years as a work of great charm, with vivid imagery and a stimulating prose style, and is now considered to be one of the greatest works of the Early Middle English period.[38] For many years its author was thought by some to be Richard Poore, Bishop of Salisbury (eleventh century), but in recent years scholars have concluded that the author was possibly an Augustinian priest or chaplain connected with Wigmore Abbey in Hertfordshire, near Worcester. It was written for the use (guidance, "*wisse*") of three sisters of noble birth, and "of one

---

[36] Verlyn Flieger, *A Question of Time: J. R. R. Tolkien's Road to Faërie* (Kent OH: Kent State University Press, 1997) 3, 4.

[37] Carpenter, *Letters*, 213–14.

[38] For a stimulating older essay on the *Ancrene Wisse*, see Richard Garnett and Edmund Gosse, *English Literature: An Illustrated Record*, vol. 1 (New York: Macmillan, 1935) 87–89. The authors call it a "work of great literary merit" and declare that it "has influenced our standard English" and is "one of the most perfect models of simple eloquent prose in our language." See also "*Ancrene Wisse*," in J. A. Burrow and Thorlac Turville-Petre, *A Book of Middle English* (Oxford: Blackwell, 1992) 104–109.

father and one mother," who had decided to become nuns (possibly at the Limesbrook convent near Worcester), and was to be an aid to meditation and right living. Sometimes called the *Ancrene Riwle* ("Rule"), it was divided into eight sections, each dealing with a single division of the rule for the inner and outer life of a recluse, such as prayer, "the control of the senses," temptations (the Seven Deadly Sins are described as beasts and courtiers of the Devil), confession, penance, love (with a picture of Christ as a lover/knight), and "practical manners."

Scholars have deduced that the author of *Ancrene Wisse* was widely read in the theological works of medieval Europe, was a master of rhetoric and language, and that the style of the manual owes much to Latin techniques of biblical interpretation. It was widely popular in its day and was translated into French and Latin.

Tolkien was interested in the *Ancrene Wisse* well before 1929, when he published an article on it in *Essays and Studies* (which has been called "the most perfect of his academic pieces"[39]), and there is correspondence from him in the Bodleian Library from 1936 regarding this edition. He had finished translating the work by 1945, and in two letters to his publisher in London in 1952 mentioned his book as overdue while he was writing the *Lord of the Rings* and working on other projects. In a letter to Raynor Unwin in 1960 he complained that the book should have been completed "many years ago," but the book was delayed until he corrected the final proofs in January 1962. In a letter to his son Michael on 19 December 1962, he mentioned that "my *Ancrene Wisse*...got between covers this week at last."

What many are not aware of today is that the *Ancrene Wisse* and its echoes found their way into and profoundly influenced several of Tolkien's popular works. In *Leaf By Niggle* and *Smith of Wootton Major*, the idea of helping one's neighbor at the expense of art is fictionalized from the *Ancrene Wisse*. Also in *Niggle*, Tolkien's "education as a Christian" paralleled the three stages

---

[39] Shippey, *Road to Middle Earth*, 36.

described in *Wisse*. His ideas about kingship in the *Hobbit* (and in the *Beowulf* essay) came at least in part from *Wisse*, and the notion of the deadly sins embodied in the evil spider Shelob and the evil wizard Saruman in the *Two Towers* was initially drawn from Tolkien's study of the section on temptation in the *Ancrene Wisse*.

A friend of Tolkien's wrote that the *Ancrene Wisse* was his "abiding love,"[40] and a colleague said in a book celebrating Tolkien that his work on the *Ancrene Wisse* "has done so much to illuminate," and that the guide's "textual superiority is as marked as its linguistic purity, the demonstration of which we owe to Professor Tolkien in the article, published over thirty years ago, which subsequent study has taken as its starting point."[41] The colleague was obviously referring here to scholarly work, but readers of Tolkien's popular books can be grateful for his abiding love of an old work that is scarcely mentioned today.

The Jerusalem Bible

In a February 1967 letter to Charlotte and Denis Plimmer, Tolkien explained that he had been "consulted on one or two points of style, and criticized some contributions" for the new *Jerusalem Bible* (January 1957).[42] The Plimmers had interviewed him for *Daily Telegraph Magazine*, sent him a draft of their article, and their interview was published 22 March 1968. Tolkien mentioned that being named as among the "principal collaborators" (of

---

[40] See J. A. W. Bennett, "*Nosce te ipsum*: Some medieval Interpretations," in Salu and Farrell, *Essays in Memoriam*, 145.

[41] E. J. Dobson, "The Affiliations of the Manuscripts of *Ancrene Wisse*," in *English and Medieval Studies Presented to J. R. R. Tolkien on the Occasion of his Seventieth Birthday*, ed. Norman Davis and C. L. Wrenn (London: Allen & Unwin, 1962) 128, 163.

[42] Deborah Rogers imaginatively suggested that "to balance things," Tolkien was asked to work on (the Catholic) *Jerusalem Bible* because famed writer and poet John Masefield was a contributor to (the Anglican) *New English Bible*. See Rogers & Rogers, *Critical Biography*, 138–39.

twenty-seven) of the Bible was an "undeserved courtesy" by the editor (Alexander Jones), and that he had originally been assigned a large amount to translate. After doing some "necessary preliminary work," he completed the book of Jonah, "one of the shortest books," after working on it sporadically for five years.[43]

The British Tolkien newsletter *Amon Hen* reported (May 1976, number 26) that Tolkien also worked on a first draft of a translation of the book of Job, and he played "an important role in establishing its final text."[44] Anthony Kenny, who was on the team of translators, wrote that Tolkien was initially asked to translate Judges and Jonah, was "a difficult collaborator," and finally "contributed only a version of Jonah," leaving Judges to another scholar, Walter Shewring.[45] When the *Jerusalem Bible* was published in 1966, Tolkien was named as a "principal collaborator in translation and literary revision," but his translation of Jonah had been considerably revised.

Another of Tolkien's colleagues in working on the translation of the *Jerusalem Bible* was Robert Speaight, the biographer of Hilaire Belloc. A later commentator gave Tolkien and Speaight high praise and said that their area of competence was "obviously that of sensitivity to the best resonances of the English language."[46]

There is a possibility that Tolkien may have used the *Jerusalem Bible* as a source for at least two of the character names in the *Lord of the Rings*. In the Old Testament, there are several references to places called "Gilgal," the most prominent being

---

[43] Carpenter, *Letters*, 378.

[44] See Wayne G. Hammond, *J. R. R. Tolkien: A Descriptive Bibliography* (New Castle DE: Oak Knoll Books, 1993) 278–79. Clyde S. Kilby reported in *Tolkien and the Silmarillion* (Wheaton IL: Harold Shaw, 1976, 54) that Tolkien learned a "considerable amount of Hebrew" to prepare for his work.

[45] Anthony Kenny, *A Path From Rome: An Autobiography* (Oxford: Oxford University Press, 1986) 117.

[46] Bruce Vawter, "The Jerusalem Bible," in *The Word of God: A Guide to English Versions of the Bible* (Atlanta: John Knox Press, 1982) 109.

near Jericho, where the Israelites camped after crossing the Jordan River and set up twelve stones in a circle as a memorial to the event (Joshua, chapter four). The word "Gilgal" means "ring of stones," and the proper name is mentioned several times in the Old Testament, including once in Deuteronomy, twelve times in Joshua (with 15:7 mentioning a "stone circle"), twice in Judges, six times in 1 Samuel, twice in 2 Kings, twice in Hosea, and once in Amos.

In the *Lord of the Rings*, the names of the characters "Gil-galad" and "Galadriel" are comparable to "Gilgal," and the similarities between "Gildad" and "Gil-galad" are striking, as is "Galadriel" with "Gildad" and "Gil-galad." It may be possible that Tolkien, while writing the *Lord of the Rings*, remembered the many instances of the name "Gildad" from his reading of the *Jerusalem Bible* and used the name in combination with other sources (and inspirations) for at least two of his characters.[47]

It has long been speculated that the origins of a ring of power in the *Lord of the Rings* may have been derived from several sources. It is well known that the Norse *Elder Edda* and Wagner's *Niebelungenlied* both contain references to rings of power that corrupt (though Tolkien denied any connections with the Ring and Wagner), and that Plato's the *Republic* and Cicero's *De Officiis* (which told the same story of the shepherd Gyges) contain references to a ring of power that makes its wearer invisible. With these as possible influences (except Wagner), it is also possible to speculate that Tolkien's use of the word "ring" may have been, in part, remembered from his reading about the ring of stones in the Old Testament biblical stories, from the *Jerusalem Bible*.

---

[47] See Paul Kocher, letter, *Mythlore 16* (vol. 4, no. 4, June 1977): 38. Professor Kocher also wrote here that Tolkien worked on the book of Proverbs.

The Old English Exodus

The *Old English Exodus* is based on Tolkien's reconstructed notes for informal lectures given to small, "specialist" classes in the 1930s and 1940s, although he began work on the English poetic version of the Old Testament book around 1925. The work has three major sections: the Anglo-Saxon text, the prose translation, and commentary, the latter being divided into an introduction and notes on the meaning of individual words and phrases. Tolkien's former student Joan Turville-Petre revised his commentary in the 1950s, deleting unnecessary material, omitting irrelevant "paleographical descriptions," and adding her own comments and notes to Tolkien's original text.

Exodus is a 590-line Old English poem dating from the eighth century, and was written by an unknown author, although a few scholars attribute it to Caedmon of the ninth century, the first English poet to be known by name. It is based on the biblical story of the exodus (13:17 through chapter 14) and was the first English treatment or interpretation of this story. It begins with praise of Moses the lawgiver, and within fifty lines skips to the tenth plague and Pharaoh's agreement to release the Israelites. Other major features of the poem include the pillars of cloud and fire, the Egyptian pursuit of the captives, the destruction of the Egyptians at the Red Sea, and a long discourse on the idea of the covenant from Noah through Abraham.

One author speculated that *Exodus* "may have been intended for use in the Holy Sunday liturgy of the Anglo-Saxon church in connection with baptism," as the Red Sea crossing was traditionally associated with baptism by such early church historians as Tertullian and St. Ambrose.[48]

Tom Shippey wrote that Tolkien was interested in this poem primarily because he thought it was older than *Beowulf* and

---

[48] See "Exodus" in David L. Jeffrey, ed., *A Dictionary of Biblical Tradition in English Literature* (Grand Rapids MI: Eerdmans, 1992) 259.

because he thought the *Exodus*-poet, like the unknown author of *Beowulf*, had known about pre-Christian mythology. In several places in *Exodus*, the poet mentions "the land of the Sigelware" (*Sigelhearwa*), usually translated as "Ethiopians." Tolkien thought this was a mistake and that the name was actually a combination of three words, two in Anglo-Saxon meaning "sun" and "jewel," and one word in Latin meaning "soot." The three words were fused into one word that meant "fire-giant." Since the poem was written in Anglo-Saxon in the "preliterate Dark Age," before anyone living then had ever heard of Ethiopia or the book of Exodus, Tolkien thought that *Sigelhearwa* meant "sons of Muspell," Muspell being the Norse fire-giant. He had suggested this thesis years before in two obscure articles and incorporated his ideas about the fire-giant into the *Silmarillion*.[49]

In her introduction, Turville-Petre mentioned that Tolkien never intended the lectures to be published, but the work is of great value to students as it shows his great skill in translation and his skillful use of colorful imagery and extensive knowledge of Anglo-Saxon prose. At the beginning of his translation, Tolkien used a word that will be forever identified with him: Middle-earth (*Middangeard*). The *Old English Exodus* is obviously not a parallel retelling of the events of the original story, but a creative and dramatic rendering based on it, and Tolkien used many "wondrous words" in this translation that showcased him as a true master of the English language. Three thousand copies of the book were published in January 1982 by Oxford's Clarendon Press.

---

[49] See Shippey, *J. R. R. Tolkien: Author of the Century* (London: HarperCollins, 2000) 85–86.

Finn and Hengest—
The Fragment and the Episode

The editor of this work, Tolkien's former student Alan Bliss, called *Finn and Hengest* Tolkien's "most significant contribution to Anglo-Saxon studies."[50] The work contains Tolkien's university lectures with notes and a glossary dating from before 1930 to after 1960 ("three separate sets"), with an introduction, preface, added notes, an appendix, the translation of the fragment, some footnotes, and some expansion of references added by Bliss. As Rawlinson and Bosworth Professor of Anglo-Saxon at Oxford, Tolkien was expected to lecture regularly on *Beowulf*, and in the twenty years he held the position (1925–1945), he lectured on the poem many times, and at least six times specifically on the story of Finn and Hengest, between 1928 and 1937. A seventh lecture was scheduled for 1939 but was canceled due to war.

The story of Finn and Hengest, two fifth-century heroes of Northern Europe, is told in two Old English poems, *Beowulf* and the *Fight at Finnesburg*. The "Fragment" is the surviving scrap of the latter poem, and the "Episode" refers to the events of the poem in *Beowulf*. The Finnesburg poem scrap (forty-seven lines) tells the story of a young Danish chieftain (Hnœf) and his followers who defend a hall under siege; one of Hnœf's most loyal followers is a man named Hengest. The scrap is of "major importance" to Anglo-Saxon studies for three reasons. First, it appears to be a fragment of a short, heroic poem called a "lay" (in Old English poetry, a song or recitation by a minstrel at a feast), and this scrap is one of only two that have survived. Second, the Finnesburg scrap is the only surviving pagan narrative poem in Old English. There is no mention of God, and the story is not told in terms of Christian ideals. And third, the story told in the scrap is closely linked to a similar story related in *Beowulf* (less than ninety lines).

---

[50] Alan Bliss, ed., *Finn and Hengest—The Fragment and the Episode* (Boston: Houghton Mifflin, 1983) dust jacket blurb.

The Finn and Hengest episode in *Beowulf* appears to have happened later than the Finnesburg story.

The Finn and Hengest episode (a tragedy) takes place after Beowulf has killed the monster Grendel. Lord Hnœf was killed in the hall siege by Finn, and Hengest has to resolve the moral dilemma of keeping a peace treaty or avenging his Lord. There are no monsters and dragons in either the episode or the fragment, only "ordinary fallible human beings, suddenly plunged into circumstances from which no issue can preserve both life and honour."[51]

Tolkien looked forward to publishing his *Finn and Hengest* lectures, as evidenced by the long version of his glossary being "carefully penned in a more formal style" and "liberally supplied with footnotes." Editor Bliss, who studied under Tolkien from 1946 to 1948 but did not attend his Finn and Hengest lectures, was planning to publish a paper on Hengest in the sixties, but discovered after conversations with friends that his old professor had come to the same (and more extensive) conclusions "many years previously." It was then impossible for Bliss to publish his paper, and in 1966 he visited Tolkien and informed him of the situation. A few days later, Tolkien wrote to Bliss, graciously offered to give him all his Finn and Hengest materials, and advised him to make use of them if he wished. Christopher Tolkien finally gave the "sorted out" materials to Bliss in 1979. Students at Oxford University, then and now, are not required to attend lectures. It is a matter of conjecture to wonder if this book would have been published at all if Bliss had attended his professor's talks.

---

[51] Ibid., 4.

Other Lectures, Stories, Art, Letters

"A Secret Vice"

"A Secret Vice" has been published only once in English, in the *Monsters and the Critics and Other Essays* (1983), and includes a revised Quenya poem, "Oilima Markirya" ("The Last Ark"). This was the title of an address Tolkien gave sometime in 1931, probably in Oxford. Christopher Tolkien stated in the foreword to *Monsters and the Critics* that its date was 1931, and he noted "that the audience was a philological society is evident" by the fact that an Esperanto Congress was held in Oxford in July 1930, and at the beginning of the essay, Tolkien mentioned an Esperanto Congress held in Oxford "a year or more ago." His original title for the manuscript was "A Hobby for the Home," adding "In other words: homemade or invented languages."

Humphrey Carpenter mentioned that when the adolescent Tolkien began making up words and inventing languages,

"Esperanto was very popular at the time."[1] Esperanto is an artificial language created during the period 1885–1887 for universal use by a Polish eye doctor named Ludwig Zamenhof (1859–1917). Meant for use as a neutral form of international communication, Esperanto (from "Doctoro Esperanto," the pseudonym Zamenhof used for an introductory booklet) today claims about one to three million users worldwide, and is the most successful artificial language in the world.[2] It is most widely used in Central and Eastern Europe, particularly the satellite nations of the old Soviet Union, and in China. Esperanto organizations were banned in Germany starting in the mid-1930s, and Adolf Hitler specifically referred to Esperanto as a "tool of Jewish world domination" in a speech in 1922 and in *Mein Kampf*. Today there are about 150 Esperanto magazines, with at least three Usenet newsgroups and several Esperanto mailing lists available on the Internet.

When Tolkien was a teenager, his cousins Mary and Marjorie Incledon invented "Animalic," a language derived from animal names. Later Tolkien learned some Animalic but was never fluent in it. Mary and Tolkien also invented another language, "Nev-bosh" ("New Nonsense," used to chant limericks), that contained English elements with Latin and French added, and he followed this with another, more serious invented language, "Naffarin," which was influenced by Spanish and Latin and had its own system on grammar and phonology (the study of sounds).

---

[1] Humphrey Carpenter, *J. R. R. Tolkien: A Biography* (Boston: Houghton Mifflin, 2000) 44.

[2] See "Esperanto" in *The Oxford Companion to the English Language*, ed. Tom MacArthur (Oxford: Oxford University Press, 1992) 379–80, and Arden R. Smith and Patrick Wynne, "Tolkien and Esperanto," in vol. 17 of *SEVEN: An Anglo-American Literary Review* (2000): 27–46. As of June 2001 there were over thirty Internet sites devoted to Esperanto. An excellent site is maintained by Donald J. Harlow, "Esperanto: An Overview," which mentions Tolkien's "Elvish Tongues" as among the "better-known constructed languages in this country" (http://www.webcom.com/~donh/efaq).

Tolkien learned Esperanto during this time (circa 1905–1911), which is shown by a page from "The Book of Foxrook." Foxrook is a small sixteen-page notebook composed when he was seventeen, and is the earliest example of one of his invented alphabets. It contains: "the key to a secret code consisting of a rune-like phonetic alphabet and a sizable number of ideographic (characters symbolizing the idea of a thing) symbols called 'monographs' representing an entire word."[3] Foxrook is mentioned in Carpenter's biography: "He was also working on invented alphabets; one of his notebooks from schooldays contains a system of code-symbols for each letter of the English alphabet."[4] A page from Foxrook is illustrated in *Tolkien: Life and Legend*, and the commentary for the illustration reads, in part: "Much of his spare time as a schoolboy henceforth became taken up with the invention of private languages and alphabets. The 'Book of Foxrook'...contains a code-alphabet and commentary in a language based on Esperanto and Spanish."[5]

In 1932, Tolkien became a member of the Board of Honorary Advisors to the Education Committee of the British Esperanto Association (BEA); he was probably offered this position due to his "Secret Vice" talk of the previous year. In 1932, he wrote a letter to the secretary of the BEA Education Committee, extracts of which were published in the May 1932 issue of the *British Esperantist*, with the title "A Philologist on Esperanto."[6]

In "A Secret Vice" Tolkien expressed his liking for Esperanto and for "artificial languages" (especially for Europe), not the least

---

[3] Smith and Wynne, "Tolkien and Esperanto," 29.

[4] Carpenter, *Biography*, 45.

[5] Judith Priestman, *Tolkien: Life and Legend—An Exhibition to Commemorate the Centenary of the Birth of J. R. R. Tolkien (1892–1973)* (Oxford: The Bodleian Library, 1992) 18.

[6] The complete text of the letter is contained in Smith and Wynne, "Tolkien and Esperanto," 35–36. It provides details of Tolkien's opinion of Esperanto and his thoughts on the international language movement and the aesthetics of invented languages.

because the one man who created it was not a philologist. Tongue in cheek, he mentioned that he "knew two people once...who constructed a language called *Animalic*," and that he was "never fully instructed in it, nor a proper Animalic speaker." He also mentioned at some length "Nevbosh" and "Naffarin" (with examples of each), talked about the influence of learnt languages, and said that the idea of using linguistic ability for amusement was deeply interesting.

The title of Tolkien's original manuscript was "A Hobby for the Home," but in a February 1967 letter he gave his essay a different name: "The amusement of making up languages is very common among children (I once wrote a paper on it, called A Secret Vice)." The manuscript was revised in the late 1940s, apparently for a second address, as Tolkien changed in the text "more than 20 years" to "more than 40 years." In a footnote in *Monsters and the Critics*, Christopher Tolkien mentioned a draft for the rewriting of the opening paragraph of the talk, saying that his father "wrote that he was 'no longer sure that [an artificial language] would be a good thing.'"[7] Further evidence that Tolkien's opinion of Esperanto had grown less favorable over the years appeared in a letter to a Mr. Thompson, 14 January 1956, in which he says that Esperanto and other similar invented languages "are dead, far deader than ancient unused languages, because their authors never invented any Esperanto legends."[8] Here Tolkien may have forgotten his words in "A Secret Vice," when he said, after approving of artificial languages in general, that "my concern is not with that kind of artificial language at all."[9] Esperanto was a public, functional language, a practical means of international

---

[7] Christopher Tolkien, ed., *The Monsters and the Critics and Other Essays* (Boston: Houghton Mifflin, 1983) 219n1.

[8] Humphrey Carpenter, *The Letters of J. R. R. Tolkien* (London: Allen & Unwin, 1981) 231.

[9] *Monsters and the Critics*, 198. Two of Tolkien's books were translated into Esperanto, *The Hobbit* and *The Lord of the Rings*, and also "A Philologist on Esperanto."

communication, and could not possibly have had a "history." Tolkien's invented languages set in a time long ago needed their histories and legends, and he created them, resulting in some of the greatest fantasy classics in all literature.

Leaf By Niggle

Tolkien wrote *Leaf By Niggle* just before World War II, after reading a preliminary version to his wife, then to friends early in 1940. In a letter to Stanley Unwin (March 1945), he wrote: "I woke up one morning (more than two years ago) with that odd thing virtually complete in my head. It took only a few hours to get down..."[10] In September 1944, the editor of an Irish literary journal wrote Tolkien and asked that he contribute a paper in order that the journal be "an effective expression of Catholic humanity." *Leaf By Niggle* (which Tolkien first called the *Tree*) was published by the *Dublin Review* in January 1945 and was later reprinted with revisions in *Tree and Leaf*.

Leaf By Niggle was the first of Tolkien's short stories to be published and is thought by many to be an autobiographical allegory.[11] Tolkien called it a "purgatorial story" and wrote once that it was "allegorical," but later that it was not "properly an

---

[10] Carpenter, *Letters*, 113.

[11] Various scholars have categorized this story in different ways. Shippey in *J. R. R. Tolkien: Author of the Century* (London: HarperCollins, 2000) calls it an autobiographical allegory (266), as does Duriez in *The Tolkien Handbook* (Grand Rapids MI: Baker, 1992) 148. Crabbe in *J. R. R. Tolkien* (New York: Continuum, 1988) calls it a prose poem (158), Pearce in *Tolkien: Man and Myth* (San Francisco: Ignatius Press, 1998) calls it a Christian allegory (171), and Kocher in *Master of Middle-earth* (Boston: Houghton Mifflin, 1972) calls it a tale with allegories and symbols (161, 162). Knowles in *A Purgatorial Flame* (Philadelphia: University of Pennsylvania Press, 1990) called it (after Tolkien) a purgatorial story (132), and Purtill in *J. R. R. Tolkien: Myth, Morality and Religion* (Sand Francisco: Harper & Row, 1984) called it an applicable story (17).

'allegory' so much as 'mythical.'"[12] In the story, Niggle, an ordinary, kindhearted, "not very successful," and rather idle painter, wanted to finish a special painting ("my real picture") before he had to go on a long journey, one he did not want to make. His painting began as a picture of a leaf caught in the wind, because Niggle "was the sort of painter who can paint leaves better than trees." But his picture of a leaf gradually became a tree, and as Niggle painted, he saw, through gaps in the leaves and boughs, a country and forest and mountains and a whole world opening up. As his canvas grew, he added smaller paintings on the edges of his bigger painting, and had to move his painting (now very large) to a shed on his potato plot.

As he observed his painting from a distance, Niggle saw it as "wholly unsatisfactory," yet the only really beautiful picture in the world. He thought that he really needed someone (particularly himself), to comment to him that his painting is "absolutely magnificent!" He tried to continue working, but there were distractions: ill friends, lame neighbors, and the like. Autumn came and went, and still Niggle worked in his shed, trying to finish his great work. One day his only really close neighbor, Parish (who Niggle did not particularly like; Tolkien once knew a gardener named Parish) stopped by and asked Niggle if he would go and fetch a doctor for his ill wife and contact a builder to repair his house—Parish could not go because he had a painful lame leg. Niggle agreed, rode his bicycle to the doctor, left a note for the builder, and on the return trip got soaking wet and caught a chill and a fever.

One day the Inspector of Houses visited Niggle. The Inspector scolded Niggle for not helping Parish repair his house, and during that time another man (dressed in black) came in, and announced himself as the "Driver." The Driver told Niggle it was time to start his journey, and the two left together. The rest of the

---

[12] See two letters by Tolkien in Carpenter, *Letters*, September 1945 (195) and 8–9 September 1962 (320).

story involved Niggle's arrival at a hospital, his being put to work as a laborer, his hearing voices discussing his "case" outside his room, and his resumption of the train journey. The journey finally led him to the world he painted long ago and to his now completed tree. As he walked toward it, he was overcome with joy: "It's a gift!" he cried. He then walked toward the forest with his neighbor, Parish, and the two of them began work in what they later learned was "Niggle's Country." Niggle left Parish, and then, with a shepherd as guide, moved to the mountains (always uphill) beyond the forest; the narrator tells the reader, "beyond that I cannot guess what became of him." The story ended with people gossiping about Niggle after his departure, and the "odd corner" of his painting was framed and put into the local museum. It was named "Leaf By Niggle" and shows a spray of leaves and a mountain peak. The reader is told that the museum burnt down, and the leaf, and Niggle, were "entirely forgotten." Niggle's Country became a popular tourist resort, used as a "holiday and a refreshment."

There is much in *Leaf By Niggle* that seems to reveal Tolkien's Christianity, or as one author noted, "his deeply religious turn of mind."[13] The story alludes to several Christian/biblical ethical ideals, including justice and mercy, grace as superior to works, and compassion and responsibility for neighbors and friends. Katharyn Crabbe wrote of Niggle's "clarity of vision," his "perception of ground and grass and, finally, the tree," and compared this to "the promise of 1 Corinthians, 'For now we see through a glass darkly; but then face to face.'"[14] Joseph Pearce called the story "the closest he [Tolkien] came to writing an overtly Christian allegory," and Paul Kocher wrote that "Niggle's world, like Tolkien's, is unmistakably Christian," and that it is governed by strict moral and Christian laws, especially when people help their needy neighbors, even at sometimes severe cost

---

[13] Crabbe, *J. R. R. Tolkien*, 162.
[14] Ibid., 163.

to themselves.[15] Richard Purtill stated that the story is "explicitly religious," and inferred this by Tolkien's use of the "Catholic" word "purgatory" and by interpreting Niggle's story through a Christian lens.[16]

In a letter to Caroline Everett (24 June 1957), Tolkien echoed his March 1945 statement to Stanley Unwin (above) by explaining that the story "arose suddenly and almost complete" and that it came from "my own preoccupation with the *Lord of the Rings*, the knowledge that it would be finished in great detail or not at all, and the fear (near certainty) that it would be 'not at all.' The war had arisen to darken all horizons. But no such analyses are a complete explanation even of a short story..."[17]

During the time of the writing of *Leaf By Niggle*, Tolkien was recuperating from a gardening injury, was deluged with writing projects, had a very heavy teaching load, was under heavy pressure (as an appointed professor holding a chair) to produce more scholarly works, and his own "internal tree," the *Lord of the Rings*, had become almost unmanageable (Tolkien says he was "dead stuck") with its "revealing endless new vistas," and the war was imminent and on everyone's mind. His words "near certainty" (above) are very revealing because, like so many in Europe at the time of the onset of the war, he assumed he might never live through another one, and that his life's work would not be completed.[18] *Leaf By Niggle* was perhaps Tolkien's cathartic response for dealing with the anxiety and fear of war, and in the story his "real self," the storyteller and the Christian, is revealed.

---

[15] See Pearce, *Man and Myth*, 171, and Kocher, *Master of Middle-Earth*, 164.

[16] Purtill, *Myth, Morality and Religion*, 22–25.

[17] Carpenter, *Letters*, 257.

[18] Ibid., 321. Tolkien also mentioned here a concern he had with a neighbor who wanted to cut down a beautiful, huge old poplar tree "with vast limbs" that he could see through his bedroom window. Tolkien always loved trees (especially this one), and his concern over the fate of the tree is believed by some scholars to have been one of the perhaps unconscious reasons for the genesis of his writing *Leaf By Niggle*.

Concerning this and Tolkien's "objective correlative" for his state of mind during the writing of the story, Ivor and Deborah Rogers commented that his "dreaming mind" helped him give in an allegorical form "a concrete image of how things are in his feelings, thoughts, and hopes."[19]

Some scholars think that *Leaf By Niggle* was Tolkien's version of Dante's *Purgatorio*, because of several seeming parallels: the journey, the driver (who is similar to Dante's angel that pilots the ship of souls), a spring that runs through the forest (the river Eunoe in Dante), and others. Sebastian Knowles wrote that *Leaf By Niggle* "follows Dante's *Purgatorio* in its general structure and in its smallest detail," and that it is "purgatorial in effect, allowing Tolkien to continue the *Lord of the Rings*. It responds to the purgatory of the time."[20]

"Valedictory Address"

Tolkien gave his Valedictory Address to the University of Oxford for a "packed house" at Merton College Hall on 5 June 1959, at the end of his final summer term as Merton Professor of English Language and Literature at Oxford. The talk was first published in *J. R. R. Tolkien: Scholar and Storyteller* (Cornell University Press, ed. Mary Salu and Robert T. Farrell) in 1979, and in 1983 from a different manuscript with alterations in the *Monsters and the Critics and Other Essays*.

At the beginning of the address, Tolkien's first "inaugural" lecture at Oxford ("34 years behind"), he showed his sense of humor by mentioning his well-known "ineffectiveness as a lecturer" and by telling his audience that he had not yet "discovered anything special to say." He continued by saying he was not giving a diagnosis of "what is wrong," or a "confident prescription

---

[19] Ivor Rogers and Deborah Rogers, *J. R. R. Tolkien: A Critical Biography* (New York: Hippocrene Books, 1980) 56.

[20] Knowles, *Purgatorial Flame*, 140, 141.

of the cure," or the "wide view," or the "masterly survey," or even "plans and prophecies." These, he said, were "never in his line," and he proceeded to tell his audience what he "had usually done."

He perhaps then contradicted himself and talked about some of the changes in the Oxford approach to English education, among them being the increased emphasis on postgraduate research, which he called "the degeneration of real curiosity and enthusiasm into a planned economy." He said this resulted in research time that is "stuffed into more or less standard skins" and turned into an assembly line of sausages "approved by our own little printed cookery book." Tolkien was complaining about the Oxford system of virtually giving away the Master of Arts degree: "the old trouble is the loss of the M. A. as a genuine degree." (For many years the Oxford M. A. degree was awarded automatically seven years after the completion of a B. A.[21]) He thought this stifled real creativity and authentic love of learning: "...those who have studied English for love...wish to spend *more time* in a university: more time in learning things..."

Tolkien followed these passionate remarks with a discussion of his feelings about the structure of the Oxford Honours School of English Language and Literature, which was often divided into two factions, "language" and "literature." In the years before Tolkien arrived at Oxford, the School syllabus placed much more emphasis on language study than most other universities. Students were required to study Anglo-Saxon or Old English, make a detailed study of *Beowulf* from the original text, learn the grammar, and study the developments of the language from Middle English through "modern" English. They also were

---

[21] From the *Handbook to the University of Oxford* (London: Oxford University Press, 1956) 407: "The degree of Master of Arts is open without further examination to candidates who have taken the Oxford degree of Bachelor of Arts and have had their names on the books of a society (i.e., have paid university and college dues) for a period of twenty-one terms." The Oxford academic year consists of three terms (Hilary, Trinity, Michaelmas) of about eight weeks each.

required to read and study many important older works, including *Sir Gawain and the Green Knight* and much or most of Chaucer, Spenser, Shakespeare, Milton, and others. Since Tolkien's arrival, the university had changed the syllabus, concentrating more on modern literature (after the Victorians), and de-emphasizing study of the older English poets. Humphrey Carpenter noted that some of the "literature people" also believed that by reading recent literature, students could in some way improve their character.[22] Tolkien strongly opposed this view and fought hard to reform the syllabus, including suggesting stopping the syllabus at 1830 and removing the study of Victorian literature (a heresy to many), but had limited success; one of his earliest opponents was C. S. Lewis.

Toward the end of his address Tolkien mentioned and thanked some of his teachers and influences, including Joseph Wright, William Craigie (his teacher of Old Norse at Exeter), Henry Bradley (his supervisor at the English Dictionary), C. T. Onions (a colleague at the *OED*), E. V. Gordon (Leeds), and Henry Wyld (a colleague at Merton). He closed the address by quoting twelve lines from his Elvish farewell poem "Namárië."

Almost six months after Tolkien's retirement, the Board of the Faculty of English sent him a letter of appreciation thanking him for his "long and invaluable service" to the university. It also expressed "its regret that it will not in future have the benefit of your wise advice and unsparing help in its deliberations. It wishes at the same time to express its sense of the distinction which your wide, meticulous, and imaginative scholarship has brought to the faculty and to the University."[23]

Pictures by J. R. R. Tolkien

This beautiful oversized book is a collection of all the pictures (paintings, drawings, designs) by Tolkien that were published in a

---

[22] Carpenter, *The Inklings* (London: HarperCollins, 1997) 25.
[23] Carpenter, *Letters*, 300, 301.

series of six calendars (Allen & Unwin in the UK and Ballantine in the US) from 1973 to 1979, with a gap in 1975. Of the nineteen calendar pictures included in or intended for inclusion in the *Hobbit*, several were pencil sketches or later colored drawings (by H. E. Riddett). Eight of the drawings were originally from the *Lord of the Rings* and eight were from the *Silmarillion*.

The book contains ninety-eight pages, which includes Christopher Tolkien's foreword and text with thirty-seven color plates and seventeen black and white plates. It has one page of floral designs, one page with three leaves from "The Book of Mazurbul" (from the *Fellowship of the Ring*), one page of three examples of Númenórean tile and textiles (as mentioned in the *Akallabêth* from the *Silmarillion*), one page of sixteen heraldic devices, one color sketch of Shelob's Lair (found on a page of an early draft of the story, from the *Two Towers*), one page of three drawings of dragons from the same period (1927–1928) as the paintings and drawings from the *Silmarillion*, one page of three examples of Elvish script (from early versions of the poems "Errantry" and "The Adventures of Tom Bombadil"), two color pages of sixteen examples of patterns (mostly flowers or flower-like forms; also heraldic devices and tapestries, doodled on newspapers/crossword puzzles), two pages of one black and white and three color trees, and one color page titled "Polar Bear had fallen from top to bottom onto his nose," which was first published in the *Father Christmas Letters* (1976).

Many of Tolkien's paintings in this book are now famous and have been reproduced many times on posters, record covers, and in other editions of his works and works about him. Some of these are: "The Hill: Hobbiton-across-the-Water," "Rivendell," "The Mountain-path," "Bilbo comes to the Huts of the Raft-elves" (made into a hugely popular poster for the fiftieth anniversary of the *Hobbit* exhibition held at the Bodleian Library, Oxford in 1987), "Conversation with Smaug," and others, including "The Tree of Amalion," which was used for the cover of the paperback edition of *Tree and Leaf* (1964).

In a review, Nancy-Lou Patterson called Tolkien a "great *naive* artist," a person without formal training who still creates powerful art.[24] Tolkien's paintings and sketches are distinctive, and their viewer recognizes his imprint, his persona, almost immediately. And while Tolkien's lack of formal art education shows itself most often in his simple (sometimes crude) drawings of human figures and architecture, his landscapes and geographical locales are nearly always evocative, luminous, and often never forgotten. And he was at his best with line drawings. He was a wonderful calligrapher (taught by his mother) who probably could have earned a living as a professional illustrator. Some Tolkien scholars believe that the illustrations and drawings in his own books have not been superseded by later artists who interpreted his work and that his art, both mature and finished (and his early drawings), are provocative and good enough to deserve to be at least as well-known as his writings.[25]

Tolkien was characteristically humble concerning his artistic abilities. In a letter to Hugh Brogan in 1954, he mentioned that he could draw only "imperfectly what I can, and not what I see,"[26] and in a letter to the Dutch artist Cor Blok, Tolkien said he was "doubtful" about the merit of his drawings and told Blok that they "had small value even as mere illustrations."[27]

Pictures was published by Allen & Unwin and Houghton Mifflin in 1979, with a new edition by HarperCollins (London) and Houghton Mifflin in 1992. Other delightful examples of Tolkien's art are from his children's stories the *Father Christmas Letters* and *Mr. Bliss*, and his original illustrated dust jackets for the British editions of the *Fellowship of the Ring*, the *Two Towers*,

---

[24] See *Mythlore 24* (Summer 1980): 32–33.

[25] See Wayne G. Hammond and Christina Scull, *J. R. R. Tolkien: Artist and Illustrator* (Boston: Houghton Mifflin, 1995) 7. This fine work is the only book that discusses Tolkien's art at length.

[26] Carpenter, *Letters*, 186.

[27] *Realms of Tolkien: Images of Middle-earth* (New York: HarperPrism, 1996), "About the Artists," no page numbers listed.

and the *Return of the King*, as well as (perhaps the most well-known) the binding and dust jacket for the *Hobbit*. The Númenórean helmet (*karma*) on the cover of the first US edition of *Unfinished Tales* was taken from an original colored drawing by Tolkien. Today most of his original drawings are preserved at the Department of Western Manuscripts of the Bodleian Library, Oxford, and the Special Collections Department of the Marquette University Library, Milwaukee.

The Letters of J. R. R. Tolkien

The *Letters of J. R. R. Tolkien* was published in hardcover by Allen & Unwin (21 August, 7,500–10,000 copies) and Houghton Mifflin (15 October, 100,000 copies) in 1981, with the first paperback edition published by Unwin Paperbacks (20 March, 7,500 copies) in 1990. The US edition did not sell well, but an additional 3,000 copies were printed in 1991 for the Tolkien Centenary. Unwin released another paperback printing of the *Letters* in 1995, and Houghton Mifflin released a paperback edition in 2000 that included a new and expanded forty-eight-page index compiled by Christina Scull and Wayne G. Hammond.

The collection contains 354 letters dated from October 1914 (to Edith Bratt) to 29 August 1973 (to Priscilla Tolkien, four days before Tolkien's death), and also included excerpts from letters and drafts with notes. It does not include letters Tolkien wrote to Edith (1913–1918) that were personal in nature, and no letters from 1925 to 1937 are included. Most of the letters fall into three categories: business letters to his publishers, letters explaining his mythology, and personal letters to members of his family. The recipients of the letters and drafts include: Allen & Unwin (102), Houghton Mifflin (seven), John Tolkien (one), Michael Tolkien (twenty-one), Priscilla Tolkien (two), Christopher Tolkien (sixty-three), Edith Bratt (four), C. S. Lewis (three), and Sam Gamgee (from London, one).

The letters were initially selected, collected, and transcribed by editor Humphrey Carpenter, and Christopher Tolkien provided comments on the selection and transcription and made suggestions for changes. Priority of selection was given to letters where Tolkien discussed and answered questions about his books, and several letters were chosen that "demonstrated the huge range of Tolkien's mind and interests, and his idiosyncratic but always clear view of the world."

The eighteen-page letter to Milton Waldman of Collins (not dated, probably late 1951) is perhaps the most interesting of the collection and is certainly one of the most informative. In it, Tolkien discussed the meanings of his mythology ("a brief sketch of my stuff that is connected with my imaginary world"), and explained that the *Lord of the Rings* and the *Silmarillion* were interdependent and inseparable. Among the many revelations of this 10,000-word letter are that he disliked "conscious and intentional" allegory but that in explaining the purpose of myths and fairy tales one must use allegorical language, and that the *Silmarillion* was primarily concerned with the "Fall, Immortality, and the Machine."

The *Letters* also reveal that Tolkien's 1911 visit to Switzerland was the inspiration for Bilbo's journey from Rivendell to the far side of the Misty Mountains in the *Hobbit*, and that the Beren and Lúthien story was inspired by his meeting with Edith in a "small woodland glade filled with hemlocks" at Roos in Yorkshire, where he was stationed as a garrison commander during the First War. Tolkien mentioned that he wrote his first story ("about a dragon") when he was seven, and described a hobbit in 1938 as having "ears only slightly pointed," which, as a reviewer noted, "set to rest forever" a controversy about hobbits and pointed ears.

There is much in the *Letters* that shed light on Tolkien's relationship with C. S. Lewis, including some that range from the gossipy (reporting that Lewis put away three pints in the morning then said he was "going short for Lent"), to the grateful (Tolkien would have never completed the *Lord of the Rings* without Lewis's encouragement). Tolkien also complained that Lewis received too much publicity, borrowed names from Middle-earth for his own writings (particularly Númenor, which Lewis misspelled "Numinor" in *That Hideous Strength*), and was prejudiced against Catholics. Tolkien praised Lewis's *Out of the Silent Planet* but called *Studies in Words* "ponderous silliness," said that Charles Williams's influence spoiled *That Hideous Strength*, objected to the Narnian stories as "outside the range of my sympathy," and amazingly found *Letters to Malcolm* "distressing and in parts horrifying."

Tolkien also praised Lewis many times for his generosity and friendship, and often recognized his lack of pretentiousness and envy. He suffered greatly when Lewis died ("an axe-blow near the roots"), called him a "great man," and complained that the "cold-blooded official obituaries" did not do Lewis justice and were superficial. Tolkien wrote that Lewis was his closest friend from 1927 to 1940, and that although they remained friends, they saw less and less of each other after Lewis "came under the dominant influence of Charles Williams" and still less after Lewis's "very strange marriage (to Joy Gresham)." In one fascinating letter (1948), after correspondence about criticisms of a paper Lewis had read aloud to the Inklings, Tolkien apologized and defined his own ideas about criticism, saying he was not really a critic and was not expressing "universally valid criticism" but only "liking" (or disliking). He also mentioned that he could write his thoughts better than he could say them, urged Lewis to publish his *Oxford History of English Literature* volume (*OHEL*), and finally apologized for missing Inklings meetings, saying his absences were not connected with his criticisms. But to get some final words in, he added in a footnote that Lewis's critical abilities got in the way of his writing and that he read too much analytically but was a born critic and writer.

Many of the letters reveal Tolkien as a wise and loving father, and his letters to his children show that he missed them when they were away and that he was always willing to give them wise advice on practical and religious matters. One remarkable letter to his son Michael (1 November 1963), who had written him asking for advice about a spiritual crisis ("his sagging faith"), is part encouragement, part loving admonishment, part Christian testimony, and part apologetic. It shows Tolkien's deep faith and knowledge of the New Testament, along with his opinions on worship and reverence for the church. Several other letters, especially to Christopher, show Tolkien's views toward the politics and culture of his day, some of which would not be "politically correct" in England today, particularly his leanings toward an "unconstitutional Monarchy" and jibes against the "State."

Many of the letters paint a picture of Tolkien's preoccupation (some might wrongly say obsession) with his literary life, with hundreds of references and answers to questions about the themes, characters, places, and events of his works, particularly the *Silmarillion*, the *Hobbit*, and the *Lord of the Rings*. A long sequence of letters to Christopher (1944) is primarily concerned with the dates of the writing and revising of the *Lord of the Rings*, with a few references to Inklings meetings and Tolkien's political ideas, which were mostly very conservative.[28]

Tolkien was a congenial friend and companion, always a cheerful gentleman, and was very well liked and respected by everyone who knew him, but several letters show his self-deprecating, sometimes sarcastic sense of humor and his pessimism toward modernity. In lighter moments he could be unintentionally funny, as in a letter to Michael (1967) when he complained, probably tongue-in-cheek, that only after his retirement did he learn that he was a successful teacher, and that his professor "friends" were always very pleased to tell him that

---

[28] Humphrey Carpenter noted that politically Tolkien was "right wing" in that he honored first monarchy and country, and that he was not a "democrat" because he believed the spiritual principles of humility and equality had been corrupted by the machine age, which led inevitably to "universal greatness and pride" and ultimately slavery. See *Biography*, 132–33.

he spoke too fast and "might have been interesting" if he had been audible. He explained this by saying that often he had too much to say in too little time, and that these comments made him even more modest and shy. Once (1964) he complained about his neighborhood and the football stadium near it, with all the "radio, tele, dogs, scooters, buzzbikes, and cars of all sizes except the smallest" that produced noise from "early morn to about 2 A.M.," and lamented the fact that three doors down a group of young men were "evidently aiming to turn themselves into a Beatle Group," and when they practiced the noise was indescribable.[29] His sarcasm concerning modern musical tastes was somewhat darker in an earlier letter to Christopher (1945), when he called "Jive and Boogie-Woogie" vulgar music "corrupted by mechanism, echoing in dreary un-nourished heads."[30]

Many of the original copies of letters in this collection are in the Tolkien-Allen & Unwin archive now held by HarperCollins (London), and in private collections. Other correspondence by Tolkien is in many collections, including the Bodleian Library (Oxford), the Pembroke College Library (Oxford), the British Library (London), the Lambeth Palace Library (London), the Marion E. Wade Center (Wheaton College, Illinois), and the Humanities Research Center (University of Texas, Austin). Tolkien's letters to Dr. Rhona Beare (who had written with several questions about the *Lord of the Rings*) were printed by the New England Tolkien Society in 1985, and many separate letters and excerpts have been published and reprinted in various books, pamphlets, booklets, newsletters, journals, and catalogues, including Sotheby's of London. One of these, to his son Michael (probably late 1960s),

---

[29] Carpenter, *Letters*, 345.
[30] Ibid., 111.

stated that Michael was one of the few people who really knew what the *Lord of the Rings* was all about.[31]

---

[31] Wayne G. Hammond, *J. R. R. Tolkien: A Descriptive Bibliography* (New Castle DE: Oak Knoll Books, 1993) 357. The excerpt was published in an article by Michael Tolkien, "J. R. R. Tolkien—The Wizard Father," in the *Sunday Telegraph* (London: :9 September 1973) and later in *Mythprint* (January 1975).

Unfinished Tales and The History of Middle-Earth

Unfinished Tales of Númenor and Middle-earth

Unfinished Tales was published by Allen & Unwin on 2 October 1980 (18 November 1980 by Houghton Mifflin) and contains Tolkien's unfinished and variant writings (stories and narratives) relating to the history of Middle-earth in the *Silmarillion* and the *Lord of the Rings*. The tales were edited by Christopher Tolkien and contain extensive notes, commentary, and two maps: Christopher's redrawing of the original accompanying the *Lord of the Rings* and a reproduction of the only map of Númenor J. R. R. Tolkien ever made.

When the *Silmarillion* was published in 1977 Christopher wrote in the foreword that "there is indeed a wealth of unpublished writing by my father concerning the Three Ages, narrative, linguistic, historical, and philosophical, and I hope that it will prove possible to publish some of this at a later date."[1] *Unfinished*

---

[1] J, R. R. Tolkien, *The Silmarillion*, ed. Christopher Tolkien (London: Allen & Unwin, 1977) 9.

Tales are those unpublished writings, and it contains much material that was composed before the *Lord of the Rings*.

This work is not for the beginning Tolkien reader, or one who has read only the *Hobbit* or perhaps some or even all of the *Lord of the Rings*. Christopher noted in the introduction that the stories in this work "constitute no whole," and that the book is "no more than a collection of writings, disparate in form, intent, finish, and date of composition." He further wrote that much in the book "will be found unrewarding" to those who do not have a good knowledge of the *Lord of the Rings*, and who do not "feel small desire for further exploration for its own sake."[2]

Nevertheless, *Unfinished Tales* contains some of Tolkien's best writing and is a book for the serious Tolkien reader who likes to explore and organize facts, places, names and themes, and who loves anything and everything to do with Middle-earth, particularly its languages, legends, politics, and kings. One Tolkien scholar wrote that much of the material in *Unfinished Tales* "is as finely crafted as anything J. R. R. Tolkien ever wrote," and it should be welcome to those readers "who find the *Silmarillion*'s style to be a little too high and distant."[3]

Unfinished Tales (472 pages) is divided into four parts (with fourteen unfinished stories), three of which are concerned with the First, Second, and Third Ages of Middle-earth, and a fourth which deals with the Drúedain, wizards, and Palantíri, or "Seeing Stones." Part One, the *First Age* (the *Silmarillion*), includes "Of Tuor and his Coming to Gondolin" (extension of part of chapter 23 of the *Silmarillion*) and "The Tale of the Children of Húrin" (Narn I Hîn Húrin—extension of chapter 21 of the *Silmarillion*). Part Two, the *Second Age* (the *Simarillion*), contains "A Description of the Island of Númenor," "Aldarion and Erendis:

---

[2] J. R. R. Tolkien, *Unfinished Tales of Númenor and Middle-earth*, ed. Christopher Tolkien (Boston: Houghton Mifflin, 1980) 1, 2.

[3] David Bratman, "*Unfinished Tales*—Review," *Mythprint* 17/6 (November 1980): 1.

The Mariner's Wife," "The Line of Elros: Kings of Númenor," and "The History of Galadriel and Celeborn." Part Three, the *Third Age* (the *Lord of the Rings*), includes "The Disaster of the Gladden Fields," "Cireon and Eorl and the Friendship of Gondor and Rohan," "The Quest of Erebor," "The Hunt for the Ring," and "The Battles of the Fords of Isen." The fourth part (the *Lord of the Rings*) includes "The Drúedain," "The Istari," and "The Palantíri."

The stories of Tuor and Túrin in Part One are much longer, detailed, and vivid than in the *Silmarillion*. The Tuor and Gondolin tale is a 1951 revision of "The Fall of Gondolin" (published in the *Book of Lost Tales*), which was written after the *Lord of the Rings* took shape and was one of the earliest parts of the *Silmarillion* (about seven pages, written 1926–1930). Tolkien intended that this story be a major part of the *Silmarillion*, and wrote its original form in 1916–1917, when he was in the army. Tuor is a hero who goes on a journey (one of Tolkien's favorite literary devices), and Tolkien repeats several times that he has a special role awaiting him in the future. "The Tale of the Children of Húrin" has many parallels with the Old Norse *Volsung Saga*, is more than three times as long as "Túrin Turambar" ("the dragon slayer") in the *Silmarillion*, and was conceived by Tolkien as a young man. Túrin's major flaws were pride and impulsive decision-making, and Tolkien may have modeled him after Beorhtnoth from the *Battle of Maldon*. This tale is a look at how Tolkien regarded evil, and how Túrin in the end succumbs to evil and becomes a monster and murderer. An unfinished narrative poem about Túrin is found in the *Lays of Beleriand*.

Paul Kocher wrote that the stories in Part Two "breathe new life into our conception of the island (Númenor) and its people."[4] In the *Silmarillion,* Númenor was the great star-shaped island in the sea of Belegaer that was "a special variety of the Atlantis

---

[4] Kocher, "J. R, R. Tolkien, *Unfinished Tales of Numenor and Middle-earth*" (review), *Mythlore 26* (vol. 7, no. 4, Winter 1981): 31.

tradition," according to Tolkien.[5] Perhaps the most interesting tale in this section is the well-developed, thirty-page partial treasure of a story, "Aldarion and Erendris: The Mariner's Wife." It is a domestic saga that includes a love-hate relationship between father (Meneldur, fifth king of Númenor), son Aldarion (his heir), and his wife Erendis. Aldarion loved the sea, and his frequent long voyages kept him away from home, which led to conflict with his father and wife. Aldarion also neglected his kingly and husbandly duties and lost the respect of his father and the love of his wife. She grew too old to bear a son who would be king. Their only child was a girl, Ancalimë, and Aldarion changed the law of succession so she could become the first female queen of Númenor. The story breaks off abruptly, but Christopher was able to piece together Tolkien's notes and supply an ending, the suicide of Erendis. This tale illustrates Tolkien's power as a storyteller as he explores the strains of family relationships and marital conflict and gives his own views, without preaching, of how families should, but often do not, live in harmony. Tom Shippey implied that "Aldarion and Erendis" may be modeled in part on Tolkien's own experience, as he "hardly knew his father" and the story "stresses the unwisdom of fathers leaving their children.[6]

The story of Galadriel ("glittering garland") and her husband Celeborn (much of it notes by Christopher Tolkien) is also provocative, as Galadriel is one of the most interesting and discussed of Tolkien's creations. A beautiful, athletic Elven princess and Queen of Lórien, she was one of the few persons from the First Age (the *Silmarillion*) to appear also in the *Lord of the Rings*. A woman of heroic moral character and courage, Galadriel is viewed as an anima figure by some,[7] and Sam's and

---

[5] Humphrey Carpenter, *The Letters of J. R. R. Tolkien* (London: Allen & Unwin, 1981) 197–98.

[6] Tom Shippey, *The Road to Middle-Earth* (London: Allen & Unwin, 1982) 217.

[7] A psychological term popularized by Carl Jung, from his *Archetypes of the Unconscious*. It means "inner personality" and when associated with people,

Gimli's devotion to her in the *Lord of the Rings* prompted several to think that Tolkien may have modeled her, in part, after the Virgin Mary. In a letter to Mrs. Ruth Austin (25 January 1971), he commented: "I think it is true that I owe much of this character to Christian and Catholic teaching and imagination about Mary, but actually Galadriel was a penitent..."[8] Galadriel was far from perfect; in her youth she was a leader in a revolt against the Valor (angelic guardians in the *Silmarillion*), at the end of the Third Age she refused forgiveness and was finally pardoned only when she refused to keep the One Ring offered to her by Frodo.[9] And although her husband Celeborn was a famous Elven lord and was called "Celeborn the Wise," he is not portrayed as especially bright in the *Lord of the Rings*.[10]

The five unfinished stories of the Third Age in Part Three were written while Tolkien was composing the *Lord of the Rings*, and published between the years 1937–1955. "The Disaster of the Gladden Fields" is mentioned briefly in the Council of Elrod (chapter two) in the *Fellowship of the Ring*, and tells of the killing by Orcs (an evil race bred by Morgoth, the "black enemy" of the *Simarillion*) of the Númenor chieftain Isildur, his three sons, and his small guard. "Cirion and Eorl" is a history of the people of Rohan (the Rohirrim, "kingdom of the horsemen") before they

---

refers to someone who is very wise, a mediator, noble, loving, and has a "second sight." An anima person also often has a "shadow" side, displaying the opposite characteristics.

[8] Carpenter, *Letters*, 407. An intriguing essay on Galadriel and Celeborn, which discusses Tolkien's treatment of them in his works of Middle-earth, is Janice Johnson, "The Celeblain of Celeborn and Galadriel," in *Mythlore 32* (vol. 9, no. 2, Summer 1982): 11–19.

[9] See Gloriana St. Clair, "An Overview of the Northern Influences on Tolkien's Works," in *Proceedings of J. R. R. Tolkien Centenary Conference, Mythlore 80*: 63–67, for a discussion of how several women from the Northern sagas could have influenced Tolkien's view of Galadriel. See also Ruth Noel, *The Mythology of Middle-Earth* (Boston: Houghton Mifflin, 1977) 118–20.

[10] Robert Foster, *The Complete Guide to Middle-Earth* (New York: Ballantine, 1978) 86.

obtained that name. Originally they were Northmen who raised horses on the plains between Mirkwood (a large forest prominent in the *Hobbit*) and the River Running.[11] "The Quest for Erebor" (perhaps written around 1950) and "The Hunt for the Ring" are stories told by Gandalf to Frodo and his friends in Minas Tirith after the crowning of King Aragorn (Strider in the *Lord of the Rings*). Erebor was a dwarf kingdom under a mountain (the *Hobbit*) that was controlled by Smaug, the winged evil dragon. In "Quest," Thoren Oakenshield is persuaded to take Bilbo with him to reoccupy Erebor and overthrow Smaug. Much of this story should be familiar to readers of the *Hobbit* and Appendix A of the *Lord of the Rings*, "Annals of the Kings and Rulers." "The Hunt for the Ring" continues the story of the search of the Black Riders (the *Lord of the Rings*, the "Nazgúl," servants of Sauron) for the Ruling Ring. The last of the unfinished stories in Part Three is "The Battles of the Fords of Isen," the river flowing south from Isengard that formed the western boundary of Rohan. Saruman, a wizard sent to Middle-earth to fight and resist Sauron, engages in several fierce battles trying to capture the kingdom of Rohan. An appendix details the military organization of the Rohirrim.

The description and short history of the unique Drúedain (or "drúgs"), was the first essay by Tolkien on these people; chronologically they make their first appearance near the end of the *Lord of the Rings*. Part Four details and explains their similarities and differences with hobbits. The "few hundred" drúgs were similar to hobbits in that they were four feet tall and "their laughter was a surprise," but dissimilar in that they were ugly, heavy, hairless, subject to great anger, could be great enemies, and loved solitude, "their capacity to utter silence and stillness."[12] "The Istari" (wizards) was written in 1954 while the *Lord of the*

---

[11] For a discussion about the Rohirrim and if they were modeled after peoples from medieval Anglo-Saxon culture, see "How Did Tolkien Actually Portray the Rohirrim?" in Michael Martinez, *Visualizing Middle-Earth*, Xlibris Corporation: 2000 (www.Xlibris.com) 78–90.

[12] See Paul Kocher, "The Drúedain," in *Mythlore 37* (Winter 1984): 23–25.

Rings was in publication, and was meant to be part of the index, but was rejected because of its length. Tolkien introduced the "blue wizards" Alatar and Pallendo (*Ithryn Luin*) in this fragment, who were "missionaries to enemy occupied lands" away from the familiar lands of the *Lord of the Rings*. This fragment also chronicles the wizard Gandalf's works and travels. "The Palantíri" were eight crystal globes, "the seeing stones," which could "see" events and places in the future, especially things near another palantír, which made them useful for communication. Richard Foster noted that "a person of strong will could learn to control the palantír and with it see where and whenever he wished."[13] Made by elves (the Noldor), the stones and their powers were prominent in the *Two Towers*, the *Return of the King*, the *Silmarillion*, and the *Road Goes Ever On*.

New hardcover and paperback editions of *Unfinished Tales* were published by Houghton Mifflin in 2001, with the cover illustrations by Ted Nasmith.

The History of Middle-Earth

The History of Middle-Earth is the collective title of twelve volumes of preliminary and unfinished manuscript materials left by Tolkien after his death and edited by his son Christopher, totaling well over 5,000 pages. These foundational works of great power, scope, and variety constitute the main body of stories, languages, geography, and other lore that initiated the *Lord of the Rings* and the *Silmarillion*, and into which the *Hobbit* evolved.[14] Christopher wrote in the introduction to the *Silmarillion* that his father conceived the work as a "compiliation, a compendious

---

[13] Foster, *Complete Guide to Middle-Earth*, 402.

[14] For a bibliographic listing and publication history of the *History of Middle-Earth* through volume nine, *Sauron Defeated*, see Wayne G. Hammond, *J. R. R. Tolkien A Descriptive Bibliography* (New Castle DE: Oak Knoll Books, 1993) 245–77.

narrative, made long afterwards from sources of great diversity (poems, and annals, and oral tales) that had survived in agelong tradition; and this conception has indeed its parallel in the actual history of the book, for a great deal of earlier prose and poetry does underlie it..."[15] The *History of Middle-Earth* brought to a good completion what Tolkien's conception of the *Silmarillion* was meant to be.

The works in this series have been of much interest to Tolkien scholars and those immersed in Middle-earth, and Christopher Tolkien has been rightly praised for his long and patient efforts in preparing them for publication. At the beginning, he wanted to give the reading public his father's mythology with all its variances, as a "continuing and evolving creation," and to include his own commentary linking it all together. Instead he carefully selected and arranged his father's materials and in certain places modified, changed (to be more coherent), and developed. His was a very difficult and painstaking task, as many of the manuscripts were very old, hard to read (often only with a magnifying glass), and many were written in pencil, which often faded over time. In addition, fragments and sections were often written on the backs of letters or other papers, or in notes attached to unrelated papers, and some passages were written in spaces in the middle of others. Also, many of the story fragments existed in more than one version and were not written in sequence, and the identification of the latest or "best" version was extremely difficult.

Although the works in the *History* were published with great care and with the best of intentions, it is interesting to consider that Tolkien may have had doubts about their usefulness as publications on the "popular" market, and that he perhaps anticipated (and dreaded) the later enormous reaction to his popular stories. Katharyn Crabbe wrote that "it does not seem to have been Tolkien's intention to provide a complete and finished

---

[15] Tolkien, *The Silmarillion* (Boston: Houghton Mifflin, 1977) 8.

version or vision of his imaginative world."[16] In his famous letter to Milton Waldman of Collins Publishing in 1951, Tolkien wrote, describing his desire to write "a body of more or less connected legend," that he "would draw some of the great tales in fullness, and leave many only placed in the scheme, and sketched. The cycles should be linked to a majestic whole, but leave scope for other minds and hands, wielding paint and music and drama. Absurd."[17]

The *History of Middle-Earth* showcases Tolkien as a writer of supreme skill, proficient and comfortable in a variety of literary genres. The series includes prose narratives ("The Lost Tales" and others), poetry and songs in octosyllabic couplets in the *Lay of Leithian* (the story of Beren and Lúthien), poetry in alliterative verse (the *Children of Húrin*), annals (year by year narratives), a cosmology of the universe (the *Ambarkanta*), time-travel stories (the *Lost Road* and the Notion Club Papers), genealogies (including diagramed family trees), and various writings about Elvish languages, including runic alphabets and words. It should be noted also that in these works, as they evolved, Tolkien sometimes changed his ideas about their final form. In the *Book of Lost Tales* he introduced some things that virtually stayed the same, such as the Music of the Ainur ("The Ainulindale," the story of creation), the treason of Melko (later Morgoth), and others. But in later accounts some things changed, such as when the Silmarils evolved from being just brilliant jewels to being the force behind the light of the Two Trees, and when Tolkien abandoned his early idea that his mythological land would correspond to the "real" world of England. In "The History of the Lord of the Rings" (the *Return of the Shadow*, the *Treason of Isengard*, the *War of the Ring*, and *Sauron Defeated*), the returning King Aragorn is a hobbit named Trotter, the love between him and Arwen had not

---

[16] Crabbe, *J. R. R. Tolkien* (New York: Continuum, 1988) 173.
[17] Carpenter, *Letters*, 144–45.

been developed, and the Ring had not yet become "the One Ring to rule them all."

The Book of Lost Tales, Part One (1983)

In his foreword to the first *Book of Lost Tales*, Christopher Tolkien wrote that his father began it in 1916–1917 "during the first War, when he was 25 years old." Tolkien left it incomplete several years later, but it was the beginning, in narrative form, of the history of Valinor (the land of Valnor in the *Silmarillion*) and Middle-earth. Before he completed the *Tales* Tolkien composed several long poems in the *History*, including the *Lay of Leithan* (the story of Beren and Lúthien) in rhyming verse and the *Children of Húrin* in alliterative verse. He started the *History* again in narrative form (a "sketch") in 1926, and this progressed until 1937, when he sent an abbreviated form of the *Silmarillion* to his publisher.

Part One includes ten short (mostly) interconnected stories, with notes and commentary, an appendix of names, and a glossary of obsolete, archaic, and rare words: "The Cottage of Lost Play" (first written out by Edith Tolkien in 1917), "The Music of the Ainur" (written when Tolkien worked at the *OED*), "The Coming of the Valor and the Building of Valinor" (originally not titled by Tolkien), "The Chaining of Melko," "The Coming of the Elves and the Making of Kór," "The Theft of Melko and the Darkening of Valinor," "The Flight of the Noldoli," "The Tale of the Sun and Moon" (the longest, twenty-two pages), "The Hiding of Valinor," and "Gilfanon's Tale: The Travail of the Noldoli and the Coming of Mankind." Poems included are "You and Me," "Over Old Hills and Far Away" (arguably the loveliest), "Why the Man in the Moon came down too soon" (first published in 1923 when Tolkien was at Leeds), and five others.

The stories in the two books of *Lost Tales* represent Tolkien's first major imaginative work. They contain the first forms of his early ideas and his attempt to put the *Silmarillion* into an accessible narrative structure, and they became the *Quenta Silmarillion* ("history of the Silmarils"), or the "Silmarillion proper." The *Book of Lost Tales* was also his first title for what later became the *Silmarillion*.

The *Book of Lost Tales* was conceived by Christopher as one work, but was divided into two parts because of its length (682 total pages) and for ease of publication, as was the *Lord of the Rings*. Christopher very honestly mentioned in the Foreword that *Part Two* contained the more interesting of the tales.

The Book of Lost Tales, Part Two (1984)

Here Christopher Tolkien completed his compilation of his father's earliest writings. As in *Part One*, this book includes notes, commentary, glossary, and a short dictionary of names. The seven stories in *Part Two* are "The Tale of Tinúvel," "Turambar and the Foalókë," "The Fall of Gondolin," "The Nauglafring," "The Tale of Eärendel," "The History of Eriol or Ælfwine and the End of the Tales," and "Ælfwine of England."

"The Fall of Gondolin" was the earliest of the *Quenta Silmarillion* stories to be written, and it (in an earlier version) was composed quickly while Tolkien was convalescing from fever in World War I, sometime in late 1916. This story of the Dark Lord Morgoth's assault on the last elvish stronghold was placed near the end of the *Silmarillion*, and its style is reminiscent of the famous British fantasy writer William Morris (1834–1896), who proceeded Tolkien at Exeter College and whose works Tolkien greatly admired.

The mariner Eriol was a fifth-century Englishman who found the Lost Road that led to the island of Tol Eressea near Valinor where the elves told him the story of the creation of the world and other tales from the *Silmarillion*. Tolkien had long wanted to create a "mythology for England," and in "The History of Eriol" and "Ælfwine of England," he tried to make a connection between his created world and his homeland.[18] In the letter (above) to Milton Waldman, he explained that he was "grieved by the poverty of his own country: it had no stories of its own." He went on to say that while the Arthurian literary world was powerful and "associated with the soil of Britain," it was not really English.[19] Unfortunately, Tolkien was never able to finalize "Ælfwine of England" (really a "framing" tale of Eriol), and the segment here, written around 1920 or possibly later, never went beyond a very short narrative.

The Lays of Beleriand (1985)

A "lay" is a short lyric or narrative poem meant to be sung, and the poems in this collection, composed between 1918 and 1931, include the elvish poem "The Lay of the Children of Húrin," "The Flight of the Noldoli," a fragment of an alliterative "Lay of Eärendel," parts of "The Lay of the Fall of Gondolin," and the elvish poem "The Lay of Leithian." Also included is a commentary by C. S. Lewis on "The Lay of Leithian," and a note by Christopher Tolkien on the original submission to Allen & Unwin of "The Lay of Leithian" and the *Silmarillion* in 1937.

The verse form of "Children of Húrin" is similar to that of *Beowulf*, and it is one of the several tales from the *Silmarillion* that can stand independently. The powerful story tells of "the flawed hero" Túrin's fostering in the house of Thingol ("Tinwelint" in the *Book of Lost Tales*) and how he became an outlaw in the wilds of

---

[18] Due to the Norman Conquest of England (beginning 1337), with the resulting influx of French and Latin learning and the destroying of English books, the country for centuries was largely bereft of its own "pure" stories, folktales, and legends. Tolkien wanted to give his country a collection of "lost legends" and epic stories similar to what it once had—tales from his imagined "far past" world reaching to the first beginnings of English history. See Shippey, *J. R. R. Tolkien: Author of the Century* (London: HarperCollins, 2000) 231–32.

[19] Carpenter, *Letters*, 144–45.

Beleriand with the great hunter Beleg. Túrin's flaws were his pride, "joylessness," and "rashness of action," similar to Beorthnoth. Katharyn Crabbe, in noting that the cursed Túrin is the opposite of most of Tolkien's characters in that he fights rather than creates, suggested that at least partly, Tolkien's vision of hell is the idea of not being able to create.[20]

Tolkien's famous heroic romance adventure of Beren and Lúthien exists in at least eight different versions, with the longest in the *Silmarillion*, and the shortest in the *Shaping of Middle-Earth*. The mortal Beren falls in love with the elven-princess Lúthien when he sees her dancing in the wood during the First Age of Middle-earth. Her father is so enraged that a mortal would dare court his daughter that he makes a condition of marriage Beren's taking of one of the enchanted Silmarils from the iron crown of the "Dark Lord" Morgoth. This version (in rhymed couplets in fourteen cantos) takes the story of their quest for the hallowed jewel to Morgoth's terrible fortress Angband, where Beren fails, is captured and rescued, then tries again and captures the Silmaril only to lose it to a wolf who bites off Beren's hand.

This story is the most passionate and emotional of all of Tolkien's tales, the first quest story he wrote. It also meant the most to him personally, as "Beren" and "Lúthien" were his pet names for himself and his wife Edith and were inscribed on their tombstones. C. S. Lewis delighted in reading and commenting on the poem and lauded its "sense of reality in the background" and its value as myth. Lewis's biographer A. N. Wilson called it "one of the most remarkable poems written in English in the twentieth century."[21]

---

[20] Crabbe, *J. R. R. Tolkien*, 186.
[21] Wilson, *C. S. Lewis: A Biography* (New York: Norton, 1990) 117.

The Shaping of Middle-Earth: The Quenta, The Ambarkanta, and The Annals (1986)

When the *Hobbit* was written and while Tolkien was working on his stories of Túrin, Beren, and Lúthien, he returned to prose for a "mythological sketch" for his poems and to provide background. "The Quenta" is sometimes called "The Quenta Silmarillion," which is another name for "The Silmarillion" ("History of the Simarils"). In this work, "The Quenta" (*Quenta Noldorinwa*, the only complete version of "The Silmarillion" Tolkien ever made) is included with "the earliest Silmarillion" (a sketch of the mythology), written by Tolkien in 1926. Also included is the first map of the Silmarillion, originally drawn on a sheet of examination paper from the University of Leeds.

Though brief (four and one-half pages of text by Tolkien and five diagrams), "The Ambarkanta" (The Shape of the World), written in the early 1930s, is significant because it is Tolkien's only account of the nature ("the fashion of the world") of his invented universe. Supposedly written by the wise First Age historian Rúmil, it discusses the cosmology of the First Age world and includes the diagrams showing the relationship of the earth (symmetrical and as a sphere) and sky. The annals of Valinor outline year 0 (the creation of the world) to the year 3000, the landing of the Noldorin prince Fingolfin in Middle-earth. Each Valian year is the equivalent of ten of our years, making this a 30,000-year chronological outline. The annals of Beleriand show an outline from Year 1, the creation of the Sun and Moon, to Year 250, the end of Morgoth's reign and the First Age. Two appendices are included, Ælfwine's translations of the *Annals of Valinor* and the *Annals of Beleriand* into Old English.

The Lost Road and Other Writings (1987)

This fifth and largest volume of the *History* completed Tolkien's writings on the First Age (and part of the Second) up till 1937, when he started work on the *Lord of the Rings*. These writings are his mythology and tales of the First and Second Ages of Middle-earth that he set aside when pressured by his publisher to write a sequel to the *Hobbit*.

Included in the *Lost Road* are "The Later Annals of Valinor" and "The Later Annals of Beleriand," later versions of the annals in the *Shaping of Middle-Earth*, and "Quenta Silmarillion," an enlarged version of "The Silmarillion." Tolkien's fascination with the story of Atlantis led him to write about the legend of the fall of Númenor, included here. "Ainulindalë" ("The Great Song") is a reframing of the account of the Music of the Ainur from the *Book of Lost Tales* that depicts the creation of the world, written by the historian Rúmil. Colin Duriez wrote that C. S. Lewis may have been inspired by the Ainulindalë in his creation of Narnia by the song of Aslan and "The Great Dance" at the end of *Perelandra*.[22] "The Lhammas" ("Account of Tongues"), also written by Rúmil, is a linguistic essay on the development and relationship between the various tongues of elves, men, and orcs. "The Etymologies" was Tolkien's last attempt to write a comprehensive vocabulary of the elvish languages. The entries, unlike a dictionary, are arranged by the primitive elve stems from which the words derived.

The origins of "The Lost Road" have been discussed frequently by both Tolkien and C. S. Lewis scholars. In a letter to Christopher Bretherton (16 July 1964), Tolkien discussed the origins of "Lost Road," which grew from his "Atlantis-haunting." Lewis agreed to write a story on space travel that eventually became *Out of the Silent Planet*, and Tolkien agreed to write a time travel story. He originally called it *Númenor*, "of which the

---

[22] Duriez, *The J. R. R. Tolkien Handbook* (Grand Rapids MI: Baker, 1992) 19.

end was to be the presence of my hero in the drowning of Atlantis."[23] "The Lost Road" was shown to Allen & Unwin in 1937 and was rejected for publication, their rationale being that even if Tolkien completed it, the work would not likely be a commercial success. Lewis's book was rejected by Allen & Unwin for the same reason.

The Return of the Shadow: The History of The Lord of the Rings, Part One (1988)

After the great popular success of the *Hobbit*, Tolkien came under considerable pressure from Allen & Unwin to write a sequel. He sent Stanley Unwin the manuscripts of the *Silmarillion, Mr. Bliss, Farmer Giles of Ham, Roverandom,* and "The Lost Road." All were read, and the children's stories were enjoyed, but all were rejected because Mr. Unwin was sure that the public "wanted more hobbits." In a letter to Unwin on 15 October 1937, Tolkien wrote that "I cannot think of anything more to say about *hobbits*...But if it is true that the *Hobbit* has come to stay and more will be wanted, I will start the process of thought, and try to get some idea of a theme drawn from this material for treatment in a similar style and for a similar audience—possibly including actual hobbits."[24]

His "process of thought" produced the material now present in the *Return of the Shadow* (an abandoned title for the first division), the first part of the *History of the Lord of the Rings*. These narrative drafts, "a sequel to the *Hobbit*," were the early versions of what was to become the first division of the *Lord of*

---

[23] Carpenter, *Letters*, 347. In a letter of 8 February 1967, he wrote that "My effort, after a few promising chapters, ran dry: it was too long a way round to what I really wanted to make, a new version of the Atlantis legend. The final scene survives as *The Downfall of Númenor*" (378).

[24] Ibid., 24.

Unfinished Tales and the 169
History of Middle-Earth

the Rings, the *Fellowship of the Ring*. The earliest version is "Concerning Hobbits," a foreword, written 1938–1939. In the *Return of the Shadow,* Bilbo has a nephew, "Bingo" (after toy koala bears owned by Tolkien's children), and Bilbo's One Ring becomes the Ruling Ring that must be destroyed before the evil Sauron can use it to control the other rings of power and thus conquer all of Middle-earth. Tolkien later added an unplanned appearance of the "Black Rider" who is searching for hobbits, the first versions of the History of the Ring as told by Gandalf to Bingo (who eventually becomes Frodo), and introduced the characters of Trotter (later Aragorn, "Strider"), "a sinister Treebeard," and "a ferocious and malevolent Farmer Maggot." Humphrey Carpenter wrote that "unconsciously, and usually without forethought," Tolkien bent this new hobbit story "away from the jolly style of the *Hobbit* towards something darker and grander," closer to the *Silmarillion*.[25]

Tolkien never found a satisfactory form for the story and never had a good idea of what it would all be about. By July 1938 his sequel "had remained where it stopped," and had "lost favour" with him. Christopher Tolkien wrote in his foreword to the *Return of the Shadow* that "the *Hobbit* was drawn into Middle-earth—and transformed it...Later, the *Lord of the Rings* in turn reacted upon the *Hobbit* itself, in published and in (far more extensive) unpublished revisions of the text..."[26]

The Treason of Isengard: The History of The Lord of the Rings, Part Two (1989)

The *Return of the Shadow* ended when the Company of the Ring (Frodo and the fellowship of hobbits, including Gandalf, which

---

[25] Carpenter, *J. R. R. Tolkien: A Biography* (Boston: Houghton Mifflin, 2000) 190.
[26] J. R. R. Tolkien, *The Return of the Shadow—The History of the Lord of the Rings Part I*, ed. Christopher Tolkien (Boston: Houghton Mifflin, 1988) 7.

accompanied him on his quest to destroy the Ring) reached the Tomb of Balin in the depths of Moria, or Khazad-dûm. Moria was a vast dwarf realm carved under the Misty Mountains. In the *Lord of the Rings*, the Company encountered a Balrog (one of Morgoth's great fire-demons), and Gandalf was killed fighting it.

In this volume, Christopher Tolkien took up his father's attempts to write a new hobbit story, one where Bilbo would have more adventures. Tolkien decided that Bilbo's ring ("the Ruling Ring") should be a terrible artifact left from an earlier age, by which the evil Sauron could control all the other rings of power and thus control and conquer all of Middle-earth. The new story then centered on the idea of destroying the ring before Sauron could recover it.

In *Isengard,* the reader is introduced to new journeys, adventures, events, and characters (including Galadriel), the earliest sketches of the history of Gondor (originally the great south kingdom of Middle-earth), and the meeting of Aragorn with Eowyn, the beautiful Rohan woman whom he heals (in the *Two Towers*) from the Nazgul-inflicted "Black Breath." Initially Tolkien had Aragorn marrying Eowyn, but eventually this idea was abandoned, and she later married Faromir. The reader is also told the account of the capture of Frodo and his rescue by his loyal friend, the hobbit Samwise Gamgee. A chapter is devoted to Frodo's "tree-adventure" with the giant Ent Treebeard (Fangorn), about which Tolkien mentioned as "writing itself."

The *Treason of Isengard* was the original title Tolkien chose for book three of the *Lord of the Rings*, the first section of the *Two Towers*. Isengard ("iron-enclosure") was the one-gated fortress tower of the wizard Saruman (the White), sent to Middle-earth and eventually controlled by Sauron. This book is engaging not only for its stories, but for learning how Tolkien "thought on paper" and worked out his ideas, often not knowing where he would eventually end. Included with the text is a complete account of the creation of the first map of the *Lord of the Rings* and an appendix describing the Runic alphabets of the time.[27]

The War of the Ring: The History of The Lord of the Rings, Part Three (1990)

This volume continued Christopher Tolkien's collection of his father's preliminary manuscripts for the *Lord of the Rings*. It is divided into three parts, "The Fall of Saruman," with five stories and a chronology; "The Ring Goes East," with eight stories; and "*Minas Tirith*," with an addendum to "The Treason of Isengard," twelve stories and a map, with notes. It includes a total of seven maps, a page from the first manuscript of "The Taming of Sméagol," three sketches of Kirith Ungol, a plan and the earliest sketch of Minas Tirith, two plans of Shelob's Lair, and seven illustrations, plus notes and commentary by Christopher Tolkien and an index of names.

Among the stories and events included in the *War of the Ring* are the Battle at Helm's Deep (the refuge of the Rohan king Helm, here totally different from the version in the *Two Towers*), the destruction of Isengard by the Ents, the journey of Frodo, Sam, and Gollum to the Path of Kirith Ungol on the eastern road past the spider Shelob's lair ("the last part of the *Lord of the Rings* for which precise dating is possible," 12–22 May 1944), the war in Gondor (the south kingdom of Middle-earth), and the conference at the Black Gate (Morannon) of Mordor between Gandalf and the Sauron ambassadors. Unplanned events included by Tolkien were Gandalf and his companions finding the palantír at Isengard (a very difficult manuscript for Christopher Tolkien), and the

---

[27] Runes were the earliest letters of the old Germanic alphabets used from the third century by Scandinavians, Icelanders, and Anglo-Saxons (Old English). For a perceptive guide to Tolkien's invented languages and a concise overview of him as a linguist, see Ruth Noel, *The Languages of Tolkien's Middle-earth* (Boston: Houghton Mifflin, 1980).

appearance in the story of a short chapter (with a "remarkable" amount of redrafting and reshaping) concerning the brave warrior Faramir, which Tolkien read to C. S. Lewis and Charles Williams on 1 May 1944.[28]

The *War of the Ring*, like the other books in this series, is interesting for its literary and critical insights into what was to become the final form of the *Lord of the Rings*, and also for its descriptions of Tolkien's struggles to find "his own best story."

Sauron Defeated: The End of the Third Age, including The History of The Lord of the Rings, Part Four (1992)

In this volume, Christopher Tolkien concluded his investigation of his father's manuscripts for the *Lord of the Rings* with "The End of the Third Age," and added two additional sections, "The Notion Club Papers," and "The Drowning of Anadûnê." Also included were thirteen illustrations, including the title page of "The Notion Club Papers" and a drawing of the volcano Mt. Doom (Orodruin) in northwestern Mordor where Sauron forged the One Ring. Christopher mentioned regretting not keeping the History of the Rings to three volumes, and allowed that the difficulties in projecting its structure and foreseeing its extent prevented him from doing so.

"The End of the Third Age" begins with Frodo being unable to throw the Ring into the volcano (the Cracks of Doom), his capture by the treacherous Gollum, and his subsequent rescue by Sam from the Dark Tower of Kirith. After the One Ring was destroyed (and thus the power of Sauron), Tolkien had problems bringing the story to a satisfying conclusion. This part ends with the inclusion of versions of a previously unpublished "Epilogue,"

---

[28] See Carpenter, *Letters*, 79. Tolkien commented about Faramir: "...I am sure I did not invent him, I did not even want him, though I like him..."

an alternate ending in which Sam answers questions from his children about Bilbo and Frodo. In a letter to the writer Naomi Mitchison (25 April 1954), Tolkien wrote that he left out his epilogue because it had been "so universally condemned," and in his notes Christopher mentioned that his father "was persuaded by others" to leave it out. The "others" might possibly have been the Inklings.

In a letter to Christopher in December 1944, Tolkien wrote, "I have been getting a lot of new ideas about Prehistory lately... and want to work them into the long-shelved time-travel story I began."[29] These ideas became "The Notion Club Papers," written in the interlude between the *Two Towers* and the *Return of the King*, 1945–1946. Tolkien wanted to turn his attention again to the story of a journey back through time to the Fall of Númenor (Atlantis), after his earlier attempt in the *Lost Road* had been abandoned. In a letter to Stanley Unwin in July 1946, he mentioned having completed three parts of the story in two weeks in December 1945, but in his introduction Christopher refuted this, saying that the size of the story and number of corrections and versions needed would have taken longer to write.

"Notion Club" is based on the Inklings meetings and two Oxford dons who are members of the club who go on a time-journey. The story is set in the 1980s, and the club has left a record of their meetings, a record that is "discovered" in 2012 in the basement of the Examination Schools at Oxford. As in "The Lost Road," the story was abandoned just after the actual time travel was described. "Imram"(Gaelic for "voyage"), a poem about St. Brendan's voyage, was one part of the story that was published, in 1955 in *Time and Tide*.

In the story, one of Tolkien's characters (Arundel Lowdham) is able to "see" and "hear" the distant past while in a trance, and the information that he receives comes to him in different languages. Most all of the information he receives tells a similar

---

[29] Ibid., 105.

story—of an island of people who long for immortality denied them, and who in seeking it end up losing everything.

Humphrey Carpenter wrote that "Notion Club" was in "the spirit of the Inklings," and that Tolkien was not attempting any "portrait of his friends, but the early drafts of the story were based on the Inklings, by name."[30] In one early draft Tolkien used several specific Inklings as characters, including himself (Latimer, later changed to Guildford), C. S. Lewis (Frankley), Hugo Dyson (Loudham, later changed to Lowdham), and Robert Havard (Dolbear). The original titles of the story, "Out of the Talkative Planet" and "Old Solar," along with references to "Lewis" and his first two space novels (including a discussion rejecting Lewis's device of using "mere machinery" to transport his characters to Mars and Venus), are further evidence that Tolkien wrote the story with Lewis's space-travel ideas in mind.[31] In the final version of the story one of the dons at the meetings, the polymath monk Dom Jonathon Markison, could have been modeled after the Benedictine priest and Inkling Fr. Gervase Mathew, himself a man of great erudition and learning. In Part Two, the "skeptical onlooker" Ranulph Stainer comes to the meetings, and his character may have been based in part on the well-known anthroposophist Rudolf Steiner, who had a vigorous devoteé in the early Inkling Owen Barfield, Lewis's lawyer and a noted philosopher and teacher. And one minor character, "old Professor Rashbold at Pembroke," is probably Tolkien ("a grumpy old bear") as "Rashbold" is a translation of "Tolkien," "*Tull-kuhn*." The last mentioned member of the club is "John Jethro Rashbold,"

---

[30] Carpenter, *Biography*, 174.

[31] For excellent discussions of Tolkien's time-travel ideas, with many references to "The Notion Club Papers," see Verlyn Flieger, *A Question of Time: J. R. R. Tolkien's Road to Faërie* (Kent OH: Kent State University Press, 1997), and John Rateliff, "The Lost Road, The Dark Tower, and The Notion Club Papers: Tolkien and Lewis's Time Travel Triad," in *Tolkien's Legendarium: Essays on the History of Middle-earth*, ed. Verlyn Flieger and Carl F. Hostetter (Westport CT: Greenwood Press, 2000).

an undergraduate of Magdalen College who never speaks; he is probably Christopher Tolkien.[32] Christopher wrote that in the final version of the story the characters probably did not have a clear association with the individual Inklings, with the possible exception being Lowdham.

No one knows exactly why Tolkien abandoned "Notion Club" and his second try at an Atlantis story, but it was probably because he felt it lacked unity, and also because he had to return to work on the *Lord of the Rings*. He did produce, in "The Drowning of Anadûnê," a discussion of Adunaic, the vernacular of the people of Númenor, and a brief third version of the story, a portion of which he read to the Inklings in August 1946.

Morgoth's Ring: The Later Silmarillion, Part One (1993)

After completing the *Lord of the Rings*, Tolkien returned again to his stories of the First Age (the "Elder Days"), and with the texts in this book it is possible to relate most of the first eleven chapters of the *Silmarillion* to their sources. These texts are "Ainulindalë," "The Annals of Aman," "The Later *Quenta Silmarillion*" (in two phases), "Athrabeth Finrod Ah Andreth," and "Myths Transformed." This book is primarily concerned with Morgoth's power, which was greater than Sauron's power and controlled, in the One Ring, all of Middle-earth.

In the writing of the *Lord of the Rings*, Tolkien introduced many new elements concerning the First Age of the Silmarillion, and these had to be reconciled with his earlier visions of that world. Before he could create a new and final *Silmarillion*, he felt he had to "satisfy the requirements of a coherent theological and metaphysical system." Among the themes and ideas he redefined that are included in this book were: the myth of light, the nature of

---

[32] Flieger, *A Question of Time*, 261.

the great western continent Aman ("the Blessed Realm"), the immortality and death of the Elves and the mode of their incarnation, the origin of the Orcs, and the power and significance of Morgoth, which resonates in all the essays.

Possibly the most frustrating revision for Tolkien was the "Ainulindalë." In his earlier version of the creation song he had created a primitive flat earth, but here he attempted a more cosmologically sound ("round earth") version that was ultimately unsatisfactory because of all the changes he would have had to make, particularly in the story of the Two Trees of Valinor and the creation of the sun and moon, created from the glowing light of the Trees. He also struggled with the nature of the orcs and other beings used as tools by Morgoth (and later for Sauron) for his evil purposes. For Tolkien, evil was only possible for creatures having a free will. The orcs, who could not make moral decisions, had to have been created, and Tolkien had to decide where they came from, and why.

Another problem for Tolkien was elves and their mortality and immortality. He reexamined their customs of marriage and family life and tried to resolve the problem of Finwë and his remarriage to Indis, after his first wife, Míriel, died after bearing her only son, Fëanor. Because elves were naturally monogamous, and no elven soul ever left the world (reincarnation), Tolkien had to reconcile Finwë's second marriage "in the manner of mortal men" with the fact that his first wife was still "alive."

This led to the remarkable "Athrabeth Finrod Ah Andreth" (probably written in 1959), which details a long debate between the wise and powerful elf Finrod and the mortal woman Andreth, with several explanatory notes by Christopher Tolkien. Here Tolkien explored the nature and origins of the ideas of Middle-earth peoples about their own mortality and reincarnation. The last section in the book, "Myths Transformed," consists of a series of short pieces (written in the late 1950s) that were concerned with the "central elements" in Tolkien's *legendarium* or mythology. These show his "prolonged interior debate," a writer struggling with and thinking and rethinking about complex ideas and trying to rework them into a coherent and manageable scheme. Some of these "central elements" include cosmology, what happened to Valinor after the Death of the Trees, the association of Varda (called Elbereth in Middle-earth) and the stars, the creation of the Sun after the Death of the Trees, a discussion of the power of Morgoth and Sauron, and further discussions about the nature and origin of Orcs and the continent Aman.

The War of the Jewels: The Later Silmarillion, Part Two (1994)

This work continued the materials presented in *Morgoth's Ring*, Tolkien's writings relating to the First Age after his completion of the *Lord of the Rings*. In *Morgoth's Ring*, the story ended when Morgoth destroyed the Trees of Light and fled Valinor with the stolen Silmarils. In this volume, the stories returned to Middle-earth and Beleriand ("the land of the Elves"), and dealt primarily with the return of the Noldor (Elves) to Beleriand. The book is divided into four parts, "The Grey Annals," "The Later *Quenta Silmarillion*," "The Wanderings of Húrin and Other Writings not Forming Part of the *Quenta Silmarillion*," and "Quendi and Eldar." The title of this book comes from an expression Tolkien used to describe the last six centuries of the First Age, the history of Beleriand after Morgoth's return to Middle-earth and the journey of the Noldor, until its end.

"The Grey Annals" (or "The Annals of Beleriand") is a parallel work to the *Quenta Silmarillion* and was never completed by Tolkien. Started around 1930, the earliest version was published in the *Shaping of Middle-earth*, and later versions were added in the *Lost Road*. This last version (nearly 100 pages) includes over sixty-five pages of commentary and notes by Christopher Tolkien and reaches the story of Húrin, where it ends.

The *Quenta* is not presented in its entirety because of length, and Christopher Tolkien commented about the changes his father made from the earlier version, published in the *Lost Road*. Following it are seven narratives, almost all of them incomplete, including "Of the Siege of Angband," "Of Beleriand and its Realms," "Concerning the Dwarves," and "Of the Coming of Men into the West."

The "major story" of Húrin, published here for the first time, is concerned primarily with his actions after the death of his son Túrin and his sister/wife, Níniel. The story of Húrin and his family is one of the most interesting and tragic in all of Tolkien's writings, and including here, exists in at least four other works: the *Book of Lost Tales II* (the story of Turambar and the Foalóke, written in 1919), the *Lays of Beleriand* ("The Lay of the Children of Húrin," written 1922–1925), the *Silmarillion* (chapter 21, probably written before 1937), and *Unfinished Tales* ("The Tale of the Children of Túrin," written after 1951).[33]

"Quendi and Eldar" consists of etymological discussions about the words that relate to Elves, Men, Dwarves, and Orcs. It includes a discussion of the linguistic elements and their developments in different languages (Quenya, Telerin, Sindarin), then moves to each language's development of the various roots. The language of the Valar (angelic beings who take on an elvish appearance) is discussed, and how this affected the elves' own language. Finally, Tolkien included a humorous elvish myth, "The legend of the Awaking of the Quendi," which showed how the elves were divided into three clans.

The Peoples of Middle-Earth (1996)

This volume of the *History of Middle-Earth* concluded Christopher Tolkien's long process of arranging and bringing together

---

[33] See Shippey, *Author of the Century*, 249.

his father's writings. It provides a close link with the *Book of Lost Tales* and the earlier *Unfinished Tales*, as it "completes" the chronology of Middle-earth's later Ages and the *Hobbit* genealogies. The first half of the book (Part One), "The Prologue and Appendices to The Lord of the Rings," shows the numerous stages of the writings, with materials changed, added, and deleted. The section on hobbits in the Prologue dates back to the earliest writings of the *Lord of the Rings* and was removed by Tolkien when he felt it would slow the pace of the narrative. Also included in this part are the genealogies of the hobbits ("The Family Trees"), the calendars of the Shire, and an appendix on the Westron language of the men and hobbits.

Part Two, "Late Writings," is a collection of papers from Tolkien's later life (some from 1967, most from 1968, and some from 1970), primarily scholarly discussions on languages and peoples, or what Christopher Tolkien calls "historical-philological" essays. This collection includes "Of Dwarves and Men," "The Shibboleth of Fëanor," "The Problem of Ros," and "Last Writings." Part Three, "Teachings of Pengolod," records the instruction of the mariner Ælfwine by Pengolo the Wise of Gondolin. Part Four, "Unfinished Tales," includes two fragmentary beginning stories, "The New Shadow" and "Tal-Elmar," a Númenórean tale. "The New Shadow" evidently was very important to Tolkien, as he wrote three versions of the story and was still concerned with it as late as January 1968. According to Humphrey Carpenter it was to be a sequel to the *Lord of the Rings*.[34] One reviewer called "The New Shadow" a "thriller piece" from Gondor in the Fourth Age, and said that it suggested what Tolkien might have produced if he had written stories in the same style as Charles Williams's "spiritual thrillers."[35] "The New Shadow"

---

[34] See *The Peoples of Middle-Earth*, ed. Christopher Tolkien (Boston: Houghton Mifflin, 1996) 409–10.

[35] See John S. Ryan, "J. R. R. Tolkien, *The Peoples of Middle-earth, Vol. 12*—Review," in vol. 14 of *SEVEN: An Anglo-American Literary Review* (1997): 115. Charles W. S. Williams (1886–1945), was an editor at the Oxford

(about eight pages) is the start of a dark tale about how bored young people abandon goodness and join a cult of evil. Tolkien probably abandoned it because Sauron and Melkor had been defeated and there was no physical incarnation of evil left in the world. And the primary character, Borlas, would have to have been at least 200 years old.

Some have suggested that the *History of Middle-Earth* should not have been published. It has been called too long and complicated, the changes and alterations and fragments show Tolkien's false starts and missteps (a disservice to him), and his sometimes archaic style and (often) "high" language are too difficult for many modern readers. Christina Scull wrote that such critics miss the point: "The *History of Middle-Earth* was conceived to illustrate not a fixed design, but a living creation, and the process by which Tolkien gave it life. It is a...fascinating insight into the work of one of the most imaginative and influential writers of the twentieth century."[36]

In a provocative essay, David Bratman listed good reasons for reading the *History of Middle-Earth*, and they are as follows, summarized: For the reader who is entranced by elves and wants to read more about them, he or she should read "The Silmarillion" (a "reader's edition of the *Silmarillion*"), the *Book of Lost Tales*, the *Shaping of Middle-earth*, and the *Lost Road*. The *Book of Lost Tales* will appeal to the reader who enjoyed the *Hobbit*, and lovers of Tolkien's poetry should obviously turn to the *Lays of Beleriand*. For the reader who enjoyed the appendices of the *Lord of the Rings*, with their details of kings and genealogies, there is *Unfinished Tales* and the *Peoples of Middle-earth*. The reader who

---

University Press, poet, Christian apologist, dramatist, novelist, Christian essayist, critic, and biographer. A friend of Tolkien and C. S. Lewis, he wrote seven novels that have been called "supernatural" or "metaphysical thrillers," among them *War in Heaven* (1930), *The Place of the Lion* (1931), and *Descent Into Hell* (1937).

[36] Scull, *"The History of Middle-Earth—Review Article,"* in vol. 12 of *SEVEN: An Anglo-American Literary Review* (1995): 105–109.

enjoys Tolkien as a pure storyteller should read *Unfinished Tales*, the *Peoples of Middle-earth*, *Morgoth's Ring*, and the *War of the Jewels*, in that order. The *Return of the Shadow* should appeal to the reader curious about the making of the *Lord of the Rings*, and the *Notion Club Papers* and the *Lost Road* are for the reader who comes to Tolkien from first reading about the Inklings, particularly C. S. Lewis and Charles Williams. And for the reader interested in linguistics and languages, the glossaries, etymologies, and linguistic essays in the *Book of Lost Tales*, the *Lost Road*, the *War of the Jewels*, and the *Peoples of Middle-earth* should have much appeal.[37]

---

[37] See Bratman, "The Literary Value of *The History of Middle-Earth*," in Flieger and Hostetter, *Tolkien's Legendarium*, 69–91.

The Impact of Tolkien's Writings

A Personal Reflection

by Joe R. Christopher

How does one tell of an impact? Was it like the Titanic hitting the iceberg? The connotations are too negative. Was it like a neutron hitting a Uranium 235 atom? Again, for all of us I am sure, too negative—although certainly a powerful impact. (My grandmother was in Las Cruces, New Mexico, when the first atomic bomb was exploded on the other side of the Organ Mountains; she told me of the early morning becoming like daylight.) Or was it like the finger of God, in the Sistine Chapel, touching the reclining body of Adam? For me, at least, that is too powerful—although perhaps not for everyone. Did an experience really bring you alive, in one sense or another? Books impact people in different ways. I want to talk about the affect of Tolkien's writings—mainly the *Lord of the Rings*—on me; but I think I am in many ways typical. For some people, Tolkien's works may have changed their lives. I cannot exactly say that, but they have certainly enriched mine.

The years 1954 and 1955 are great ones for Tolkien fans. I was in those days a cover-to-cover reader of the *Magazine of Fantasy and Science Fiction*, and that included the "Recommended Reading" of the editor, Anthony Boucher. In the April 1955 issue, Boucher said that among fantasy novels, the *Fellowship of the Ring* "may be the major achievement of the year or even the decade." Obviously, he was not about to commit himself completely on the first third. He made a comparison, which he repeated later, of the *Lord of the Rings* to E. R. Eddison's the *Worm Ouroboros*—although at this point he believed Eddison to be Tolkien's superior in characterization and narrative form. (Later he seemed to think the works were at the same level.) He praised the creation of an elaborate world, the humor, the adventure, and the style. In the August 1955 issue Boucher, as he would in all the reviews, complained of the books being too long, but he was no longer tentative about the merits, including "some of the most sheerly beautiful prose (and occasional verse) that this harsh decade has seen in print." Finally, in the July 1956 issue, Boucher tried to suggest the greatness of the *Lord of the Rings* with the appearance of the *Return of the King*. One of his comments is on its "world bound and ruled by Rings of Power which symbolize Lord Acton's maxim; the purpose of quest, journey, and war (to oversimplify) is the destruction of the ultimate Ring and the return of free will." I noticed in Tom Shippey's *J. R. R. Tolkien: Author of the Century* (2001) an emphasis on Lord Acton also. When Boucher wrote, "anyone with the faintest interest in imaginative literature must at least sample the *Lord of the Rings*," what could I do? I managed to scrape together the huge amount of fifteen dollars and bought all three volumes.

I realize that for many Tolkien fans the first reading occurred when Ace Books released the cheap (and unauthorized) paperbacks in 1965. They were seventy-five cents each. That was the beginning of the Tolkien craze. But the exact year we first read the *Lord of the Rings* does not matter—the impact matters. Diane Duane wrote in her essay "The Longest Sunday" (2001) that "[I] ran to our little town's main street, and caught the bus to the next town, where the bookstore was. I threw myself in through its door and went straight to the rack where I found the first two books, and found the third one, and seized it as if it was the heart out of my body, and just barely remembered to pay for it, for I was already reading it as I got to the door." Lisa Goldstein wrote in "The Mythmaker" (also 2001), "I ended up reading the series every year of my adolescence. I read it until those first paperbacks wore out; I read it until I practically had it memorized." I first read the *Lord of the Rings* in my early twenties, so the impact was not quite as strong—but my hardcovers have their dust jackets held together by transparent tape.

Unlike Duane and Goldstein, who went on to become writers (their essays are in Karen Haber's *Meditations on Middle-Earth*, a book of essays by authors on Tolkien), I went to become an academician. So it is appropriate that while I was at the University of Oklahoma, Dr. John Marlin Raines offered one of the first, if not the first, graduate seminars that included the *Lord of the Rings*. It was titled "Mystical Literature," which was more appropriate for Charles Williams and others who were considered than for Tolkien—this was in the fall of 1962. I had finished my course work for my doctorate, and so I just sat in on the seminar. I remember Dr. Raines, that staunch churchman, making a Freudian comment. "Something is wrong with the elves' sexuality," he said in those or similar words. "Look at Elrond, a male elf [actually a half elf], ruling over the vulvar Rivendell, and Galadriel, a female elf, essentially ruling over the phallic mellryn of Lórien. No wonder the elves are fading."

Scholarship is simply a response to literature, much as compulsive rereading, literary imitation, parody, or competition is. Those who are analytic tend to respond with critical discussions. Like all responses, it can be poorly done—especially when a writer is doing it not out of love for the literary work but (for example) for a publication needed for one's dossier. But reading can be done in order to be a member of a fad, or an imitation can be hacked out to make money. Poor responses do not deny the validity of the work. Likewise, I am not the person to judge the value of my pieces of criticism—but I have written on Tolkien always because I wanted to. My main essay on Tolkien's main work is "The Moral Epiphanies of the *Lord of the Rings*" (1995)—the essay seems drily written when I look back on it, but it was not intended to be. Also, I have written on some of the poems in the *History of Middle-Earth* in "Tolkien's Lyric Poetry" (2000), and have produced at least two substantial biographical essays in large part on Tolkien: "J. R. R. Tolkien, Narnian Exile" (1988), and "Roy Campbell and the Inklings" (1997). These and other essays are simply one way I express my appreciation of Tolkien's sub-creation, acknowledging the enrichment he has given my life. There are other writers on Tolkien far better known than I am, and with more to say—particularly the writers of major books on him—but we are all responding analytically out of appreciation.

But I have also responded in a way more like the authors I quoted earlier. In 1981, mainly for an Inkling convention at which I was one of the guests of honor, I produced a chapbook of my Tolkienian verse (given away to the members freely)—verse that previously, or in one case belatedly, appeared in the fan periodicals *Niekas, Anduril, Mathom, Amon Hen, Mythlore, Minas Tirith Evening-Star, Ravenhill,* the *Mythic Circle,* and the *Charles Williams Society Newsletter*. (Surely the last is also, in one sense, a fan magazine.) Should I mention that I was part of science-fiction and fantasy fandom? I never had money enough to attend many fan conventions—I got to a World Science Fiction Convention between my junior and senior years in high school, and I attended a World Fantasy Convention many years later when it was held nearby—but I have contributed to fanzines off and on since my early years out of grad school and I have attended a number of the conventions of the Mythopoeic Society (dedicated to Tolkien, C. S. Lewis, and Charles Williams)—and one glorious combined convention of the Mythopoeic Society and the Tolkien Society, held for a week in Oxford. My chapbook of verse, *Musings Beneath a Tree of Amalion*, was later republished in an augmented form by the New England Tolkien Society (that is, mainly by Gary Hunnewell) in 1993; perhaps the most recognizable of my parodies is "Ents," which has these first and last couplets:

> I think that I could ne'er invent
> A verse as grandiose as an ent—
> .....
> Verses are made by fools with a bent,
> But only Eru can make an Ent.

Some of my verses are more serious than this sub-sub-creation, but none of these will compete with the major novels by the authors in Haber's book, who for the most part *reacted to Tolkien with competition*. Robin Hobb says, "To discover that someone has already written the most amazing books that could possibly exist raised the bar to an almost impossible height for me" and "Raising that bar was the most wonderful thing that anyone could have done for an ambitious young writer." Unlike Hobb and her peers, competing with the *Lord of the Rings*, I am only competing with the *Adventures of Tom Bombadil*.

In the dedication to the first edition of my chapbook, I spoke, in part, of my "love for the works of J. R. R. Tolkien, / which drive me to song, not to scholarship." (My scholarship on Tolkien came later.) I went on to refer, in a rather ungrammatical way, to the "applicability" of Tolkien's works for the production of verses. The use of "applicability" refers to Tolkien's foreword to the second edition of the *Lord of the Rings*, where he said he disliked allegory but liked "history, true or feigned, with its varied applicability to the thought and experience of readers." He was thinking of the readers' discovery of the meaning of a work for themselves. In a larger sense, scholarship is one application; the writing of fantasy novels or verses (or painting of pictures) is another application. But the enhancement of being that Tolkien offers does not have to have any more than a psychological product, any more than a psychological applicability. Further, different people will respond to different aspects of Tolkien's work. For example, the battles in the latter part of the book have never spoken strongly to me. That is because my only experience of the military was two years of compulsory ROTC at the University of Oklahoma—and I was of draftable age during the early years of the Vietnam war, before the major build-ups. Intellectually, I understand the need for battles. Tolkien had served in World War I and lost most of his close friends in that war; he knew, from Old English literature and history, how wars are a common human experience; he was writing in part during World War II. I do not argue that the battles are out of place, simply that those episodes do not speak to my condition. But, oh, Lothlórien and its trees! In spring, "when the boughs are laden with yellow flowers, and the floor of the wood is golden, and golden is the roof, and its pillars are of silver, for the bark of the trees is smooth and grey." And, likewise, Fangorn Forest and Treebeard! "The drink was like water, indeed very like the taste of the draughts [Merry and Pippin] had drunk from the Entwash near the borders of the forest, and yet there was some scent or savour in it which they could not describe: it was faint, but it reminded them of the smell of a distant wood borne from afar by a cool breeze at night." For a basically urban dweller, I am moved by Tolkien's trees. It is true that I grew up in a region where the trees are taller than in the Cross Timbers region of Texas where I live now, but that is not the full explanation. All I can suggest is that there is something perhaps numinous, at least mysterious, in Tolkien's arboreal presentations. These are archetypal forests.

If Lothlórien and Fangorn are images that often come to my mind, then there are still other aspects of the *Lord of the Rings* that mean much to me. Morally, I find a short conversation important. Éomer asks Aragorn, "How shall a man judge what to do in such times?" Aragorn replies, "As he ever has judged. Good and ill have not changed since yesteryear; nor are they one thing among Elves and Dwarves and another among Men." During the Modernistic period, in which the *Lord of the Rings* was published, the main tradition of Existentialism assumed mankind could create its individual moralities, if finding morality at all. In popular belief, that one philosophical system or religious system was as good as another was widely assumed ("whatever does it for you"). Tolkien's statement of Natural Law (in the older sense of the term) does not, of course, "prove" anything—as in logical or scientific proof. It is simply a statement of an ancient tradition, going back at least to the Stoics, that sees the universe as morally shaped. (Some branches have a moral God in their system; others do not.) Tolkien's is a moral universe caught in a moral conflict. Not that his characters are simply bad or good, but their ultimate concern (in Paul Tillich's phrase) is. When Frodo knows what he should do at Amon Hen, but hesitates to do it, I can identify with him all too often.

Finally, I find the journey of Frodo toward Mount Doom in the latter part of the *Lord of the Rings* to be deeply moving. I understand Michael Swanwick's symbolic reading of Sam and Gollum in those episodes as good and bad aspects of Frodo (in another essay from Haber's book, "A Changeling Returns"). I also understand something that he does not say: when Frodo fails ("I do not choose now to do what I came to do"), then his bad side, his evil aspect, takes over—that is, Gollum attacks and takes the Ring. When Gollum dies, then Frodo is left incomplete—and will soon leave this world. This is not the same thing as an allegory, for a true allegory would not have Frodo as well as Sam and Gollum, and it would have thematic names for the two characters remaining. Instead, it is part of an ancient tradition of the compound hero. Sir Artegall and Talus in the *Fairie Queene* illustrate the idea (and also illustrate Spenser's moral limitations as an Englishman in Ireland). A curious example of the compound hero is in the parallelism of Pip and Orlick in *Great Expectations*. I understand all this, but this is not what moves me. Rather, it is the literal story of the suffering hero—the hero who really tries, through all the pain and exhaustion, and who ultimately fails. Tolkien, his imagination fed on Germanic myth, in which the heroes fight and die and are rescued by the Valkyrie in order that they may fight and die again at Ragnarök, knew that no success is complete, and many failures come to those who try hardest. "Work without Hope" is the title of one of Coleridge's epigrams; he suggests that such work is meaningless (it is gathering "nectar in a sieve"). Tolkien depicts a moral imperative that goes beyond such a reaction all the way to utter failure.

I am a Christian, and I live with hope—hope of an afterlife. If my emotions were better Christianized than they are, no doubt I would respond strongly to the eucatastrophe in Tolkien's story—to the coming of the eagles to rescue Sam and Frodo. I would read into Frodo's departure at Grey Havens an image of salvation. (The tone is wrong for a simple reading of salvation into it, however.) But I am speaking in this essay of the impact of Tolkien on my imagination. I do not think of eagles when I think of Tolkien. Rather, it is the image of Sam and Frodo toiling across the plain of Mordor, without hope. There is Tolkien's power (for me) revealed.

I do not expect that every reader will agree with even some of my choices of aspects of the *Lord of the Rings* that create an impact, and maybe no reader with all of them. They are my "applicability." As I have suggested, those with military backgrounds may find the battles more meaningful. Tolkien's great prose romance has many virtues—many aspects that different readers will find and love. Perhaps if I have stimulated a reader to think about just what it is that has impacted him or her, I have done enough.

APPENDIX ONE

A CHRONOLOGY OF THE LIFE AND CAREER OF J. R. R. TOLKIEN

1892 John Ronald Reuel Tolkien born 3 January in Bloemfontein, South Africa. Parents Arthur and Mabel Suffield Tolkien.
1894 February, younger brother Hilary born.
1895 Spring, Ronald returns to England with mother and brother.
1896 February, father Arthur dies of rheumatic fever in South Africa. Summer, Mabel Tolkien rents a cottage at Sarehole Mill, near Birmingham. She and boys live there for four years. Ronald loves reading the Curdie stories of George MacDonald.
1900 June, Mabel Tolkien received into the Catholic Church with sister May. She and boys move to Birmingham

	suburb of Moseley. Ronald attends King Edward's School.
1901	Mabel and boys move to Hagley Road, King's Heath, less than a mile from Moseley.
1902	Mabel and the boys move to Oliver Road, Edgbaston, a suburb of Birmingham. Ronald and Hilary attend St. Phillip's Grammar School.
1903	Ronald obtains a scholarship to King Edward's and returns there in autumn.
1904	November, mother dies of complications from diabetes, aged 34. Father Francis Morgan of King Edward's becomes the boys' guardian.
1905	The boys move into their Aunt Beatrice Suffield's home on Stirling Road, Edgbaston.
1908	The boys move to Mrs. Faulkner's boarding home on Duchess Road. Ronald meets future wife Edith Bratt at the home.
1909	Autumn, Ronald's romance with Edith discovered by Father Morgan, and is forbidden to see or speak to her until he is 21. Ronald fails to gain scholarship to Oxford.
1910	January, Ronald and Hilary move to lodgings near Mrs. Faulkner. March, Edith moves to Cheltenham. December, Ronald wins an Exhibition at Exeter College, Oxford.
1911	Enters Exeter College, Oxford University. Formation of "The T.C.B.S"—"Tea Club & Borravian Society," a reading and talking club of Tolkien and three friends from King Edward's. They meet and write until the war. Summer, Ronald travels to Switzerland. Autumn, his first term at Oxford. First published work, poem "The Battle of the Eastern Field," published in *The King Edward's School Chronicle*.
1912	Christmas with relatives near Birmingham, wrote and performed in a family play, "The Bloodhound, the Chef, and the Sufragette."

A Tolkien Chronology 193

1913   January, Ronald reunited with Edith. February, takes Honor Moderations and is awarded a Second Class degree. Summer, begins to read for the Honour's School of English Language and Literature. Visits France.

1914   January, Edith is received into the Catholic Church. She and Ronald are engaged. Summer, Ronald visits Cornwall.

1915   Summer, Ronald is awarded First Class Honours in his final examination. Is commissioned as a second lieutenant in the Lancashire Fusiliers; begins training in Bedford and Staffordshire. Poem "Goblin Feet" published by Blackwell's.

1916   22 March, marries Edith at Catholic church in Warwick. After honeymoon in Clevedon, Somerset, she moves to Great Haywood. June, Tolkien goes to war in France, invalided home in November to Great Haywood with trench fever.

1917   Begins writing his mythology, which is to become *The Silmarillion*. November, son John born. Family moves to village of Roos, Humberside.

1918   War ends; "all but one of my close friends dead." November, returns to Oxford with family and joins the staff of the New English Dictionary as assistant lexicographer; he works on the letter "w." Family moves to 55 St. John's Street.

1919   Begins work as freelance tutor with women students. Family moves to 1 Alfred Street.

1920   Autumn, assumes teaching post as Reader in English Language at Leeds University. Son Michael born in Oxford. Family lives for a few months at Hollybank House in Leeds, a home rented from a relative of Cardinal Newman.

1921   Family moves to 11 St. Mark's Terrace, near the university.

1922 Tolkien and colleague E. V. Gordon begin work on their edition of *Sir Gawain and the Green Knight* and *A Middle English Vocabulary*, Ronald's first published book.

1924 Becomes Professor of English Language at Leeds; family moves to Darnley Road. Son Christopher born.

1925 *Sir Gawain and the Green Knight* published. Autumn, assumes professorship (Rawlinson and Bosworth Professor of Anglo-Saxon) at Pembroke College, Oxford. Family moves to 22 Northmoor Road, Headington.

1926 May, meets and becomes friends with C. S. Lewis. Formation of "The Coalbiters" literary club.

1927 Strenuous teaching load: gives 136 classes and lectures in year; minimum required at Oxford is 36 per year. Favorite lectures are on *Beowulf* and *Sir Gawain and the Green Knight*; J. I. M. Stewart says that Tolkien "can turn the lecture room into a mead hall."

1929 Daughter Priscilla born.

1930 Family moves one house down to 20 Northmoor Road, former home of bookseller Basil Blackwell. Begins early work on *The Hobbit*.

1932 Tolkien purchases first family car, a Morris known as "Old Jo," followed shortly by updated model "Jo 2." Family makes several visits to countryside around Worminghall, later to become setting for the "Little Kingdom" in *Farmer Giles of Ham*.

1936 Delivers famous lecture "Beowulf: The Monsters and the Critics." Susan Dagnall of Allen & Unwin reads unfinished manuscript of *The Hobbit*, and suggests Tolkien finish it. It is accepted for publication.

1937 Autumn, *The Hobbit* published. Stanley Unwin suggests Tolkien write a sequel, which becomes *The Lord of the Rings*.

1939 8 March delivers famous Andrew Lang lecture *On Fairy-Stories* at St. Andrew's University. Becomes friends with Charles Williams at Inklings meetings.

1945 Elected Merton Professor of English Language and Literature at Oxford. Begins work on "The Notion Club Papers," based on experiences with C. S. Lewis and Inklings meetings.
1947 The Tolkien family moves to home on 3 Manor Road owned by Merton College.
1949 *The Lord of the* Rings completed. *Farmer Giles of Ham* published by Allen & Unwin.
1950 Tolkien offers *The Lord of the Rings* to Collins Publishing. The family moves to a home on 99 Holywell Street owned by Merton College.
1952 Collins rejects *The Lord of the Rings* and Tolkien offers it to Allen & Unwin.
1953 The Tolkien family moves to 76 Sandfield Road, Headington.
1954 The first two volumes of *The Lord of the Rings* published by Allen & Unwin.
1955 The third volume of *The Lord of the Rings* published by Allen & Unwin.
1957 Receives medal of the Royal Society of Literature.
1958 March, is guest of honor at a "Hobbit meal" in Rotterdam, Holland, the first and only time he accepted such an invitation.
1959 Retires from Oxford professorship. Gives valedictory address to the University on 5 June.
1962 *The Adventures of Tom Bombadil* published by Allen & Unwin.
1963 Great friend C. S. Lewis dies on 22 November.
1964 *Tree and Leaf* published by Allen & Unwin.
1965 June, Ace Books unauthorized paperback publication of *The Lord of the Rings*. Autumn, authorized Ballantine paperback. Start of Tolkien "boom."
1966 Tolkien and wife Edith celebrate their golden wedding anniversary. In their honor composer Donald Swann performs his song cycle *The Road Goes Ever On* at

Merton College, based on Tolkien's poems from *The Hobbit* and *The Lord of the Rings*.

1967   *Smith of Wootton Major* published by Allen & Unwin.

1968   Ronald and Edith move to 19 Lakeside Road, Poole, near Bournemouth; they stay often at the Miramar Hotel. They worship often at Sacred Heart Church in the Richmond Hill section of the city.

1971   Edith dies in a Bournemouth nursing home on 29 November, aged 82.

1972   Tolkien returns to Oxford; lives in rooms in 21 Merton Street. Is awarded the C.B.E. Oxford University awards him an honorary Doctorate of Letters.

1973   June, receives honorary degree from University of Edinburgh. On 28 August returns to Bournemouth to stay with friends. Is taken ill and dies in nursing home of complications due to an acute bleeding ulcer on 2 September, age 81. Requiem mass held at Church of St. Anthony of Padua, in Headington, with son John chief celebrant. Tolkien buried beside wife Edith in Wolvercote Cemetery.

1975   Translations of *Sir Gawain*, *Pearl*, and *Sir Orfeo* published by Allen & Unwin and Houghton Mifflin; edited by son Christopher.

1976   *The Father Christmas Letters* published by Allen & Unwin; edited by son Christopher's wife Baillie Tolkien. Brother Hilary dies.

1977   *The Silmarillion* published by Allen & Unwin; edited by son Christopher. Humphrey Carpenter writes authorized biography; published by Allen & Unwin.

1979   *Pictures by J. R. R. Tolkien* published by Allen & Unwin; forward and text by son Christopher.

1980   *Poems and Stories* published by Allen & Unwin. *Unfinished Tales* published by Allen & Unwin; edited by son Christopher.

1981   *The Letters of J. R. R. Tolkien* published by Allen & Unwin; edited by Humphrey Carpenter with assistance of son Christopher.

1982   *Mr. Bliss* published by Allen & Unwin. *Finn and Hengest: The Fragment and the Episode* published by Allen & Unwin; edited by Alan Bliss. *The Old English Exodus* published by Clarendon Press, edited by Joan Turville-Petre.

1983   *The Monsters and the Critics and Other Essays* published by Allen & Unwin and Houghton Mifflin; edited by son Christopher.

1983-1996   The twelve volumes comprising *The History of Middle Earth* published by Allen & Unwin, Unwin Hyman, and HarperCollins; edited by son Christopher: *The Book of Lost Tales, Part One*; *The Book of Lost Tales, Part Two*; *The Lays of Beleriand*; *The Shaping of Middle-Earth: The Quenta, The Ambarkanta, and the Annals*; *The Lost Road and Other Writings*; *The Return of the Shadow: The History of the Lord of the Rings, Part One*; *The Treason of Isengard: The History of the Lord of the Rings, Part Two*; *The War of the Ring: The History of the Lord of the Rings, Part Three*; *Sauron Defeated: The End of the Third Age, including The History of the Lord of the Rings, Part Four*; *Morgoth's Ring: The Later Silmarillion, Part One*; *The War of the Jewels: The Later Silmarillion, Part Two*; *The Peoples of Middle-Earth*.

1984   Son Michael dies of leukemia. Memorial service in honor of Tolkien at Bloemfontein Cathedral, South Africa.

1986   Tolkien's former student Simonne d'Ardenne dies in Belgium; she gives to daughter Priscilla over forty years' worth of letters from Tolkien.

1992   *The Tolkien Family Album* published by Houghton Mifflin; text by son John and daughter Priscilla.

1997   *Tales from the Perilous Realm* published by HarperCollins, a reprint of *Farmer Giles of Ham*, *The Adventures* of *Tom Bombadil*, *Leaf By Niggle*, and *Smith of Wootton Major* (without illustrations).

1998 *Roverandom* published by HarperCollins; edited by Wayne Hammond and Christina Scull. The Royal Mail (UK) issues a Tolkien postcard and postage stamp (*The Hobbit*) as part of the "Magical Worlds" series in honor of the C. S. Lewis Centenary.

APPENDIX TWO

THE PUBLISHED WORKS OF J. R. R. TOLKIEN

1911 "The Battle of the Eastern Field" (poem). *The King Edward's School Chronicle* 26/186 (March). Reprinted in *Mallorn*, 1978.

1913 "From the many-willow'd margin of the immemorial Thames" (poem, signed "J"). *The Stapledon Magazine* 4/20 (December). Published for Exeter College by B. H. Blackwell, Oxford.

1915 "Goblin Feet" (poem). In *Fifty New Poems for Children: An Anthology*. Edited by G. D. H. Cole and T. W. Earp. Oxford: Basil Blackwell.

1918 Introductory note (signed "J. R. R. T."). In *A Spring Harvest*. Poems by G. B. Smith. London: Erskine Macdonald. Tolkien helped edit this collection of Smith's poetry.

1920 "The Happy Mariners" (poem, signed "J. R. R. T."). *The Stapledon Magazine* 5/26 (June). Published for Exeter College by B. H. Blackwell, Oxford.

1922 *A Middle English Vocabulary.* Oxford: Clarendon Press. Originally designed for use with Kenneth Sisam's *Fourteenth Century Verse & Prose*; in subsequent editions of which it appears as glossary. It was also reprinted separately several times.

1923 "Iumona Gold Galdre Bewunden" (poem, a line from *Beowulf*). *The Gryphon* 4/4, New Series (January). Unsigned but Tolkien's authorship verified by entry in his diary.

"Holy Maidenhood" (poem). *Times Literary Supplement* (Thursday, 26 April).

"The City of the Gods" (poem). *The Microcosm* 7/1 (Spring). Edited by Dorothy U. Ratcliffe. Issued privately in Leeds.

"Henry Bradley, 3 December 1845–23 May 1923" (obituary). *Bulletin of the Modern Humanities Research Association* 20 (October): 4–5. Signed "J. R. R. T."

"The Eadigan Saelidan: The Happy Mariners." Revised from version in *The Stapledon Magazine*, 1920.

"Why the Man in the Moon Came Down Too Soon," and "Enigmata Saxonica" (poems). In *A Northern Venture: verses by members of the Leeds University English School Association.* Leeds: Swan Press.

"The Cat and the Fiddle: A Nursery-Rhyme Undone and its Scandalous Secret Unlocked" (poem). *Yorkshire Poetry* 2/19 (October–November). Leeds: Black Swan Press. An early version of poem in the *Lord of the Rings*, book 1, chapter 9, and in the *Adventures of Tom Bombadil* as "The Man in the Moon Stayed Up Too Late."

1924 "An Evening in Tavrobel," "The Lonely Isle," and "The Princess Ni" (poems). In *Leeds University Verse 1914–24.* Leeds: Swan Press.

Chapter on "Philology, General Works." *The Year's Work in English Studies* 4 (1923): 20–37. London: Oxford University Press.

1925 "Some Contributions to Middle-English Lexicography." *Review of English Studies* 1/2 (April): 210–15. London: Sidgwick & Jackson.

"Light as Leaf on Lindentree" (poem). *The Gryphon* 6/6, New Series (June). An early version of poem in the *Lord of the Rings*, book 1, chapter 11. Reprinted in the *Lays of Beleriand*; incorporated in "The Lay of the Children of Hurin."

"The Devil's Coach-Horses." *Review of English Studies* 1/3 (July): 331–36. London: Sidgwick & Jackson.

Sir Gawain and the Green Knight. Edited by J. R. R. Tolkien and E. V. Gordon. Oxford: Clarendon Press. Second edition revised by Norman Davis, Oxford, 1967.

1927 Chapter on "Philology, General Works." *The Year's Work in English Studies* 5 (1924): 26–65. London: Oxford University Press.

"The Nameless Land" (poem). In *Realities: An Anthology of Verse*. Edited by G. S. Tancred. Leeds: Swan Press; London: Gay & Hancock.

"Adventures in Unnatural History and the Medieval Metres, being the Freaks of Fisiologus" (poems, signed "Fisiologus"). *The Stapledon Magazine* 7/40. Published for Exeter College by B. H. Blackwell, Oxford.

Chapter on "Philology, General Works." *The Year's Work in English Studies* 6 (1925). London: Oxford University Press.

1928 Foreword to *A New Glossary of the Dialect of the Huddersfield District* by Walter E. Haigh. London: Oxford University Press.

1929 "Ancrene Wisse and Hali Meiðhad." *Essays and Studies* 14 (1929): 104–26. Oxford: Clarendon Press.

1930 "The Oxford English School." *Oxford Magazine* 48/21 (Thursday, 29 May 1930): 778–82. Oxford: The Oxonian Press. An article proposing a reformed syllabus.

1931 "Progress in Bimble Town" (poem, signed "K. Bagpuize"). *The Oxford Magazine* 50/1 (October). Oxford: Oxonian Press.

1932 Appendix I: "The Name 'Nodens' in *Report on the Evacuation of the Prehistoric, Roman, and Post-Roman Sites in Lydney Park, Gloucestershire.*" Reports of the Research Committee of the Society of Antiquaries of London 9: 132–37.

"Sigelwara Land": Part I in *Medium Ævum* 1 (December): 183–96; Part II in *Medium Ævum* 3 (June 1934): 95–111. Oxford: Basil Blackwell, 1933.

1933 "Errantry" (poem). *The Oxford Magazine* 52/5 (November). Oxford: The Oxonian Press. Later published in the *Treason of Isengard* and (a revised version) in the *Adventures of Tom Bombadil*.

1934 "Firiel" (poem). *The Chronicle* 4. Roehamptom: Covenant of Sacred Heart. An early version of poem by the same title in the *Adventures of Tom Bombadil*. Reprinted 1978 in pamphlet by Bangor, Wales.

"Looney" (poem). *The Oxford Magazine* 52/9 (January). Oxford: The Oxonian Press. An early version of poem in the *Adventures of Tom Bombadil* as "The Sea-bell."

"The Adventures of Tom Bombadil" (poem). *The Oxford Magazine* 52/13 (February). Oxford: The Oxonian Press. An early version of poem by same title in the *Adventures of Tom Bombadil.*

"Chaucer as a Philologist: The Reeve's Tale." In *Transactions of the Philological Society*, 1–70. London: David Nutt.

1936 *Songs for the Philologists* by J. R. R. Tolkien, E. V. Gordon, and others. Privately printed in the Department of English at University College, London. A collection of humorous poems originally written and circulated in typescript when Tolkien was at Leeds University. Tolkien wrote thirteen of the poems, including "Flower of the Trees" and "Across the Broad Ocean."

1937 "The Dragon's Visit" (poem). *The Oxford Magazine* 55/11 (February). Oxford: The Oxonian Press. Reprinted in *Winter's Tales for Children I*, 1965.

"Knocking at the Door: Lines induced by sensations when waiting for an answer at the door of an Exalted Academic Person" (poem, signed "Oxymore"). *The Oxford Magazine* 55/13 (February). Oxford: The Oxonian Press. Original version of "The Mewlips."

"Iumonna Gold Galdre Bewunden" (poem). *The Oxford Magazine* 55/15 (March). Oxford: The Oxonian Press. Revised from version in the *Gryphon*, 1923. Further revised as "The Hoard" in the *Adventures of Tom Bombadil.*

Corrections and contributions to *The Battle of Maldon* by E. V. Gordon. London: Meuthen's Old English Library. Professor Gordon in his preface thanks Tolkien for "reading the proofs," making "many corrections and contributions," and for his "characteristic generosity" in giving him the solution "to many of the textual and philological problems" in the book.

"Beowulf: The Monsters and the Critics." *Proceedings of the British Academy* 22 (1936): 245–95. London: Oxford University Press. Reprinted many times (see below), and separately as the Sir Israel Gollancz Memorial Lecture.

The Hobbit, or There and Back Again, London: George Allen & Unwin. Reprinted many times, and from the second impression in 1942 onward, four color plates were included. The first US edition was published in 1938 by Houghton Mifflin. The Swedish edition (1947) was the first Tolkien book to be translated into a foreign language. Other notable versions include the 1987 Houghton Mifflin fiftieth anniversary edition in green and gold slipcases (with a foreword by Christopher Tolkien), a lovely oversized annotated Houghton Mifflin edition by Douglas Anderson in 1988 (revised and expanded in 2002), a special Houghton Mifflin edition in 1994 with illustrations by Michael Hague, a 1995 HarperCollins (London) edition with corrected text ("represents as closely as possible Tolkien's final intended form"), a sixtieth Houghton Mifflin anniversary edition in 1997 with illustrations by Allan Lee, and a 1999 HarperCollins (London) mass market edition, the first paperback printing of the corrected text version of 1995. In 2001 a new hardcover edition was published by Houghton Mifflin, with cover art by Caldecott Award winner Peter Sis.

1938 Letter about *The Hobbit*. *The Observer* (20 February). London. Reprinted in *The Letters of J. R. R. Tolkien*.

1940 Preface to *Beowulf and the Finnesburg Fragment: A Translation into Modern English Prose* by John R. C. Hall, revised by Charles L. Wrenn. London: George Allen & Unwin.

1944 *Sir Orfeo*. Oxford: The Academic Copying Office. A mimeographed booklet, in Middle English, used in an English course that Tolkien organized and directed.

1945 "Leaf by Niggle," *Dublin Review* 432 (January): 46–61. London: Burns Oates & Washbourne. Reprinted many times—see below.

"The name Coventry" (letter). *The Catholic Herald* (23 February). Reply to letter by "H. D." published 9 February.

"The Lay of Aotrou and Itroun." *The Welsh Review* 4/4 (December). Cardiff: Penmark Press.

1947 "'Ipplen' in Sawles Warde." *English Studies* 28 (6 December): 168–70. Edited by R. W. Zandvoort, Groningen. In collaboration with S. T. R. O. d'Ardenne.

"On Fairy-Stories." *Essays Presented to Charles Williams*. Edited by C. S. Lewis. London: Oxford University Press, 38–39. Reprinted—see below.

1948 "MS. Bodley 34: A Re-collation of a Collation." *Studia Neophilogica* 20 (1947–1948): 65–72. Uppsala. In collaboration with S. T. R. O. d'Ardenne.

1949 *Farmer Giles of Ham*. London: George Allen & Unwin. (First US edition, Boston: Houghton Mifflin, 1950. In 1991 Houghton Mifflin published a new American edition, with illustrations by Roger Garland. In 1999 Houghton Mifflin published in a fiftieth anniversary edition, edited by Christina Scull and Wayne G. Hammond, with illustrations by Pauline Baynes.)

1953 "A Fourteenth-Century Romance." *Radio Times*. London: 4 December. Foreword to the BBC "Third Programme" broadcasts of Tolkien's translation of "Sir Gawain and the Green Knight."

"The Homecoming of Beorhtnoth Beorhthelm's Son." *Essays and Studies*. London: John Murray, 1–18.

Pearl. Edited by E. V. Gordon. Oxford: The Clarendon Press. Tolkien contributed notes, corrections, and part of the introduction.

"Middle English 'Losenger.'" *Essais de Philologie Moderne* (1951): 63–76. Universitie de Liege. Paris: Les Belles Lettres.

1954 *The Fellowship of the Ring: Being the First Part of the Lord of the Rings*. London: George Allen & Unwin. First US edition, Boston: Houghton Mifflin, 1954.

The Two Towers: Being the Second Part of the Lord of the Rings. George Allen & Unwin. First US edition, Boston: Houghton Mifflin, 1955.

1955 *The Return of the King: Being the Third Part of the Lord of the Rings*. London: George Allen & Unwin. First US edition, Boston: Houghton Mifflin, 1956.

"Imram" (poem). *Time and Tide* 36/49 (December). London. Appeared in unpublished ms *The Notion Club Papers* as "The Death of St. Brendan."

Preface to *The Ancrene Riwle*. Translated into Modern English by Mary R. Salu. London: Burns & Oates.

1958 Prefatory note to *The Old English Apollonius of Tyre*. Edited by Peter Gooden. London: Oxford University Press, iii.

1960 Letter to *Triode* 18 (May). Comments on article by Arthur K. Weir in previous issue.

1962 *The Adventures of Tom Bombadil and Other Verses from The Red Book*. London: George Allen & Unwin. Illustrated by Pauline Baynes. First US edition, Boston: Houghton Mifflin, 1962. (In 1991 Houghton Mifflin published a new edition, illustrated by Roger Garland.)

Ancrene Wisse: The English Text of the Ancrene Riwle. Edited from MS Corpus Christi College Cambridge 402 by J. R. R. Tolkien. With an introduction by N. R. Ker. Early English Text Society, volume 249. London: Oxford University Press.

1963 "English and Welsh." *Angles and Britons: O'Donnell Lectures.* Cardiff: University of Wales Press, 1–41. Published in the United States by Verry, Lawrence, 1963.

1964 *Tree and Leaf.* London: George Allen & Unwin. Reprint of "On Fairy-Stories" and "Leaf By Niggle." First US edition, Boston: Houghton Mifflin, 1965. The third Allen & Unwin edition (1988) included the poem "Mythopoeia."

1965 "Once Upon a Time" and "The Dragon's Visit" (poems). In *Winter's Tales for Children I.* Edited by Caroline Hiller. London: Macmillan. First US edition, New York: St. Martin's Press, 1965. Reprinted in *The Young Magicians*, edited by Lin Carter, New York: Ballantine Books, 1969. "The Dragon's Visit" is revised from the version in the *Oxford Magazine*, 1937.

1966 "Tolkien on Tolkien." *Diplomat* 18/197 (October): 39. Taken from a statement Tolkien prepared for his publishers, this is a brief summary of his life and his motives as a writer.

The Jerusalem Bible. London: Darton, Longman & Todd. Published in the US, New York: Doubleday. Tolkien is named as "principal collaborator in translation and literary revision," but his primary contribution was to write the original draft of the translation of the book of Jonah, later revised by several others before publication.

The Tolkien Reader. New York: Ballantine Books. (A reprint of Tolkien's "The Homecoming of Beorhtnoth," *Tree and Leaf* [containing "Leaf by Niggle" and "On Fairy-Stories," with an introductory note by Tolkien], *Farmer Giles of Ham*, and the *Adventures of Tom Bombadil*, introduction by Peter Beagle ["Tolkien's Magic Ring"]; illustrated by Pauline Baynes.)

1967 *Smith of Wootton Major.* London: George Allen & Unwin. First US edition, Boston: Houghton Mifflin, 1967.

Illustrations by Pauline Baynes. In 1991 Houghton Mifflin published a new American edition, with illustrations by Roger Garland.

"For W. H. A." (poem). *Shenandoah: The Washington and Lee University Review* 18/2 (Winter). Poem in Anglo-Saxon with modern English translation in honor of sixtieth birthday of W. H. Auden.

The Road Goes Ever On: A Song Cycle. Poems by J. R. R. Tolkien, set to music by Donald Swann. Boston: Houghton Mifflin. First UK edition, London: George Allen & Unwin, 1968. Includes six poems from the *Lord of the Rings* and one from the *Adventures of Tom Bombadil.*

1969 Letter describing the origins of "The Inklings." In *The Image of Man in C. S. Lewis* by William Luther White. Nashville and New York: Abingdon Press, 221–22. First UK edition, London: Hodder & Stoughton, 1970.

1971 Passage in *Attacks of Taste.* Compiled and edited by Evelyn B. Byrne and Otto M. Penzler. New York: Gotham Book Mart. Tolkien describes his reading habits as a young man.

1972 "Beautiful Place because Trees are Loved" (letter). *The Daily Telegraph* (4 July). About forests in Middle-earth, in response to editorial of 29 June. Letter reprinted in the *Letters of J. R. R. Tolkien.*

Calendar containing Tolkien drawings issued by Ballantine Books. In 1973 Allen & Unwin and Ballantine issued calendars using the same drawings. In 1976, 1977, and 1978 Allen & Unwin issued calendars using other drawings by Tolkien; several were illustrated by Tim Kirk. Several of these have been issued as postcards and posters. The calendar art was reprinted in *Pictures by J. R. R. Tolkien,* 1979. Since the 1970s Tolkien calendars have been produced by various other publishers, including Unwin Paperbacks (1984–1991), Grafton Books (1992–present), *Beyond Bree* (1989, 1992, 1994), and HarperCollins in the 1990s. Illustrators have included Pauline Baynes, Roger Garland, Michael Hague, Tim and Greg

Hildebrandt, John Howe, Tim Kirk, Allan Lee, Ted Nasmith, and many others.

1974 "Bilbo's Last Song" (poem). Published on poster, with decorations by Pauline Baynes. London: George Allen & Unwin. First US edition, Boston: Houghton Mifflin (with photographic background). (*Bilbo's Last Song* in book form was published in 1990—see below.)

1975 "Guide to the Names in *The Lord of the Rings*." In *A Tolkien Compass*, edited by Jared Lobdell. LaSalle IL: Open Court. Notes on the terminology of the story, originally written for guidance of translators.

Sir Gawain and the Green Knight, Pearl, and Sir Orfeo. Translated into Modern English by J. R. R. Tolkien. Edited and with a preface by Christopher Tolkien. London: George Allen & Unwin.

Letter in *Mythlore* 10. Volume 3, number 2. Letter of 17 November 1957 to Dr. Herbert Schiro; included in article by G. GoodKnight. Tolkien says that the *Lord of the Rings* "is about Death and the desire for deathlessness." Reprinted in part in the *Letters of J. R. R. Tolkien*.

1976 *The Father Christmas Letters*. Edited by Baillie Tolkien. London: George Allen & Unwin. First US edition, Boston: Houghton Mifflin. Included in the several reprints of this work were three miniature volumes, published by HarperCollins (London) in 1994, a one-volume version with pull-out letters by Houghton Mifflin in 1995, and a one-volume miniature version by HarperCollins in 1998. In 1999 HarperCollins and Houghton Mifflin published *Letters From Father Christmas*, an enlarged edition of the 1976 publication, with previously unpublished letters, illustrations, and facsimiles.

1977 *The Silmarillion*. Edited by Christopher Tolkien. London: George Allen & Unwin. First US edition, Boston: Houghton Mifflin. In 1997 Houghton Mifflin published a special edition of the *Silmarillion*, with illustrations by Ted Nasmith.

J. R. R. Tolkien: A Biography. Humphrey Carpenter. London: George Allen & Unwin. Includes previously unpublished letters, poetry, and prose by Tolkien.

1978 "The Lonely Mountain" (drawing). Reproduced in *The Tolkien Scrapbook*. Edited by Alida Becker. New York: Grossett & Dunlap.

The Inklings. Humphrey Carpenter. London: George Allen & Unwin. Includes previously unpublished letters, diaries, and manuscripts by Tolkien.

1979 *Pictures by J. R. R. Tolkien*. Foreword and notes by Christopher Tolkien. London: George Allen & Unwin; new edition, London: HarperCollins, 1992. First US edition, Boston: Houghton Mifflin; new edition, 1992. A collection of Tolkien's paintings, drawings, and designs that were published in calendars from 1973–1979, with a gap in 1975. One painting, titled "Fanghorn Forest," is a scene from the *Silmarillion*. Also included are the original pen and ink drawings published in the *Hobbit*.

"Valedictory Address to the University of Oxford, 5 June 1959." In *J. R. R. Tolkien, Scholar and Storyteller*. Edited by Mary Salu and Robert T. Farrell. Ithaca and London: Cornell University Press.

1980 *Poems and Stories*. London: George Allen & Unwin. Boxed volume, containing reprints of *The Adventures of Tom Bombadil*, "The Homecoming of Beorhtnoth Beorhthelm's Son," "On Fairy-Stories," "Leaf by Niggle," *Farmer Giles of Ham* and *Smith of Wootton Major*. Illustrations (old and new) by Pauline Baynes.

Unfinished Tales of Numenor and Middle-earth. Edited by Christopher Tolkien. London: George Allen & Unwin. First US edition, Boston: Houghton Mifflin.

1981 *The Letters of J. R. R. Tolkien*. Edited by Humphrey Carpenter with assistance of Christopher Tolkien. London: George Allen & Unwin. First US edition, Boston: Houghton Mifflin. Includes 354 letters from every adult period of Tolkien's life except 1917–1922, 1924, 1926–1936, with the first dated October 1914 to his fiancee and later wife Edith Bratt, and the last dated 29 August 1973, four days before his death, to his daughter Priscilla. In 2000 Houghton Mifflin published a paperback edition with an expanded index, compiled by Wayne G. Hammond and Christina Scull.

The Old English Exodus. Text, translation, and commentary by J. R. R. Tolkien. Edited by Joan Turville-Petre. Oxford: Clarendon Press.

The Lord of the Rings. Silver anniversary edition (twenty-fifth anniversary of first American edition of the *Return of the King*). Three-volume boxed set. Boston: Houghton Mifflin.

1982 *The Lord of the Rings.* Boston: Houghton Mifflin; reprinted numerous times. Notable versions include the Houghton Mifflin 1982 collector's edition in one volume, in slipcase, with notes on the text by Douglas Anderson, a special 1991 one-volume centenary edition priced at sixty dollars (illustrations by Allan Lee), the 1994 HarperCollins (London) three-volume edition (with numerous corrections, "the best text"), and the 1999 Houghton Mifflin edition, priced at twenty dollars, the first American one-volume paperback edition. "Movie versions" of this edition, both hardcover and paperback, with a scene from the December 2001 *Lord of the Rings* film (New Line Cinema) on the covers, were published by Houghton Mifflin on 1 June 2001, with a teacher's guide forthcoming. These versions are the same edition published in 1994 by HarperCollins. Houghton Mifflin released individual movie versions of the work, starting with the *Fellowship of the Ring*, in September 2001. In 1999 HarperCollins (with CD) and in 2000 Houghton Mifflin (no CD) published a Millennium edition seven-volume set in slipcase.

Mr. Bliss. London: George Allen & Unwin. First US edition, Boston: Houghton Mifflin.

Finn and Hengest: The Fragment and the Episode. Edited by Alan Bliss. London: George Allen & Unwin. First US edition, Boston: Houghton Mifflin.

The Old English Exodus. Oxford: Clarendon Press. Tolkien contributed the text, translation, and commentary.

1983 *The Book of Lost Tales, Part I.* Edited by Christopher Tolkien. London: George Allen & Unwin. First US edition, Boston: Houghton Mifflin.

The Monsters and the Critics and Other Essays. Edited by Christopher Tolkien. London: George Allen & Unwin; Boston: Houghton Mifflin, 1984. Includes "Beowulf: The Monsters and the Critics," "On Translating Beowulf," "Sir Gawain and the Green Knight," "On Fairy-Stories," "English and Welsh," "A Secret Vice," and "Valedictory Address."

1984 *The Book of Lost Tales, Part II.* Edited by Christopher Tolkien. London: George Allen & Unwin. First US edition, Boston: Houghton Mifflin.

1985 *The Lays of Beleriand.* Edited by Christopher Tolkien. London: George Allen & Unwin. First US edition, Boston: Houghton Mifflin. Includes a fifteen-page commentary by C. S. Lewis on the "Lay of Leithian."

1986 *The Shaping of Middle-earth.* Edited by Christopher Tolkien. London: George Allen & Unwin. First US edition, Boston: Houghton Mifflin.

1987 *The Lost Road and Other Writings.* Edited by Christopher Tolkien. London: Unwin Hyman. First US edition, Boston: Houghton Mifflin.

1988 *The Return of the Shadow.* Edited by Christopher Tolkien. London: Unwin Hyman. First US edition, Boston: Houghton Mifflin.

1989 *The Treason of Isengard.* Edited by Christopher Tolkien. London: Unwin Hyman. First US edition, Boston: Houghton Mifflin.

1990 *Bilbo's Last Song.* Boston: Houghton Mifflin. Illustrated by Pauline Baynes. Quotations from second hardcover edition of the *Lord of the Rings* and the fourth hardcover edition of the *Hobbit.* A private printing, with music by Donald Swann, was issued by Albert House Press, England, 1992. A new, smaller, slightly revised edition was published by Alfred A. Knopf (New York) in 2002.

The War of the Ring. Edited by Christopher Tolkien. London: Unwin Hyman. First US edition, Boston: Houghton Mifflin.

C. S. Lewis: A Biography. A. N. Wilson. London: Collins; New York: Norton. Includes excerpts from previously unpublished remarks by Tolkien on C. S. Lewis.

1992 *Sauron Defeated.* Edited by Christopher Tolkien. London: HarperCollins. First US edition, Boston: Houghton Mifflin. Includes "The Notion Club Papers," 182 pages. In 2000 Houghton Mifflin published in paperback the first separate edition of *Sauron Defeated*, titled *The End of the Third Age*, in a set with *The Return of the Shadow*, *The Treason of Isengard*, and *The War of the Ring*, collectively titled *The History of the Lord of the Rings.*

1993 *Morgoth's Ring.* Edited by Christopher Tolkien. London: HarperCollins. First US edition, Boston: Houghton Mifflin.

Poems of J. R. R. Tolkien. London: HarperCollins. Three volumes in slipcase.

Poems from The Hobbit. London: HarperCollins; Boston: Houghton Mifflin, 1997. Miniature.

1994 *The War of the Jewels.* Edited by Christopher Tolkien. London: HarperCollins. First US edition, Boston: Houghton Mifflin.

1996 *The Peoples of Middle-earth.* Edited by Christopher Tolkien. London: HarperCollins. First US edition, Boston: Houghton Mifflin.

1998 *Roverandom.* Edited by Christina Scull and Wayne G. Hammond. London: HarperCollins. First US edition, Boston: Houghton Mifflin.

2002 *A Tolkien Miscellany.* Science Fiction Book Club, special edition. Contains *Smith of Wootton Major*, *Farmer Giles of Ham*, *Tree and Leaf* ("On Fairy Stories," Leaf by Niggle), *The Adventures of Tom Bombadil*, *Sir Gawain and the Green Knight.*

APPENDIX THREE

Resource Bibliography

*Recommended

Abromaitis, Sue, C. N. "The Distant Mirror of Middle-Earth: The Sacramental Vision of J. R. R. Tolkien." *Touchstone* 15/1 (January/February 2002): 33–40.

*Allan, James, editor. *An Introduction to Elvish and to Other Tongues and Proper Names and Writing Systems of the Third Age of the Western Lands of Middle-earth as Set Forth in the Published Writings of Professor John Ronald Reuel Tolkien.* Hayes Middlesex: Bran's Head Books, 1978.

*Anderson, Douglas A. (introduction and notes). *The Annotated Hobbit.* Boston: Houghton Mifflin, 1988. Details Tolkien's revisions to the text, and discusses his folk, mythic, and linguistic sources for the story. A must for the serious Tolkien fan and scholar. In 2002 Houghton Mifflin published a revised and expanded edition of this work.

Auden, W. H. "Good and Evil in *The Lord of the Rings*." *The Tolkien Journal* 3/1 (1967): 5–8.

Beare, Rhona. *J. R. R. Tolkien's The Silmarillion*. New Lambton, Australia: Nimrod Publications, 2000. Part of the *Babel Handboooks on Fantasy and SF Writers 10* series.

Beaumont, John. "The Catholic Witness of J. R. R. Tolkien." *The Downside Review* 407 (April 1999): 115–32.

Becker, Alida, editor. *A Tolkien Treasury*. Philadelphia: Courage Press, 1989. Formerly titled *The Tolkien Scrapbook*. Fun and fannish, with very good and not so good essays.

Begg, Ean C. M. *The Lord of the Rings and the Signs of the Times*. London: Greaves, 1975.

Bergmann, Frank. "The Roots of Tolkien's Tree: The Influence of George MacDonald and German Romanticism Upon Tolkien's Essay 'On Fairy-Stories.'" *Mosaic* 10/2 (Winter 1977): 5–15.

Berman, Ruth, and Ken Nahigian, editors. *The Middle-earth Songbook*. Rancho Cordova CA: AJD Graphics, n.d. [1975].

Birzer, Bradley J. "The Christian Gifts of J. R. R. Tolkien." *New Oxford Review* (November 2001): 25–29.

———. *J. R. R. Tolkien's Sanctifying Myth*. Wilmington DE: ISI Books, 2002.

*Blackwelder, Richard E. "The Great Copyright Controversy." *Beyond Bree* (September 1995). This eleven-page essay explains the copyright controversy concerning the publication of the *Lord of the Rings* and the "unauthorized" Ace Books reprints of 1965.

Bloom, Harold, editor. *J. R. R. Tolkien*. Philadelphia: Chelsea House, 2000.

———, editor. *Modern Critical Interpretations of The Lord of the Rings*. Philadelphia: Chelsea House, 2000.

Bradley, Marion Zimmer. *Men, Halflings, and Hero Worship*. Baltimore: T-K Graphics, 1973.

Bratman, David. "The Order to Read Tolkien's Books." Internet. (http://www.stanford.edu/~dbratman/tolkien_order).

Bruner, Kurt, and Jim Ware. *Finding God in the Lord of the Rings*. Wheaton IL: Tyndale House, 2001.

Burns, Marjorie J. "Echoes of William Morris's Icelandic Journals in J. R. R. Tolkien." *Studies in Medievalism* 3/3–4 (Winter, Spring 1991): 367–73.

*Carpenter, Humphrey. *J. R. R. Tolkien: A Biography*. Boston: Houghton Mifflin, 2000. The authorized biography of Tolkien, written with access to his papers, including private diaries. First published in 1977.

*———. *The Inklings*. London: HarperCollins, 1997. Mostly about C. S. Lewis, Charles Williams, and Tolkien. The only book-length study of the group; biased against Lewis.

*———, editor. With the assistance of Christopher Tolkien. *The Letters of J. R. R. Tolkien*. London: Allen & Unwin, 1981; new edition, Boston: Houghton Mifflin, 2000. An indispensable and very informative and entertaining collection. Contains 354 letters.

———, and Mari Prichard. *The Oxford Companion to Children's Literature*. Oxford: Oxford University Press, 1991. Nearly 600 pages; 2,000 entries; more than 150 illustrations.

Carter, Lin. *A Look Behind the Lord of the Rings*. New York: Ballantine, 1969.

———. *Imaginary Worlds: The Art of Fantasy*. New York: Ballantine, 1973.

Chance, Jane, and David D. Day. "Medievalism in Tolkien: Two Decades of Criticism in Review." *Studies in Medievalism* 3/3–4 (Winter, Spring 1991): 375–87.

*———. *Tolkien's Art: A Mythology for England*. Revised edition. Lexington KY: The University Press of Kentucky, 2001. Traces sources and influences that formed Tolkien's literary, philosophical, and moral foundations.

*———. *The Lord of the Rings: The Mythology of Power*. Revised edition. Lexington KY: The University Press of Kentucky, 2001.

*Clark, George, and Daniel Timmons, editors. *J. R. R. Tolkien and His Literary Resonances: Views of Middle-earth*. Westport CT: Greenwood Press, 2000.

*Clute, John, and Peter Nichols, editors. *The Encyclopedia of Science Fiction*. New York: St. Martin's, 1993.

*———, and John Grant, editors. *The Encyclopedia of Modern Fantasy*. New York: St. Martin's, 1997.

Colbert, David. *The Magical Worlds of* The Lord of the Rings. New York: Berkeley Books, 2002.

Colebatch, Hal. *Return of the Heroes: The Lord of the Rings, Star Wars, and Contemporary Culture*. Perth: Australian Institute, 1990.

Collins, David R. *J. R. R. Tolkien: Master of Fantasy*. Minneapolis: Lerner Publications, 1992. Perhaps the best biography for younger readers.

Cooper, Susan. "There and Back Again: Tolkien Reconsidered." *The Horn Book* (March/April 2002): 143–50.

Coren, Michael. *J. R. R. Tolkien: The Man Who Created The Lord of the Rings*. Toronto: Stoddart, 2001. Toronto: Scholastic, 2001. A movie tie-in for younger readers.

*Crabbe, Katharyn W. *J. R. R. Tolkien*. Revised and expanded edition. New York: Continuum, 1988. One of the best of the critical studies on Tolkien.

Crawford, Edward. *Some Light on Middle-Earth*. London: Peter Roe Memorial Booklet No. 1, The Tolkien Society, 1985.

Curry, Patrick. *Defending Middle-Earth: Tolkien: Myth and Modernity*. London: HarperCollins, 1998. Often more Curry than Tolkien but still compelling reading.

Davenport, Guy. "Hobbits in Kentucky." *New York Times*. 23 February 1979, A27.

Davis, Erik. "The Fellowship of the Ring." *Wired*. (October 2001): 116–32. Perhaps the best of the many "fanzine" articles devoted to Tolkien and the making of the new movie.

*Davis, Norman and C. L. Wrenn, editors. *English and Medieval Studies Presented to J. R. R. Tolkien on the Occasion of his Seventieth Birthday*. London: George Allen & Unwin, 1962.

Day, David. *A Tolkien Bestiary.* New York: Ballantine, 1979. A moderately attractive book with pictures. Several of this author's works contain the same material, reworked.

———. *Tolkien: The Illustrated Encyclopedia.* New York: Macmillan, 1992.

———. *The Tolkien Companion.* London: Mandarin in association with Michael Beazley, 1993.

———. *Tolkien's Ring.* London: HarperCollins, 1994. Superficial at best.

———. *The Hobbit Companion.* Atlanta: Turner Publishing, 1997. Only for the youngest of readers.

DeKoster, Katie, editor. *Readings on J. R. R. Tolkien.* San Diego: Greenhaven Press, 2000.

Deyo, Steven M. "Niggle's Leaves: *The Red Book of Westmarch* and Related Minor Poetry of J. R. R. Tolkien." *Proceedings of the Sixteenth Annual Convention of the Mythopoeic Society. Mythlore* 27 (July 1985): 48–65.

*Drollinger, Frank. "J. R. R. Tolkien & the 20th Century." *CSL—The Bulletin of the New York C. S. Lewis Society* 376 (vol. 32, no. 2, February 2001): 1–8.

Drury, Roger. "Providence at Elrond's Council." *Mythlore* 25 (vol. 7, no. 3, Autumn 1980): 8–9.

*Duriez, Colin. *Tolkien and the Lord of the Rings: A Guide to Middle-earth.* Mahwah NJ: Hidden Spring, 2001. Formerly *The J. R. R. Tolkien Handbook* (Baker, 1992). Good overview and well organized. Some themes and works are given only passing reference, particularly the *History of Middle-Earth.*

———. "The Theology of Fantasy in Lewis and Tolkien." *Themelios* 23/2 (February 1998): 32–50.

———, and David Porter. *The Inklings Handbook.* St. Louis: Chalice Press, 2001. Uneven; riddled with errors, omissions, and strange entries.

Ellwood, Gracia Faye. *Good News from Tolkien's Middle Earth.* Grand Rapids: Eerdmans, 1970.

Etkin, Anne, editor. *Eglerio! In Praise of Tolkien.* Greencastle PA: Quest Communications, 1978.

Evans, Robley. *J. R. R. Tolkien.* New York: Warner Paperback Library, 1972.

Fisher, Jude (Jane Johnson). *The Lord of the Rings: The Fellowship of the Ring Visual Companion.* Boston: Houghton Mifflin, 2001.

*Flieger, Verlyn. *Splintered Light: Logos and Language in Tolkien's World.* Grand Rapids MI: Eerdmans, 1983. Discusses Owen Barfield's *Poetic Diction* as a key to understanding Tolkien's use of language and symbol. One of the best critical studies written on Tolkien.

*——. *A Question of Time: J. R. R. Tolkien's Road to Faërie.* Kent OH: Kent State University Press, 1997. Examines closely Tolkien's concern with time—past and present, real and "fairie."

*——, and Carl F. Hostetter, editors. *Tolkien's Legendarium: Essays on the History of Middle-earth.* Westport CT: Greenwood Press, 2000. A superlative collection, written in honor of and recognition of Christopher Tolkien's monumental editing achievement.

*Fonstad, Karen W. *The Atlas of Middle-Earth.* Revised edition. Boston: Houghton Mifflin, 1991. *Mythprint* called this book "absolutely indispensable...a masterful work."

*Foster, Robert. *The Complete Guide to Middle-Earth.* New York: Ballantine, 2001. A detailed glossary of all the people, places, and things from the *Hobbit* through the *Silmarillion.* No Tolkien student or fan should be without it. In 2002 Andrews McMeel Publishing (Kansas City, MO) issued a 2003 calendar, "A Guide to Middle-Earth," based on entries in Foster's book.

*Garbowski, Christopher. *Recovery and Transcendence for the Contemporary Mythmaker: The Spiritual Dimension in the Works of J. R. R. Tolkien.* Lublin Poland: Marie Curie-Sklodowska University Press, 2000. Explores the spiritual and theological aspects of Tolkien's writings in relation to authority, revelation, and eschatology.

Geist, Brandon, editor. *The QPB Companion to the Lord of the Rings*. New York: Quality Paperback Club, 2001. A reprinting of older book reviews and pieces, by C. S. Lewis, Edmund Wilson, Tom Shippey, and others. The same publisher (1995) produced *A Reader's Companion to The Hobbit and The Lord of the Rings* with some of the same material.

Giddings, Robert, and Elizabeth Holland. *J. R. R. Tolkien: The Shores of Middle-earth*. London: Junction Books, 1982.

———, editor. *J. R. R. Tolkien: This Far Land*. London: Vision Press, 1983.

Gillam, James H. *Treasures from the Misty Mountains: A Collector's Guide to Tolkien*. Burlington Ontario: Collectors Guide Publishing, 2001. Great fun.

Glover, Christopher. "The Christian Character of Tolkien's Invented World." *Mythlore* 10, vol. 3, 2 (1975): 3–8.

Gray, Rosemary, editor. *A Tribute to J. R. R. Tolkien*. Johannesburg: University of South Africa Press, 1992. Includes a foreword by Priscilla Tolkien.

*Green, Roger Lancelyn, and Walter Hooper. *C. S. Lewis: A Biography*. New York and London: Harcourt Brace, 1974. The first biography of Lewis, and still one of the best.

Green, William H. *The Hobbit: A Journey Into Maturity*. New York: Twayne, 1994.

Greenberg, Martin H., editor. *After the Ring: Stories in Honor of J. R. R. Tolkien*. New York: Tor Fantasy, 1992. Tales by such luminaries as Gregory Benford, John Brunner, Stephen Donaldson, and Jane Yolen.

Grotta, Daniel. *J. R. R. Tolkien: Architect of Middle Earth*. Philadelphia: Courage Books, 1992. A revision of the first biography (unauthorized) of Tolkien (1976). Some of the errors have been corrected and art has been added by the Brothers Hildebrandt, but this is *not the biography to consult on*

Tolkien. Contains many inaccuracies in fact and omits much pertinent information.

Guadalupi, Gianni, and Alberto Manguel. *The Dictionary of Imaginary Places* (updated and expanded edition). Orlando: Harcourt, 2000.

*Haber, Karen, editor. *Meditations on Middle-Earth*. New York: St. Martin's, 2001. Includes fifteen personal essays on Tolkien and his impact, some moving and nearly all illuminating.

*Hadfield, Alice Mary. *Charles Williams: An Exploration of His Life and Work*. New York: Oxford University Press, 1983. The only full-length treatment of Williams.

*Hammond, Wayne G. With assistance from Douglas A. Anderson. *J. R. R. Tolkien A Descriptive Bibliography*. New Castle DE: Oak Knoll Books, 1993. A monumental and indispensable work. Should be supplemented with issues of the *Tolkien Collector* (see Appendix Four).

*————. "Whose *Lord of the Rings* is It, Anyway?" *The Canadian C. S. Lewis Journal* 97 (Spring 2000): 59–65.

*————, and Christina Scull. *J. R. R. Tolkien Artist & Illustrator*. Boston: Houghton Mifflin, 1995. The only book treatment of Tolkien's art and extremely well written and illustrated.

*————. "J. R. R. Tolkien: The Achievement of His Literary Life." *Mythlore* 22, 3 (Winter 1999): 27–37.

*————. *J. R. R. Tolkien: A Companion & Guide*. London: HarperCollins, forthcoming in 2003. Similar in style and length to W. Hooper's *Companion* to C. S. Lewis. A much anticipated work.

*Hansen, J. T. et al., editors. "The Tolkien Papers." *Mankato Studies in English* 2. Mankato State College Studies, volume 2, February 1967.

Harvey, David. *The Song of Middle-Earth: J. R. R. Tolkien's Themes, Symbols and Myths*. London: Allen & Unwin, 1985.

*Heaney, Seamus, translator. *Beowulf*. New York: Norton, 2001.

Hein, Rolland. *Christian Mythmakers.* Chicago: Cornerstone Press, 1997.

Helms, Randel. *Tolkien's World.* Boston: Houghton Mifflin, 1974.

*———. *Tolkien and the Silmarils.* Boston: Houghton Mifflin, 1981. The best short introduction to the *Silmarillion.*

Hildebrandt, Gregory Jr. (text), and Glenn Herdling (editor). *Greg and Tim Hildebrandt—The Tolkien Years.* New York: Watson-Guptill, 2001. An expanded version of this work was published in 2002 by Watson-Guptill.

Hillegas, Mark, editor. *Shadows of Imagination.* Revised edition. Carbondale: Southern Illinois University Press, 1979.

Honegger, Thomas, editor. *Root and Branch: Approaches Toward Understanding Tolkien.* Zurich and Berne: Walking Tree Publishers, 1999.

*Hooper, Walter, editor. With a memoir by W. H. Lewis. Revised and enlarged edition. *Letters of C. S. Lewis.* Orlando: Harcourt Brace, 1988.

———. *C. S. Lewis: Companion & Guide.* San Francisco: HarperSanFrancisco, 1996.

*Isaacs, Neil D., and Rose A. Zimbardo, editors. *Tolkien and the Critics.* Notre Dame: Notre Dame University Press, 1968. This and the collection below are still worth reading.

*———, editors. *Tolkien: New Critical Perspectives.* Lexington KY: University Press of Kentucky, 1981. A follow-up version of *Tolkien and the Critics* (above).

*Johnson, Judith A. *J. R. R. Tolkien—Six Decades of Criticism.* Westport CT: Greenwood Press, 1986.

*Kilby, Clyde S. *Tolkien and the Silmarillion.* Wheaton IL: Harold Shaw, 1976. Dated with respect to the *Silmarillion,* but still a warm, intimate little book that sheds light on Tolkien as a writer and human being.

*———, and Marjorie Lamp Mead. *Brothers and Friends: The Diaries of Major Warren Hamilton Lewis.* San Francisco: Harper & Row, 1982.

_____. "Mythic and Christian Elements in Tolkien," in John W. Montgomery, ed., *Myth, Allegory, and Gospel: An Exploration of J. R. R. Tolkien, C. S. Lewis, G. K. Chesterton, Charles Williams* (Minneapolis: Bethany, 1974) 142.

Knight, Gareth. *The Magical World of the Inklings: J. R. R. Tolkien, C. S. Lewis, Charles Williams, Owen Barfield*. Longmead Dorset: Element Books, 1990.

_____. *The Magical World of J. R. R. Tolkien*. Oceanside, CA: Sun Chalice, 2001.

Knowles, Sebastian D. G. *A Purgatorial Flame: Seven British Writers in the Second World War*. Philadelphia: University of Pennsylvania Press, 1990.

*Kocher, Paul H. *Master of Middle-earth: The Fiction of J. R. R. Tolkien*. Boston: Houghton Mifflin, 1972. An excellent older study.

_____. *A Reader's Guide to the Silmarillion*. London: Thames and Hudson, 1980. For the *Silmarillion* read Helms (above) before this book.

*Lewis, C. S. "The Hobbit" and "Tolkien's *The Lord of the Rings*." In C. S. Lewis, *Of This and Other Worlds*. Edited with a preface by Walter Hooper. London: Fount, 1989, 111–21.

*Lobdell, Jared, editor. *A Tolkien Compass*. LaSalle IN: Open Court, 1975. Includes Tolkien's "Guide to the Names in *The Lord of the Rings*," written originally for his translators.

_____. *England and Always: Tolkien's World of the Rings*. Grand Rapids MI: Eerdmans, 1981.

Maker of Middle-Earth. Charlottesville VA: Mars Hill Audio, 2002. Audiocassette. Conversations with Tom Shippey, Joseph Pearce, Ralph Wood.

Manlove, Colin. *Modern Fantasy*. Cambridge: Cambridge University Press, 1975.

_____. *The Impulse of Fantasy Literature*. Kent OH: Kent State University Press, 1983.

_____. *Christian Fantasy: From 1200 to the Present*. Notre Dame IN: University of Notre Dame Press, 1992.

Martin, Philip, editor. *The Writer's Guide to Fantasy Literature: From Dragon's Lair to Hero's Quest*. Waukesha WI: The Writer Books, 2002.

*Martinez, Michael. *Visualizing Middle-Earth*. Xlibris Corporation. (www.Xlibris.com): 2000. Some of these Internet articles are better than you would think, and the author writes well. Fannish.

*Martsch, Nancy, editor. "List of Tolkienalia." Sherman Oaks CA: Beyond Bree, 1992. Sixty pages; from the *Beyond Bree* newsletter. A must for the serious Tolkien collector.

*Matthews, Richard. *Lightning from a Clear Sky*. Van Nuys CA: Borgo Press, 1978. One of the best short books about Tolkien, with a great title, taken from a quote from C. S. Lewis.

Miller, Miriam Y. "The Lord of the Rings and Sir Gawain and the Green Knight." *Studies in Medievalism* 3/3–4 (Winter, Spring 1991): 345–65.

Mills, David. "The Writer of Our Story: Divine Providence in *The Lord of the Rings*." *Touchstone* 15/1 (January/February 2002): 22–28.

Milward, Peter. "Perchance to Touch—Tolkien as Scholar." *Mythlore* 22 (vol. 6, no. 4, Fall 1979): 31–32.

Mooney, Chris. "Kicking the Hobbit." *The American Prospect* (on-line) <<www.jrtolkien.org.uk/kicking_the_hobbit_chris_mooney>>. Volume 12, issue 10 (4 June 2001): 1–6.

Moorman, Charles W. *Precincts of Felicity: The Augustinian City of the Oxford Christians*. Gainesville: University of Florida Press, 1966.

Morse, Robert E. *Evocation of Virgil in Tolkien's Art: Geritol for the Classics*. Oak Oark IL: Bolchaz-Carducci, 1986.

_____. *Bilbo's Birthday and Frodo's Adventure of Faith*. Lincoln, NE: Writers Club Press, 2002.

Moseley, Charles. *J. R. R. Tolkien*. Plymouth England: Northcote House, 1997.

Neimark, Anne E. *Myth Maker: J. R. R. Tolkien*. Orlando: Harcourt Brace, 1996. For young readers.

Nichols, Peter, editor. *The Science Fiction Encyclopedia*. New York: Doubleday, 1979. Includes an essay on Tolkien by John Clute.

*Noel, Ruth S. *The Mythology of Middle-Earth*. Boston: Houghton Mifflin, 1977.

*———. *The Languages of Tolkien's Middle-earth*. Boston: Houghton Mifflin, 1980.

Norton, Jack E. (text). *The Fantasy Art Techniques of Tim Hildebrandt*. London: Paper Tiger, 2000 (reprint).

O'Neill, Timothy R. *The Individuated Hobbit: Jung, Tolkien and the Archetypes of Middle-Earth*. Boston: Houghton Mifflin, 1979.

*Parker, Douglass. "Hwaet We Holbytla...." *The Hudson Review* 9:4 (Winter 1956–1957): 598–609. A response to Edmund Wilson's notorious review of *The Lord of the Rings* ("Oo, Those Awful Orcs!") in *Nation*, 14 April 1956.

Parks, Louis B., and Bruce Westbrook. "From Middle-Earth to Silver Screen." *Houston Chronicle*, 16 December 2001, 8–11, 27.

Pearce, Joseph. *Tolkien: Man and Myth*. London: HarperCollins (in US, San Francisco: Ignatius Press), 1998. Focuses primarily on Tolkien as a Catholic Christian.

*———, editor. *Tolkien: A Celebration*. London: Fount (HarperCollins), 1999. Includes fourteen essays and one interview that discuss Tolkien's literary legacy and spiritual values.

Petty, Anne C. *One Ring to Bind Them All: Tolkien's Mythology*. Tuscaloosa AL: University of Alabama Press, 1979.

*Priestman, Judith. *Tolkien: Life and Legend—An Exhibition to Commemorate the Centenary of the Birth of J. R. R. Tolkien (1892–1973)*. Oxford: The Bodleian Library, 1992. Beautiful book.

Purtill, Richard L. *Lord of the Elves and Eldils: Fantasy and Philosophy in C. S. Lewis and J. R. R. Tolkien*. Grand Rapids MI: Zondervan, 1974.

———. *J. R. R. Tolkien: Myth, Morality and Religion*. San Francisco: Harper & Row, 1984.

Ready, William. *The Tolkien Relation*. Chicago: Regnery, 1968. Also published as *Understanding Tolkien and The Lord of the Rings*, New York: Paperback Library, 1969. One of the two worst books on Tolkien, with Simpson (below).

Realms of Tolkien: Images of Middle-earth. London: HarperCollins (in the US, New York: HarperPrism), 1996.

Reilly, R. J. *Romantic Religion*. Athens: University of Georgia Press, 1971.

*Reynolds, Patricia, and Glen H. GoodKnight, editors. *Proceedings of the J. R. R. Tolkien Centenary Conference—Keble College, Oxford, 1992*. Published as *Mythlore* 80 (vol. 21, no. 2, Winter 1996), and *Mallorn* 33. Altadena CA: The Mythopoeic Press, 1995. An indispensable work for the serious Tolkien reader. All of the sixty plus articles are excellent!

*Rogers, Ivor and Deborah Rogers. *J. R. R. Tolkien: A Critical Biography*. New York: Hippocrene Books, 1980. Still a very useful work, and great fun to read. Based on D. Rogers's dissertation.

Rosebury, Brian. *Tolkien: A Critical Assessment*. London: St. Martin's, 1992.

Rossi, Lee D. *The Politics of Fantasy: C. S. Lewis and J. R. R. Tolkien*. Ann Arbor MI: UMI Research Press, 1984.

Russell, Gary. *The Lord of the Rings: The Art of the Fellowship of the Ring*. Boston: Houghton Mifflin, 2002. "...not published with the approval of the Estate of the late J. R. R. Tolkien."

Sage, Alison. *The Lord of the Rings: The Fellowship of the Ring Photo Guide*. Boston: Houghton Mifflin, 2001. Includes photos from the new movie.

*Salu, Mary, and Robert T. Farrell, editors. *J. R. R. Tolkien, Scholar and Storyteller*. Ithaca NY: Cornell University Press, 1979. Includes Tolkien's Valedictory address.

*Sayer, George. *Jack: A Life of C. S. Lewis*. Second edition. Wheaton IL: Crossway Books, 1994. The best biography of C. S. Lewis by his former student and good friend.

Schindler, Tim. *Concerning Hobbits and Other Matters: Tolkien Across the Disciplines*. St. Paul, MN: University of St. Thomas, 2001.

*Scull, Christina. "*The Hobbit* considered in relation to Children's Literature Contemporary with its Writing and Publication." *Mythlore* 52, (vol. 14, no. 2, Winter 1987): 49–56.

*Shippey, Tom A. *The Road to Middle-Earth*. London: George Allen & Unwin, 1982 (second edition, London: Grafton, 1992). A superb and learned work; perhaps the best critical study of Tolkien.

*———. *J. R. R. Tolkien: Author of the Century*. London: HarperCollins, 2000; New York: Houghton Mifflin, 2001. A fine popular study of Tolkien that examines the *Lord of the Rings* as a linguistic and cultural map and as a response to the meaning of myth.

Shorto, Russell. *J. R. R. Tolkien: Man of Fantasy*. New York: Kipling, 1988.

Sibley, Brian. *The Map of Tolkien's Middle-Earth*. With images by John Howe. London: HarperCollins, 1994.

———. *There and Back Again: The Map of the Hobbit*. With images by John Howe. London: HarperCollins, 1995.

———. *The Map of Tolkien's Beleriand and the Lands of the North*. With images by John Howe. London: HarperCollins, 2000.

———. *The Lord of the Rings Official Movie Guide*. Boston: Houghton Mifflin, 2001. A 120-page guide to the new film.

———. *The Lord of the Rings: The Fellowship of the Ring's Insider's Guide*. Boston: Houghton Mifflin, 2001. For young readers.

Sirridge, Mary. "J. R. R. Tolkien and Fairy Tale Truth." *The British Journal of Aesthetics* 15/1 (Winter 1974): 81–91.

Smith, Mark E. *Tolkien's Ordinary Virtues: Exploring the Spiritual Themes of The Lord of the Rings*. Downers Grove IL: InterVarsity Press, 2002.

*Stanton, Michael N. *Hobbits, Elves, and Wizards*. New York: St. Martin's Press, 2001.

Stevens, David, and Carol D. Stevens. *J. R. R. Tolkien*. Mercer Island WA: Starmont House, 1992.

Stimpson, Catherine R. *J. R. R. Tolkien*. Columbia Essays on Modern Writers 41. New York: Columbia University Press, 1969. One of the worst books ever on Tolkien; ranks with Ready (above). Snide, condescending, ill-informed.

*Strachey, Barbara. *Journeys of Frodo: An Atlas of J. R. R. Tolkien's The Lord of the Rings*. New York: Ballantine, 1981.

Sturch, Richard. *Four Christian Fantastists: A Study of the Fantastic Writings of George MacDonald, Charles Williams, C. S. Lewis and J. R. R. Tolkien*. Zollikofen Switzerland: Walking Tree Publishers, 2001.

*Suckling, Nigel (text). *Garlands of Fantasy: The Art of Linda and Roger Garland*. Limpsfield Surrey: Dragon's World, 1994.

Tolkien, Christopher. *A History of Middle-Earth Index*. London: HarperCollins, 2002.

*Tolkien, John and Priscilla Tolkien. *The Tolkien Family Album*. Boston: Houghton Mifflin, 1992. A delightful and charming book. The pictures alone make it worthwhile.

**Tolkien's World—Paintings of Middle-earth*. London: HarperCollins, 1992; New York: MJF Books, 1992.

**Leaves From the Tree: Tolkien's Shorter Fiction*. London: Peter Roe Memorial Booklet No. 2, The Tolkien Society, 1991.

Tyler, J. E. A. *The Tolkien Companion*. New York: St. Martin's Press, 1976. Inferior to Foster (above).

Urang, Gunnar. *Shadows of Heaven: Religion and Fantasy in the Fiction of C. S. Lewis, Charles Williams and J. R. R. Tolkien.* London: SCM, 1971.

Veldman, Meredith. *Fantasy, the Bomb, and the Greening of Britain.* Cambridge: Cambridge University Press, 1994.

West, John G., editor. *Celebrating Middle-earth: The Lord of the Rings as a Defense of Western Civilization.* Seattle: Inkling Books, 2002.

*West, Richard C. *Tolkien Criticism: An Annotated Checklist.* Revised edition. Kent OH: Kent State University Press, 1981. Lists and summarizes works by and about Tolkien.

White, Michael. *J. R. R. Tolkien.* Indianapolis: Alpha Books, 2002.

Wood, Ralph. *The Gospel According to J. R. R. Tolkien.* Louisville KY: Westminster/John Knox Press, forthcoming, 2003.

Wyatt, Joan. *A Middle-Earth Album: Paintings.* New York: Simon & Schuster, 1979.

*Wyke-Smith, E. A. *The Marvelous Land of Snergs.* Baltimore: Old Earth Books, 1996.

Zaentz, Saul, Production Company. *The Film Book of J. R. R. Tolkien's The Lord of the Rings.* New York: Ballantine, 1978.

*Zipes, Jack, editor. *The Oxford Companion to Fairy Tales.* Oxford: Oxford University Press, 2000.

APPENDIX FOUR

Tolkien Journals, Newsletters, Societies, And Archives

Amon Hen (first issue December 1972) is the bimonthly bulletin of the Tolkien Society and contains reviews, announcements, and references to Tolkien collectibles. Its cost is about $41.00 US, and it can be ordered the Tolkien Society web link (www.tolkiensociety.org/index.html) or from Trevor Reynolds (membership secretary), 65 Wentworth Crescent, Ash Vale GU1Z 5LF, Surrey, England. The annual academic publication of the Society is *Mallorn*.

Arda is the quarterly journal of the Swedish Tolkien Society. For information, contact: Anders Stenstrom (editor), Stiernheilmsgatan 5 B, 753 33, Upsala, Sweden, or the US Regional agent: Gary Hunnewell, 2030 San Pedro Dr., Arnold, MO 63010.

Athelas is the magazine of the Danish Tolkien society. It can be ordered from Peter Jacome, Nedenomsvej 14, Hosterkob, 2970 Horsholm, Denmark.

Beyond Bree is the monthly newsletter of the Tolkien special interest group of American Mensa, a high IQ society. It contains short articles on Tolkien and his works, plus reviews of books, games, films, and events by, about, or inspired by Tolkien and his works, and general fantasy that might of interest to the Tolkien fan. Cost: $12.00 per year. Order from Nancy Martsch, P.O. Box 55372, Sherman Oaks, CA 91413. Online: beyondbree@yahoo.com

The Bodleian Library in Oxford (UK) houses the bulk of Tolkien's vast literary and manuscript legacy. Contact Dr. Judith Priestman, Department of Western Manuscripts, Broad Street, Oxford OX1 3BG, England; (01865) 277046. E-mail: modern.papers@bodley.ox.ac.uk; online: http://rsl.ox.ac.uk

The Canadian C. S. Lewis Journal is published bi-annually (May and October), and publishes reviews, news, and scholarly articles on (mostly) Lewis, Tolkien, and the other Inklings. Edited by Dr. Roger Stronstad. Yearly subscriptions are $15.00 (US) and inquiries should be made to the *Canadian C. S. Lewis Journal*, c/o Western Pentecostal College, Box 1700, Abbotsford, British Columbia V2S 7E7, Canada, or to PO Box 70, Sumas, WA 98295.

CSL: The Bulletin of the New York C. S. Lewis Society is published monthly. The society publishes semi-scholarly articles primarily on Lewis and his friends, including Tolkien. Includes reviews, society meeting news, announcements, letters, and miscellanea. The editor is Robert Trexler, and the cost is $12.00 per year. Contact Clara Sarrocco for subscriptions and back issues at 84-23 77th Ave., Glendale, NY 11385.

Eredain is the Swiss Tolkien Society, founded in 1986. It edits a fanzine, "Aglared" (German and English) and a newsletter on a regular basis. For information, contact The Swiss Tolkien Society, EREDAIN, Postfach 1916, CH-8021 Zurich; e-mail: swisstolkiensociety@usa.net

Forodrim is the Stockholm Tolkien Society, founded in 1972, and is a "non-confessional, non-political" association for people who love Tolkien. For information, contact The Stockholm

Tolkien Journals, Societies, Newsletters and ARchives

Tolkien Society, Agnegatan 45, SE 11229, Stockholm, Sweden. E-mail: curatrix@hotmail.com; online:www.algonet.sel/~arador/foroden

The Italian Tolkien Society was founded in February 1994. It publishes two journals, *Terra di Mezzo* (March and September) and *Minas Tirith* (September and June). Offers articles, surveys, and studies on Tolkien, his work, and his sources. Once a year the Society sponsors a Hobbiton, which includes lectures, meetings, talks, dances, theatrical performances, games, and costumes "related to Middle-earth." The Silmaril Prize is awarded yearly for paintings and drawings; the best pictures are published in a calendar.

The Marquette University Special Collections—J. R. R. Tolkien, is the American archive of many Tolkien manuscripts and rare editions. Contact: Matt Blessing, Acting department Head/University Archivist, Marquette University Libraries, 1415 W. Wisconsin Ave., PO Box 3141, Milwaukee, WI 53201-3141; 414 288-7256. E-mail: matt.blessing@marquette.edu

Mythlore is the quarterly journal of the Mythopoeic Society. Founded in 1969, edited by Dr. Ted J. Sherman. Contains reviews and mostly scholarly essays covering the genre of fantasy and myth, with emphasis on C. S. Lewis, Charles Williams, and Tolkien. *Mythprint* is the Society's monthly newsletter, and *Mythic Circle* is its literary magazine. All (plus back issues) can be ordered from Lee Speth, The Mythopoeic Society Orders Department, 920 N. Atlantic Blvd., #E, Alhambra, CA 91801. Information: Edith Crowe, Mythopoeic Society, P.O. Box 320486, San Francisco, CA 94132-0486. E-mail: ecrowe@email.sjsu.edu; online: http://www.mythsoc.org/

Orcrist is the journal of the University of Wisconsin Tolkien Society. Appears irregularly and has not been published in some years, but an index of the contents of all issues can be viewed online (http://www.sit.wisc.edu/~tolksoc). Contact Dr. Richard West via e-mail (rwkfw@macc.wisc.edu).

Parma Eldalamberon is a journal of linguistic studies of fantasy literature, "especially of the Elvish languages and nomenclature in the works of J. R. R. Tolkien." Published at irregular intervals, and "publishes new primary materials from the Tolkien manuscript archives." Back issues: Chris Gilson, 500-C North Civic Dr., Walnut Creek, CA 94596; (510) 945-6351; E-mail: harpwire@netcom.com; online: http://www.eldalamberon.com/parma9

Ravenhill is the newsletter of the New England Tolkien Society and can be ordered from Gary Hunnewell, 2030 San Pedro, Arnold, MO 63010; e-mail: sgh1@cec.wustl.edu

SEVEN: An Anglo-American Literary Review is an annual journal published by the Marion E. Wade Center of Wheaton College. Contains scholarly articles on C. S. Lewis, Charles Williams, G. K. Chesterton, George MacDonald, Dorothy L. Sayers, Owen Barfield, and Tolkien, plus reviews and announcements. Cost: $12.50. Order from The Marion E. Wade Center, Wheaton College, Wheaton, IL 60187-5593.

The Tolkien Collector is a quarterly magazine that covers all aspects of Tolkien collecting, with emphasis on non-English collectible books/publications. Cost: $11.00 per year US; $12.00 surface mail outside the US; $14.00 airmail worldwide. Order: Christina Scull, 30 Talbott Road, Williamstown, MA 01267. E-mail: W. Hammond wayne.g.hammond@williams.edu

Tolkien Studies is a new annual journal and is scheduled to begin publication in Autumn 2002. It will be edited by Verlyn Flieger, Douglas Anderson, and Michael Drout. E-mail inquiries to Dr. Michael Drout at mdrout@wheatoncollge.edu

Unquendor is the Danish/Flemish Tolkien society, founded in 1981. Information: Rene van Rossenberg, Unquendor Information, Seringen Straat 140, 2404 ET Alphen a/d Rijn, Holland (or e-mail: rene@tolkienshop.com). Rossenberg owns The Tolkien Shop, one of the largest Tolkien (books, games, tapes, memorabilia, art, etc.) mail-order businesses in the world.

Vinyar Tengwar is the quarterly newsletter of the Tolkien Elvish Linguistic Society. An academic journal, it includes articles, conference announcements, and news of new publications. It can be ordered from Carl F. Hostetter at 2509 Ambling Circle, Crofton, MD 21114; E-mail to aelfwine@erols.com

APPENDIX FIVE

Tolkien On The Internet

Tolkien web sites usually fall into three general categories: (1) sites devoted to Middle-earth works, particularly the *Lord of the Rings*;(2) sites that focus on Tolkien's life and career, including the overall body of his work; and (3) sites that focus on and discuss (reviews, chats, opinions, etc.) the recent movie directed by Peter Jackson, the *Lord of the Rings: The Fellowship of the Ring*.

The J. R. R. Tolkien Information page: www.csclub.uwaterloo.ca/u/relipper/tolkien/rootpage

Ultimate Tolkien Fan-site: http://hem1.passagen.se/josa99/tolkien

Grey Havens—Ultimate Tolkien Resource Web Page: www.bayside.net/users/Tolkien/

A Guide to Tolkien Discussion on the Web: www.xenite.org/talk/Tolkien

The LOR Official Movie Site: www.lordoftherings.net

Tolkien Enterprises: www.tolkien-ent.com

Tolkien Language Mailing List: www.dcs.ed.ak.uk/misc/local/TolkLang

Elvish Linguistic Fellowship: www.elvish.org

Middle-earth role-playing & Tolkien research: http://dcs.ed.ak.uk/misc/local/TolkLang/articles

Annotated Tolkien Index: www.yahoo.com/Arts/Humanities/Literature/Genres/Science_Fiction_Fantasy_and_Horror/Authors/Tolkien_J_R_R_/

Hypertextualized Tolkien FAQ: www.daimi.aau.dk/~bouvin/tolkienfaq

Tolkien Timeline: gollum.usask.ca/tolkien/index

Australian Tolkien Page: www.dcscomp.com.au/jewell/tolkien/oxford/index

Stockton Retreat Center: www.idiscover.co.uk/stockton/tolkien

The Tolkien Shop: www.xs4all.nl/~rossnbrg/

Tolkien Music List: www.vikings.lv/~witchcraft/jrrt/; Contains the lyrics of 376 individual songs and 130 "larger works" based on Tolkien and Middle-earth.

Tolkien Collecting Resources: www.tolkiencollector.com

Gazing Upon Everlasting Day: The Catholic Vision of JRRT: www.geocities.com/Athens/Column/7573/

Middle-earth Toys: www.middlearthtoys.com

History of Middle-earth: www.gofree.indigo.ie/~warren/Tolkien/History/History.html

The Tolkien Trail: tolkientrail.com

The Encyclopedia of Arda: www.glyphweb.com/arda

Middle-Earth Vault: mevault.ign.com

Tolkien in Oxford: www.jrrtolkien.org.uk

Usenet Newsgroups: www.alt.fan.tolkien & www.rec.arts.books.tolkien

The Tolkien Archives: www.tolkien-archives.com

Listing of recordings by/about Tolkien and his works: www.planet-tolkien.com

A chronological bibliography about Tolkien: www.hem.passagen.se/annuvin/tolklist

www.marquette.edu/library/collections/archives/mss/jrrt/mss-jrrt-sc

APPENDIX SIX

A Listing Of Recordings By And About Tolkien And His Works Including Films

At the Tobacconist's. Earliest known recording of Tolkien, with Professor A. Lloyd James (University of London), English Lesson 20, London, Linguaphone Conversational Course: English. Sixteen 78 rpm long-playing records with four teaching booklets. Tolkien reads and dramatizes in lessons 20 and 30, of 30 total. London: The Linguaphone Institute, June 1930.

J. R. R. Tolkien Interviewed. CD format, interview by Denis Gueroult in 1964, 27 minutes 40 seconds. London: BBC, 1980. The same recording as *The Author Speaks: Basil Bunting and J. R. R. Tolkien*, BBC Study Tapes (audiocassette), 1960.

The Homecoming of Beorhtnoth—Read by J. R. R. Tolkien. CD format, preceded by a commentary by Christopher Tolkien and a later reading by him of the sequel, "Beorhtnoth's Death." Distributed by Spitter Spatter Sounds, Holland.

J. R. R. T: A Portrait of J. R. R. Tolkien. PAL/VHS videocassette, 110 minutes. Includes interviews with Christopher, John, and Priscilla Tolkien, Rayner Unwin, Tom Shippey, Father Robert Murray, Verlyn Flieger, and Queen Margrethe of Denmark, plus excerpts from an interview with Tolkien, made from *Tolkien in Oxford*, made for the BBC in 1968. Narrated by Judi Dench, directed by Derek Bailey. Produced by the Tolkien Partnership by Landseer Film & Television Productions, London, 1992. Contains 50 minutes more material than the earlier 60-minute Central Television version broadcast on cable in the US and made in 1984. A superlative video. Films for the Humanities and Sciences (Princeton, NJ) produced in 1996 a 38-minute edited version of the 1992 Landseer production.

National Geographic Beyond the Movie—The Lord of the Rings: The Fellowship of the Ring. VHS videocassette, DVD, 60 minutes. Produced by Arden Entertainment (New Line Cinema, an AOL Time Warner company) for National Geographic Television, 2002.

J. R. R. Tolkien: Master of the Rings. Issued in two VHS videocassettes (80 minutes total), a DVD/Booklet set with music by Rick Wakeman, and a single DVD package; by Eagle Media, 2002. Contains scenes from Tolkien calendars and books illustrated by the Brothers Hildebrandt.

J. R. R. Tolkien: Origin of the Rings. Issued in one VHS videocassette (63 minutes) by Trinity Home Entertainment, 2002. Directed by Sean Buckley. Labeled as an "unauthorized version."

J. R. R. Tolkien: An Audio Portrait. Two CD format (110 minutes), presented by Brian Sibley. Published by the BBC Radio Collection (London), distributed by Dell Audio Publishing (New York), 2002. Interviews with Tolkien and people who knew him.

The Hobbit

Gandalf the Grey & The Grey Wizard Am I. LP records. Independently produced and probably made in the 1960s.

The Hobbits, Down to Middle-earth. LP format, Decca Records, circa 1968.

Two Sides of Leonard Nimoy. 45 PM recording and LP format; includes "The Ballad of Bilbo Baggins." Dot Records, c. 1968. Re-released on CD format by Rev-Old Records, 1993, under new title *Highly Illogical.*

In 1975 Caedmon published (TC 1477) a long-playing record, "J. R. R. Tolkien Reads and Sings his The Hobbit and The Fellowship of the Ring," with J. R. R. Tolkien reading sections from his works. This record (liner notes by George Sayer) was originally recorded in Sayer's home in Malvern in 1952. Several abridged editions have been produced by Caedmon (the latest 1999) on audiocassette, titled "J. R. R. Tolkien Reads The Hobbit and The Fellowship of the Ring."

In 1997 BBC Worldwide Ltd. issued a sixtieth anniversary "newly mastered collector's edition" of the *Hobbit* on compact disk, with "an original score written for Renaissance-era instruments, outstanding ensemble acting, and innovative sound techniques."

The Hobbit. Animated film, Rankin/Bass productions, 1977, 76 minutes, color. Voices for characters include Orson Bean, John Huston, Otto Preminger, and Glenn Yarbrough. Music by Maury Laws, lyrics written and adapted by Jules Bass, distributed by Warner Brothers. Video version published in 1991 by Warner Home Video.

The Hobbit. 33 1/3-rpm record, produced by Disneyland/Vista Records, 1977. "Based on the original version of The Hobbit written by J. R. R. Tolkien" and the Rankin/Bass animated movie. Includes twenty-four-page read-along booklet.

The Hobbit. Produced by The Mind's Eye, audiocassette and CD format, six cassettes and four CDs each. Novato CA: Soundelux Audio Publishing, 1994.

There and Back Again: Harp Music Inspired by J. R. R. Tolkien's The Hobbit. CD format, harp music composed and played by Kim Skovbye and others, 67 minutes. Fonix Music, 1997.

In a Hole in the Ground There Lived a Hobbit. Audiocassette format, radio play by Tolkien's biographer Humphrey Carpenter on Tolkien's years in Leeds. Distributed by Spitter Spatter Sounds, Holland, 1992.

The Hobbit. Read by Martin Shaw, abridged, four audiocassettes, six hours playing time. Harper Collins Audio Books, 1993. Also published on four audiocassettes by Durkin Hayes Audio, Ontario, 1993 and titled *The Hobbit—Performance by Martin Shaw.*

There and Back Again: Harp Music Inspired by J. R. R. Tolkien's The Hobbit. CD format, 67.26 minutes, composed and played by Kim Skovbye and others. Arhus: Fonix Music, 1997.

BBC Radio Presents The Hobbit. Four audiocassettes, BBC Audio, London, and BDD Publishing, New York, 1988. Also produced in CD format, 1997, a dramatization by Michael Kilgariff on four CDs, with a fifth included with theme and incidental music. Produced by John Powell, 1997.

Bilbo, Music Inspired by The Hobbit—Composed by Psr Lindh & Bjsrn Johannsson. CD format, Sweden, Crimsonic Label.

The Hobbit. Unabridged, CD format, 10 CDS, 11 hours and 15 minutes, read by Rob Inglis, BBC. Was re-released by Recorded Books in July 2001 in audio format, 7 cassettes, 11 hours.

The Hobbit. Four CD format (290 minutes), adapted and directed by Bob Lewis. Published by the High Bridge Co., St. Paul, MN. Cover art by John Howe.

The Lord of the Rings

Music Inspired by the Lord of the Rings. Music by Bo Hansson. LP record with Tolkien poster, Buddha Records, 1972. Also produced on CD format, Albany NY: One Way Records.

In 1975 Caedmon published (TC 1478) a long-playing record, "J. R. R. Tolkien Reads and Sings his Lord of the Rings—The Two Towers and The Return of the King," with J. R. R. Tolkien reading sections from his works. Much of this record, with liner notes by George Sayer, was originally recorded in Sayer's home in Malvern in 1952. An abridged version was produced by Caedmon in 1999 on audiocassette, titled "J. R. R. Tolkien—The Lord of the Rings." In 1992 Caedmon produced the "J. R. R. Tolkien Audio Collection" in four cassettes, which combined Tolkien's readings from "Poems and Songs of Middle-earth" and "The Road Goes Ever On" with Christopher Tolkien's readings of the *Silmarillion*; these were released in CD format in 2001. In 1978 Fantasy Records published a two-record music album based on the *Lord of the Rings* animated film, composed and conducted by Leonard Rosenman.

J. R. R. Tolkien's The Lord of the Rings. 1978, animated movie produced by Saul Zaentz, directed by Ralph Bakshi, Republic Pictures and Fantasy Films, Los Angeles. Released through United Artists, 130 minutes, color. Many reviewers called this film disappointing, primarily because of superficiality, names of characters being changed, alterations in Tolkien's original text and scenes (bad plotting), "dreadful music," and poor editing. Published as video by Republic Pictures, 1993.

The Original Motion Picture Soundtrack from J. R. R. Tolkien's The Lord of the Rings. From the Saul Zaentz production, directed by Ralph Bakshi, screenplay by Chris Conkling and Peter S. Beagle. Two picture LP records, Fantasy Records, 1978. Fifteen selections composed and conducted by Leonard Rosenman, including "Theme from *The Lord of the Rings*" and "Escape to

Rivendell." Also published on regular LP, cassette tape, 8-track, and CD formats.

The Return of the King. Animated film, Rankin/Bass productions, 1979, 96 minutes, color. Voices for characters include Orson Bean, Theodore Bickel, William Conrad, John Huston, and Glenn Yarbrough. Music by Maury Laws, lyrics written and adapted by Jules Bass, distributed by Warner Brothers. Video version published in 1993 by Warner Home Video.

The Return of the King. 33 1/3-rpm record, produced by Disneyland/Vista Records, 1980. "Based on the original version of The Hobbit and The Return of the King by J. R. R. Tolkien" and the Rankin/Bass animated movie. Includes twenty-four-page read-along booklet.

The Lord of the Rings—The Dutch Royal Military Band, Conducted by Pierre Kuijpers. CD format, KMK & Ottavo Recordings, The Hague, The Netherlands, 1989.

The Return of the King. Unabridged, 11 audiocassettes, 15 1/2 hours. Read by Rob Inglis. Recorded Books, Prince Frederick, MD, 1990.

The Music of Middle-Earth. 88-minute audiocassette, "Instrumental Music for J. R. R. Tolkien's The Lord of the Rings." Instrumental settings of fifty songs and poems from the *Lord of the Rings* and *The Adventures of Tom Bombadil* by Gene Hargrove; Old Forest Sounds, 1991.

Journey of the Dunadan. CD format, combines music with narration and sound effects. Based on *The Lord of the Rings*, by the progressive rock group Glass Hammer, Arion Records, 1993.

J. R. R. Tolkien's Classic Trilogy The Lord of the Rings—Produced by The Mind's Eye. Audiocassette and CD format, twelve cassettes and nine CDs each. Novato CA: Soundelux Audio Publishing, 1994.

The Lord of the Rings—Symphonie no 1. Composed by Johan de Meij, conducted by Rene Joly, Ensemble Vents et Percussion de Quebec. CD format, ATMA Records, Quebec, 1997. Also performed by the US Air Force Band of Flight in 1993, by the

Osaka Japan Symphonic Band in 1992, by the Danish Concert Band in 1995, and by La Aristica Bunol (Mexico) in 1999. Reissued in 2001 as *Symphony No. 1—Inspired by The Lord of the Rings*, composed by de Meij, the London Symphony Orchestra, conducted by David Warble. CD format, Madacy Entertainment Group, 2001. Added "The Sorcerer's Apprentice" by Paul Dukas.

The Lord of the Rings. BBC Radio Collection, 13 audiocassettes, dramatization by Brian Sibley and Michael Bakewell, starring Ian Holm and twenty-five other performers. Originally broadcast on BBC Radio 4 in 1981. Reissued in CD format (13 CDs) by the BBC in 1995.

Enteli Live. CD format, Amigo Misik AB, 1997. Enteli is a Swedish group, and the CD includes an improvisation based on Enteli's score for the Swedish National Radio Theatre performance of the *Lord of the Rings*.

The Return of the King—The Soundtrack of the Rankin-Bass Production. CD format, from the LP recording of 1980. Distributed by Spitter Spatter Sounds, Holland.

An Evening in Rivendell With the Tolkien Ensemble: Selected Songs from The Lord of the Rings by J. R. R. Tolkien. Composed by Caspar Reiff & Peter Hall, CD format. The Ensemble is composed of graduates and final year students of the Royal Danish Academy of Music and professional musicians from the Danish folk-music scene. Denmark: ClassicO Records, 1997. In 2001 ClassicO released *A Night in Rivendell with the Tolkien Ensemble*, and in 2001 both CDs were released in a pack as *J. R. R. Tolkien—24 Songs from The Lord of the Rings*.

The Starlit Jewel—Songs from J. R. R. Tolkien's The Lord of the Rings and The Hobbit—Music by Marion Zimmer Bradley. Performed by Avalon Rising, CD format, Flowinglass Music, 2000. A limited edition of 2,000 copies, endorsed by the estate of Tolkien. Was produced on one audiocassette tape by Flowinglass Music in 1996. Avalon Rising is a San Francisco area medieval/folk ensemble, and most of the songs were performed at the 1996 Mythopoeic Conference in Boulder, Colorado.

The Fellowship of the Ring and *The Two Towers*. Both unabridged, 12 audiocassettes, 20 hours, "includes the original author Forward"; read by Rob Inglis. Prince Frederick MD: Recorded Books, July 2001.

The Fellowship of the Ring. A "full-cast dramatization" on 4 CDs. BBC Radio (Random House Audio), 2001.

Lord of the Rings Trilogy. 3 CDs, "Lord of the Rings Overture," "Legend of the Hobbit," and "March of the Dark Lords." Composed and directed by Sir James Pitton-Smith. Dressed to Kill Music, 2001.

The Lord of the Rings—The Fellowship of the Ring. One CD, original motion picture soundtrack. Music composed, orchestrated and conducted by Howard Shore, Reprise Music, 2001.

Music Inspired by Middle Earth. One CD, 13 songs, featuring David Arkenstone. Neo Pacifica, 2001.

The Fellowship of the Ring. Three CD format (210 minutes), adapted by Bernard Mayes. Published by the High Bridge Co., St. Paul, MN. Cover art by John Howe. "The Original American Production."

The Two Towers. Three CD format (210 minutes), adapted by Bernard Mayes. Published by the High Bridge Co., St. Paul, MN. Cover art by John Howe. "The Original American Production."

The Return of the King. Three CD format (210 minutes), adapted by Bernard Mayes. Published by the High Bridge Co., St. Paul, MN. Cover art by John Howe. "The Original American Production."

The Lord of the Rings—The Fellowship of the Ring. Issued in one VHS videocassette and two DVD format. The Peter Jackson movie (Full Screen version, 178 minutes), produced and distributed by New Line Home Entertainment, 2002, soundtrack by Enya. The DVD version contains a 10-minute preview of The *Lord of the Rings—The Two Towers* (December 2002), "original theatrical trailers and TV spots," a preview of Electric Arts' video game *The Lord of the Rings—The Two Towers* (November 2002), "featurettes of the locales and locations of Middle-earth" (including interviews with the actors), and an "inside look" at the Special Extended DVD version (four discs) of the movie, due in December, 2002.

The Silmarillion

In 1977 and 1978 Caedmon Records issued two recordings by Christopher Tolkien reading selections from the *Silmarillion: Of Beren and Lúthien* (TC 1564, reissued by Caedmon in 1977 in the *J. R. R. Tolkien Soundbook*, with booklet and poster map) and *Of the Darkening of Valinor and of the Flight of the Noldor* (TC1579).

The Silmarillion. Audiocassette and CD format, read by Robert Shaw, unabridged. Five packages of four cassettes and four CDs each, about 15 hours. HarperCollins Audio (London). The titles of the individual packages are volume one, *Of the Valor and the Valinor before the Darkening* (chapters 1–8); volume two, *Of Elves and Men in Middle-earth* (chapters 9–16); volume three, *Of Beren and Luthien and the Ruin of Beleriand* (chapters 17–20); volume four, *Of Turin and Tuor and the Fall of Beleriand* (chapters 21–24); and volume five, *Of the Fall of Numenor and the Rings of Power*. In October of 1998 a boxed set of all five volumes was published as the *Silmarillion Gift Pack*. In the US, Bantam Doubleday Dell issued the recording on audiocassette and CD, in three volumes, each with four cassettes or five CDs.

Other Works

The Road Goes Ever On: A Song Cycle. Published as "Poems and Songs of Middle Earth" on long-playing stereo record by Caedmon Records (TC 1231), New York, 1967. Includes Tolkien reading from "The Adventures of Tom Bombadil," with "The Road Goes Ever On" sung by William Elven and Donald Swann at piano. Liner notes by W. H. Auden. In 1997 a CD of the performance was published by Jan Krediet Music Productions, Rotterdam, the Netherlands. The cover painting of the music notes booklet, "Weathertop," was by the Dutch artist Cor Blok, whose work was much admired by Tolkien. The music was performed by the choir and baritone Jan Krediet of the Pilgrim Fathers Church in Delfshaven, The Netherlands, 10 June 1995. Includes booklet that contains the text of a lecture about Tolkien by Rene van Rossenberg (Dutch Tolkien Society) and the texts of the music in English and Dutch.

The Inklings: C. S. Lewis, J. R. R. Tolkien, Charles Williams, and Their Friends. The book by Humphrey Carpenter, unabridged, nine 90-minute audiocassettes, read by Bernard Mayes. Produced in 1989 and distributed by Blackstone Audio Books (www.blackstoneaudio.com) and North Star Audio Books, PO Box 129, Van Wyck, SC 29744, (800) 522-2979.

Donald Swann's Alphabetaphon. Three audiocassettes, a musical autobiography of Swann. Includes "Bilbo's Last Song" and "I Sit Beside the Fire" (from Book Two of the *Fellowship of the Ring*). Albert House Cassettes, 1990.

The Only Flanders & Swann Video. Includes "I Sit beside the Fire"; VHS (European format), Picture Music International, 1992.

Tales From the Perilous Realm. Two audiocassettes, Brian Sibley's dramatizations of *Farmer Giles of Ham*, *Leaf By Niggle*, *Smith of Wootton Major*, and *The Adventures of Tom Bombadil*. BBC Radio Collection, 1993.

The Hobbitons Singing 3 Songs from the Shire. Audiocassette, semi-professional recording by the Dutch Tolkien Society *Unquendor* smial Ar Caras, Nijmegen, The Netherlands, 1993. The three songs are "Trollsong," "The Man in the Moon," and "The Bath Song." In 1996 the group produced a CD called *Songs from Middle Earth* (Ar Caras).

J. R. R. Tolkien's Songs from Middle-earth. Sung by the Hobbitons (Dutch singing group), music by Ron Ploeg, Willem van Wordragen, and Stephen Oliver. CD format, 16 of Tolkien's poems, including "Bilbo's Song," "Goblin Town," and "The Man in the Moon Stayed up too Late." *Unquendor*, Nijmegen, The Netherlands, 1996.

Letters From Father Christmas. Two audiocassettes, a reading (about two hours) by Derek Jacobi of the *Father Christmas Letters*, with John Moffatt as Polar Bear and Christian Rodska as Ilbereth. HarperCollins Audio, 1997.

Pearl and Sir Orfeo. Two audiocassettes, a reading (about two hours) of Tolkien's translations of the Middle English poems by Terry Jones. HarperCollins Audio Books, 1997.

Sir Gawain and the Green Knight. Two audiocassettes, a reading (about 2 1/2 hours) of Tolkien's translation of the Middle English poem by Terry Jones. HarperCollins Audio Books, 1997.

Roverandom. Two audiocassettes, an abridged reading (about 21/2 hours) by Derek Jacobi. HarperCollins Audio Books, 1998; also published by Houghton Mifflin, 2001.

Farmer Giles of Ham & Other Stories. Two audiocassettes, an unabridged reading (about three hours) of *Farmer Giles of Ham, Smith of Wootton Major*, and *Leaf By Niggle* by Derek Jacobi. HarperCollins Audio Books, 1999; also published by Houghton Mifflin, 2001.

Index

"A Elbereth Gilthoniel" 98
A Finnish Grammar (C. N. E. Eliot) 76
A Middle English Vocabulary 106-107
"A Secret Vice" 134-38
Ace Books 20, 63-64, 183
The Adventures of Tom Bombadil 19, 94-97, 98, 145, 186
"Ælfwine of England" 164
"Ainulindalë" 82, 161, 167, 175, 176
"Akallabeth" 82
"Aldarion and Erendis: The Mariner's Wife" 156
Alice's Adventures in Wonderland (Carroll) 4, 30
"The Ambarkanta" 82, 161, 166
Amon Hen 118, 128, 185
The Ancrene Wisse 12, 18, 19, 125-27
Andersen, Hans Christian ("The Steadfast Tin Soldier") 53
Angles and Britons: O'Donnell Lectures 123

The Annals of Beleriand 12, 166
The Annals of Valinor 12, 166
The Annotated Hobbit 91
"Aotrou and Itroun" 12
Apolaustics (club) 7
Aragorn 158, 161, 169, 170, 188
Arwen 6, 161
"Athrabeth Finrod Ah Andreth" 176
At the Drop of Another Hat (Swann) 98
Auden, W. H. 9, 26, 43, 59, 95, 98, 125
Austin, Ruth 157

Baggins, Bilbo 28, 34, 35, 36, 68, 73, 94, 102, 169, 173
Barfield, Owen 13, 174
Barrett, Anne 85
The Battle at Helm's Deep 171
The Battle of Maldon 92, 155
Battle of the Somme 8
Baynes, Pauline 40, 43, 90, 95, 102
Bent, William O. 30

Beare, Rhona 151
Beren 148, 162, 165, 166
Beowulf 26, 31, 32, 39, 93, 113, 114, 115, 116, 117, 131, 132, 133, 143, 164
Beowulf and the Finnesburg Fragment 14
"Beowulf: The Monsters and the Critics" 14, 39, 113-18
"Bilbo's Last Song at the Grey Havens" 99, 101-103
Birmingham 2, 3, 4
Bliss, Alan 132, 133
Bloemfontein 2, 3
Blok, Cor 146
Boccaccio 111
The Bodleian Library 54, 117, 145, 147, 151
Boethius 112
The Book of Fairy Poetry 91
"The Book of Foxrook" 136
The Book of Lost Tales 7, 8 53, 80, 89, 154, 161, 162-64, 167, 178, 179, 180, 181
"The Book of the Silmarils" 76
Boucher, Anthony 183
Bournemouth 21, 22
"The Bovadium Fragments" 19
Bradley, Henry 104, 106, 144
Bratman, David 180
Bretherton, Christopher 167
Brewerton, George 5
The British Library 151
Brogan, Hugh 146
The Brothers Grimm 31
Burchfield, Robert 106

Campbell, Joseph (*The Hero With a Thousand Faces*) 70-71
Carpenter, Humphrey 24, 33, 46, 80, 101, 109, 134, 136, 144, 148, 169, 174
Carr, Charlie 22
Castell, Daphne 21
Celeborn 156
Chance, Jane 45
Chapman, Vera 110
Chaucer 107, 144
Chesterton, G. K. 120
The Children of Húrin 161, 162
Cicero (*De Officiis*) 129
"Cirion and Eorl" 21
Clevedon, Somerset 6
Coalbiters (club) 10
Coghill, Nevill 79
Coleridge 6, 189
Crabbe, Katharyn 39, 70-71, 121, 140, 160, 165
Cragie, William 106, 144
Crist 77

Dagnall, Susan 27, 28
Dante, 111
d'Ardenne, Simonne 11, 32
Davis, Norman 108
The Denham Tracts (Denham) 33
Dickens, Charles 120
"The Disaster of the Gladden Fields" 21
Drout, Michael 117
"The Drowning of Anadûnê" 175
Duane, Diane 184
Duriez, Colin 167

Dyson, H. V. D. ("Hugo") 13, 16, 60, 79, 99, 174

Eagle and Child (pub) 13, 16
The Earthly Paradise (Morris) 78
Eaton, Anne 30
Eddison, E. R. 15, 183
The Elder Edda 31, 129
Elven, William 20, 98
"English and Welsh" 18, 122-25
English School Syllabus 12
Eriol 163
"Errantry" 13, 145
Esperanto 135
Essays Presented to Charles Williams (Lewis) 118
Essays and Studies 12, 93, 126
Everett, Caroline 141
Exeter College 7, 19, 77, 79, 144, 163

The Fairie Queene 188
"The Fall of Arthur" 13
"The Fall of Gondolin" 79, 155, 163
Farmer Giles of Ham 13, 14, 37-42, 44, 63, 82, 83, 84, 95, 96, 105, 168
Farrell, Robert T. 142
Farrer, Austin 20
Farrer, Katharine 20
The Father Christmas Letters 32, 47-50, 145, 146
The Fellowship of the Ring 18, 57, 95, 97, 98, 145, 146, 157, 169

Fifty New Poems for Children 91
The Fight at Finnesburg 132

Finn and Hengest - The Fragment and the Episode 132-33
Five Children and It (Nesbit) 53
Flanders, Michael 98
Flieger, Verlyn 13, 97
"The Flower of the Trees" 92
'The Fords of Isen" 20

Foster, Mike 74
Foster, Richard 159
Fourteenth Century Verse and Prose (Sisam) 106

Galadriel 69, 129, 156, 157, 170
Gandalf 6, 31, 34, 35, 36, 68, 73, 158, 169, 170, 171
Gamgee, Sam 147
Gilson, Robert 6, 8
"Goblin Feet" 91
The Golden Key (MacDonald, story and book) 20, 42, 46
Goldstein, Lisa 184
Gollum 21, 31, 35, 59, 69, 172, 188
"Good Luck to You" 92
Gordon, E. V. 8, 92, 108, 144
Gordon, Ida L. 109
Graves, Robert 91
Great Expectations (Dickens) 189
Green, Roger Lancelyn 42
Greeves, Arthur 26, 81

Gresham, Joy 17, 18, 149
Griffiths, Elaine 11, 27, 28
Gulliver's Travels 105

Hall, John R. Clark 116
Hammond, Wayne 39, 48, 49, 54, 61-62, 84, 147
Hardie, Colin 23
Havard, R. E. 13, 174
Heaney, Seamus 113
Hill, Joy 22, 84, 85, 98, 101, 102, 103
The History of Middle-Earth 159-81, 185
Hitler, Adolf 135
Hobb, Robin 186
The Hobbit 14, 16, 20, 22, 26-37, 40, 53, 55, 56, 57, 58, 63, 66, 78, 81, 82, 89, 91, 95, 102, 126, 145, 147, 150, 154, 158, 159, 166, 168, 169, 179, 180
Holy Trinity Church 20
"The Homecoming of Beorhtnoth Beorhthelm's Son" 44, 92-94
The House of the Wolfings (Morris) 77, 78
Humanities Research Center (University of Texas) 151
Huxley, Julian 32

Incledon, Mary and Marjorie 135
The Inklings 13, 15, 150, 173, 175, 181

The Jerusalem Bible 20, 127-29

"J. R. R. Tolkien: Narnian Exile" (Christopher) 185
J. R. R. Tolkien: Scholar and Storyteller (Salu and Farrell) 142
J. R. R. Tolkien: Author of the Century (Shippey) 183

The Kalevala 76
Keble College 25
Kenny, Anthony 128
Ker, W. P. 114
Kilby, Clyde S. 21, 46, 51
King Edward's School 4
Knowles, Sebastian 142
Kocher, Paul 45, 94, 140, 155

Lambeth Palace Library 151
Lang, Andrew 4, 119
"The Lay of Eärendil" 77
"The Lay of Leithian" 10, 80, 82, 161, 164
The Lays of Beleriand 80, 89, 155, 164-65, 178, 180
"Leaf By Niggle" 11, 15, 44, 126, 138-42
Leeds University 8, 47, 80, 92, 106, 107
"The Legend of Worming Hall" 38
"Leithian" 14
Letters to Malcolm (Lewis) 149
The Letters of J. R. R. Tolkien 56, 59, 69, 76, 85, 147-52
Lewis, C. S. 10, 11, 13, 14, 15, 16, 17, 18, 19, 36, 62, 80, 81, 99, 118, 144, 147, 148, 164, 165, 167, 172, 181, 186
Lewis, Sinclair (*Babbitt*) 31, 32

Lewis, Warren ("Warnie") 13, 60
"The Lhammas" 14
The Lord of the Rings 2, 14, 15, 16, 17, 18, 20, 21, 22, 23, 31, 38, 53, 56-75, 83, 88, 89, 91, 95, 97, 102, 116, 126, 129, 141, 142, 145, 148, 149, 150, 153, 154, 155, 156, 157, 158, 159, 167, 172, 174, 175, 177, 179, 181, 182, 183, 184, 186, 187, 188, 189
The Lord of the Rings: The Fellowship of the Ring (movie) 68
"The Lost Road" (story) 14, 15, 168
The Lost Road (book) 80, 82, 110, 138-42, 161, 167, 177, 180
Lúthien 6, 148, 162, 165, 166

MacDonald, George 4, 31 (*The Princess and the Goblin* and *The Princess and Curdie*)
Madlener, Josef 6
The Magazine of Fantasy and Science Fiction 183
Magdalen College 99
The Marion E. Wade Center 151
Marquette University 51, 147
Martin, Phillip 36
Martsch, Nancy 25
Mathew, Gervase 174
McIntosh, Angus 23
Mere Christianity (Lewis) 15

Meditations on Middle-Earth (Haber) 184
Merton College 10, 16, 17, 19, 20, 22, 98
"Middle English 'Losenger'" 18
Milton 144
Mirkwood 158
The Misty Mountains 170
Mitchison, Naomi 173
The Monsters and the Critics and Other Essays 113, 116, 118, 123, 134, 137
"The Moral Epiphanies of *The Lord of the Rings*" (Christopher) 185
Morgan, Fr. Francis 4, 5
Morgoth's Ring 175-77, 181
Morris, William 77-78, 163
Mr. Bliss 37, 50-52, 63, 82, 146, 168
Murray, Sir James 11, 106
Murray, Rosfrith 11
"Mythopoeia" 99-101
Mythopoeic Society 186
Mythlore 185

"Namárië" 144
"The Nameless Land" 110
Narnian stories (Lewis) 16, 149
Neave, Jane 6, 19, 77, 95
The New England Tolkien Society 151, 186
The New English Dictionary 8
Newman, John Henry 4
"The Notion Club Papers" 16, 161, 172, 173-75, 181
Númenor 153, 154, 155, 156, 167

"Of Beren and Lúthien" 79
"Oilima Markirya" 134
The Old English Exodus 130-31
Old Testament 128, 129
"On Fairy Stories" 42, 43, 106, 118-22
Onions, C. T. 105, 106, 144
Out of the Silent Planet (Lewis) 14, 149, 167
Ovid, 112
The Oxford English Dictionary (OED) 11, 30, 39, 104-106, 162
The Oxford History of English Literature (Lewis) 149
Oxford Poetry 1914-1916 91

"The Palantir" 20
Patterson, Nancy-Lou 146
Pavlac, Diana L. 81
Pearce, Joseph 25, 101, 140
Pembroke College 9
Pembroke College Library 151
The Peoples of Middle-Earth 178-81
Perelandra (Lewis) 15, 167
Peter Pan 53
Pictures By J. R. R. Tolkien 144-47
The Pilgrim's Regress (Lewis) 13
Poems and Stories 40, 44, 92, 96
Poetic Diction (Barfield) 13
Poetry 88-103
Poore, Richard 125
Potter, Beatrix 52
Plato (*The Republic*) 129

Plimmer, Charlotte and Denis 127
Proceedings of the J. R. R. Tolkien Centenary Conference (Reynolds & Goodknight) 25
Purgatorio (Dante) 142
Purtill, Richard 141

"Quenta Noldorinwa" 12, 166
Quenta Silmarillion 14, 80, 82, 163, 177

Raines, John Marlin 184
The Return of the King 18, 57, 122, 147, 159, 173, 183
The Return of the Shadow 161, 168-69
Reynolds, Patricia 25
Riddett, H. E. 145
The Road Goes Ever On - A Song Cycle 20, 65, 97-99, 159
"The Road Goes Ever On and On" 89
Rogers, Deborah 25, 142
Rogers, Ivor 142
Roverandom 52-55, 168
"Roy Campbell and the Inklings" (Christopher) 185
Ruskin, John 105

Salu, Mary 11, 23, 142
Sarehole Mill 3
Sauron Defeated 161, 172-75
Scott, Sir Walter 105
Scull, Christina 39, 48, 49, 54, 147, 180
Selby, G. E. 26

Index   253

Sendak, Maurice 43
Shakespeare 144
The Shaping of Middle-Earth
    80, 82, 165, 166, 167, 177, 180
Shelob 21, 70, 145, 171
Shippey, Tom 72, 73, 85, 88, 91, 92, 112, 116-17, 130
"The Shores of Faëry" 78
The Silmarillion 13, 20, 21, 22, 31, 60, 76-87, 95, 145, 148, 150, 153, 154, 155, 156, 159, 160, 162, 163, 164, 165, 168, 169, 175, 178, 180
"the Silmarillion proper" 87
Sir Gawain and the Green Knight 5, 18, 19, 39, 107-10, 144
Sir Orfeo 15, 31, 111-12
Sisam, Kenneth 9, 105, 106, 116
Sitwell, Edith 91
"Sketch of a Mythology" 10
Smith, Geoffrey 6, 8
Smith, Mark 70
Smith of Wootton Major 11, 20, 42-47, 65, 126
Snowmane 89-90
"Songs for the Philologists" 92
Sotheby's 151
Speaight, Robert 128
Spenser 144
St. Ambrose 130
St. Anne's Church 4
Stanton, Michael 59, 71
Steiner, Rudolf 174
The Story of the Amulet (Nesbit) 53
Studies in Words (Lewis) 149

Suffield, Beatrice 5
Swann, Donald 20, 97, 98, 99, 102
Sylvie and Bruno (Carroll) 53

Tales of the Arabian Nights 58
The Taming of the Shrew 105
T.C.B.S. 6, 23, 80
That Hideous Strength (Lewis) 149
Through the Looking Glass (Carroll) 30
Tolhurst, Denis and Jean 24
Tolkien, Arthur Reuel (father) 2, 3, 4
Tolkien, Baillie (daughter-in-law) 49
Tolkien, Christopher (son) 9, 15, 16, 17, 26, 47, 50, 60, 76, 85, 86, 87, 100, 111, 112, 121, 123, 134, 137, 145, 147, 148, 150, 151, 153, 156, 159, 160, 162, 163, 164, 169, 170, 171, 173, 175, 179
Tolkien, Edith Bratt (wife) 5, 10, 11, 12, 17, 19, 21, 22, 24, 79, 80, 91, 147, 148, 165
Tolkien, Hilary (brother) 3, 4
Tolkien, John (son) 8, 24, 26, 47, 106, 147
Tolkien: Life and Legend 136
Tolkien, Mabel Suffield (mother) 2, 3, 4
Tolkien, Michael (son) 8, 26, 31, 47, 50, 52, 58, 88, 94, 106, 126, 147, 150, 151, 152
Tolkien, Priscilla (daughter) 12, 16, 17, 40, 47, 49, 147

The Tolkien Reader 43, 92, 96
Tolkien Society 185
"Tolkien's Lyric Poetry" (Christopher) 185
The Treason of Isengard 161, 169-71
Tree and Leaf 20, 44, 65, 118, 138, 145
Treebeard 169, 170, 187
Turville-Petre, Joan 130, 131
The Two Towers 18, 57, 95, 126, 145, 146, 159, 170, 171, 173

UK Tolkien Society 110
Unfinished Tales 147, 153-59, 178, 179, 180, 181
Unwin, David ("David Severn") 38
Unwin, Raynor 17, 28, 54, 60, 61, 83, 84, 126
Unwin, Stanley 28, 38, 58, 82, 83, 94, 95, 96, 138, 141, 168, 173

"Valedictory Address" 142-44
Virgil 112
The Volsung Saga 77, 155
"The Voyage of Eärendil, the Evening Star" 76

Wagner 129
Waldman, Milton 83, 84, 148, 161, 164
Wales 1
The War of the Jewels 177-78, 181
The War of the Ring 161, 171-72

Wells, H. G. 105
Welsh language 1, 4
Wilkinson, Colonel C. H. 42
Williams, Charles 15, 149, 172, 179, 181, 186
Wilson, A. N. 165
Wiseman, Christopher 5, 6, 23, 80
Wodehouse, P. G. 43
The Worm Ouroboros (Eddison) 183
Wrenn, Charles 9, 116
Wright, Joseph 7, 123, 144
Wright, Mrs. Joseph 106
Wyke-Smith, E. A. (*The Marvelous Land of Snergs*) 10, 31, 118
Wyld, Henry 144

"You and Me and the Cottage of Lost Play" 7

Zamenhof, Ludwig 135

www.ingramcontent.com/pod-product-compliance
Lightning Source LLC
Chambersburg PA
CBHW020751160426
43192CB00006B/294